PREACHING TO THE CONVERTED

PREACHING TO THE CONVERTED

*On Sundays and Feast Days
Throughout the Year*

Richard Leonard, SJ

PAULIST PRESS
New York/Mahwah, NJ

Cover design by Cindy Dunne
Book design by Lynn Else

Library of Congress Cataloging-in-Publication Data

Leonard, Richard, 1963-
    Preaching to the converted : on Sundays and Feast Days throughout the year / Richard Leonard.
        p.   cm.
    Short homilies for each Sunday for all three cycles in one volume.
    ISBN 0-8091-4416-6 (alk. paper)
    1. Church year sermons. 2. Catholic Church—Sermons. I. Title.
BX1756.L453P74 2006
252'.6—dc22

                                                              2006021816

Published by Paulist Press
997 Macarthur Boulevard
Mahwah, New Jersey 07430

www.paulistpress.com

Printed and bound in the
United States of America

CONTENTS

FEASTS AND SOLEMNITIES

INTRODUCTION

There are three gripes I constantly hear about sermons: They are too long, they are over the heads of the congregation, and they do not intersect with the assembly's daily lives.

We have all sat listening to a preacher who is just about to land his or her homily when all of a sudden he or she goes into full throttle again and takes off for another circuit. It never ceases to amaze me that preachers seem to have very little accurate idea about how long they preach. On inquiry, most underestimate their sermons' length and breath—and sometimes their height and depth too! A good rule of thumb is that one hundred words take about a minute to deliver. An even better rule to preach by is that, for every minute a homily goes, an hour's preparation should have been invested in it. It's amazing how that rule prunes the verbiage!

I am not denying that there is a place for a rather lengthy homily, though the deacon, priest, or bishop had better have something decent to say, and then say it well. Or that in a very biblically literate congregation the use of professional jargon is appropriate, though there are only a handful of those congregations in the country. But there is never a reason for a homily that does not explicitly connect the word of God to the lived experience of the gathered assembly.

The liturgy documents of the Catholic Church tell us that, while preaching should provide a commentary on the word that gives the listener an accurate picture of the biblical message, it is also meant to nurture faith and help Christians to live their daily lives.

What preachers seem to be either oblivious to, or resistant toward, is the context in which people now listen. Speakers' Corner in Hyde Park, London, demonstrates my point. Once, people in London used to flock to Speakers' Corner to hear the brilliant and the raving mad. It was a way to be informed and participate in free speech. Now, Speakers' Corner is a free tourist attraction, and a dying one at that. People do not go out anymore to listen to sermons, speeches, orations, toasts, addresses, lectures, and political or union tirades, as they did just a generation or two ago.

Preaching is getting harder and harder. We are up against some tough opposition. Whether we like it or not, the media now determines what our congregations listen to, and how they listen. For a normal Western churchgoer, a homily could be the only regular time he or she sits, on a modern version of the rack, and does nothing else but listen to a single voice for several minutes. And there are no ad breaks or, usually, accompanying pictures, music, canned laughter or applause, and no restroom stop at the end. Just by listening to the radio or watching television, our congregations have been trained to expect that if a "talking head" goes on for longer than a minute, then he or she has a good story to tell and a dynamic way of presenting it.

We can resent this development all we like, but we do so at our peril, or worse still at the gospel's peril. People no longer listen to sermons that are too long, over their heads, or not in touch with their daily lives.

This book comes out of a commission I received to provide a weekly homily for an international liturgy Web site. The requirements were clear: The homily had to be 550–750 words, it could not refer too specifically to any country so as to be helpful in several English-speaking nations, and it had to be submitted seven weeks in advance. Because there was an exegete commentating on the scriptural readings, I was commissioned to write "story-based" reflections, bouncing off the gospel rather than mining it for the richness of its exegetical message.

Given that the best homily I have ever heard was one sentence long, the first requirement was a good challenge: to briefly say something engaging and intelligent. It meant, however, that I almost always had to stay focused on the gospel of the day, though there were several times when I could not leave the first and second readings alone. The entire exercise robbed me of a local church in which to situate my preaching, so that removed the more specific appeals to national issues I wanted to use. The third requirement tested my gifts for prophecy. A good preacher relies on the relationship with the worshipping community to whom he or she is preaching, and regularly enough uses local or international events to focus where the word might best speak to the congregation. Because of these obstacles, the homilies here are not "model homilies" that a preacher can copy on Saturday and give out as his or her own. Far from it.

Adaptation is the key to how helpful this book may prove to be. And my hope is that will be of value not only to preachers and homilists, but also to those communities who have to have Sunday celebrations in the absence of a priest, to teachers in classrooms, people preparing reflection sessions on the Sunday gospel, those who want to prayerfully prepare for the Sunday or feast-day liturgy, and those who seek to publish a written reflection on the gospel in their parish, school, or CCD bulletin or newsletter.

The best way to use this homiletic smorgasbord is as a resource of stories and ideas that enable the one who preaches to help Christ's converts hear the word of God, alive and active in the here and now.

Cycle A

FIRST SUNDAY OF ADVENT

ISAIAH 2:1–5
ROMANS 13:11–14
MATTHEW 24:37–44

Given the rich way Paul and Matthew use the theme of day and night as a metaphor for the coming of Christ, we should sing "Night and Day" by Cole Porter! Sung to Christ, it might just work.

The moments before dawn are often special: Everything is still, the air is damp, noise is at a minimum, and, at least on clear days, there is an anticipation of the sun bursting forth into daylight.

But these days we can experience night bursting forth into day in unexpected ways. It must have been frightening being in New York City when the recent power surge led to a blackout of the entire city. Still traumatized from the events of 9/11, tens of thousands of people did what many of us would do in the circumstances—they hit the road until it was clear that it was fine to return.

In the developing world, power failures are a fairly routine way of life. People refer to them as a "brownout," because the shutdown isn't quite complete and usually lasts a predictable period of time. The real difference is how people respond to the darkness caused by a power failure.

In developing countries, brownouts are so regular that people are prepared for them. They have flashlights, generators, candles, gas cookers, and lamps. In the developed world, we're so used to an uninterrupted power supply that most offices and homes are ill prepared for darkness overcoming the light. It can be the same with our spiritual life as well. And preparation is the key there too.

Being in the light is not just about what we see; it is about what we do. St. Ignatius Loyola often spoke about the things we keep buried in the dark. For Ignatius the experience we won't speak about, the sins we won't confess, and the memories we suppress are the signs of the bad spirit. They gain an inordinate power over us and we displace a lot of energy keeping them buried in the dark. Ignatius always saw the hand of the good spirit when these things came into the light. Every time someone says to me, "I've never told anyone this before, but I want to talk about it now," I thank God that the good spirit is alive and active.

St. Ignatius encourages us to be alert to all the ways we con ourselves that keeping secrets hidden in the dark is a necessary or acceptable way to live. He was a great fan of preparation. He was convinced that the best spirituality was one that kept reflecting on daily existence to see the pattern of God's goodness drawing us into the light, and the sometimes unexpected moments in the day when we are plunged into darkness.

The season of Advent is the time when we, the church, remember what it was like to wait and hope and long for the Messiah to come. It parallels all those moments in our lives when we wait for Christ to break in upon our day with his gifts of saving love. In this season may we bring to consciousness and to God all the things that stop us from being fully alive, and bask in the freedom and light Christ wants us to have.

SECOND SUNDAY OF ADVENT

 Isaiah 11:1–10
Romans 15:4–9
Matthew 3:1–12

Even in church circles these days, it is quite common to engage a management-consultancy company to help find people for a particular church job. This is a good idea and often these companies find excellent people for the task.

I recently saw a consultancy profile, however, for a diocese seeking a lay chancellor. We all know these people must be upright citizens, but I am convinced that Jesus himself may have been challenged to fill this job description! Apart from having degrees in civil and canon law, the desired applicant had to have "outstanding Catholic faith, an exemplary moral character and have an unimpeachable character."

A couple of days later I came across a tongue-in-cheek summary of a management consultant's report on those who had applied to lead the earliest Christian church:

> JOHN: Says he is a Baptist, but definitely doesn't dress like one. Has slept in the outdoors for months on end, has a weird diet, and picks fights in public with religious leaders.

> PETER: Has a bad temper, even has been known to curse. Had a big run-in with Paul in Antioch. Aggressive. A loose cannon.

> PAUL: Powerful, CEO type of leader and fascinating preacher. However, short on tact, unforgiving with young ministers, harsh and has been known to preach all night.

> JESUS: Has been popular at times, but once when his following grew to 5000 he managed to offend them all and it dwindled down to some faithful women and his best friend. Seldom stays in one place very long.

> JUDAS: His references are solid. Conservative. Good connections. Knows how to handle money. Great possibilities here.

In today's Gospel we hear what a fierce character John the Baptist was. He lets the Pharisees and Sadducees have it with both barrels. These groups were the publicly devout churchgoers of their day. They were often hypocrites, professing one thing and doing another. We know they regularly demanded observances of ordinary Jews that they did not live out themselves. No wonder John disliked them so much.

Their religious observance was a charade, focused on their needs, their souls, their salvation. They were going to get to heaven, and everyone else be damned! They even come out to the wilderness to get baptized. This was like going to a salvation megastore and buying a little of everything, just to be sure. John attacks them violently and, in doing so, condemns their privatized religion and lack of social responsibility.

In Christianity there is an important distinction between personal and private faith. Personal faith knows that God is close and intimate, which is what we celebrate at Christmas. We should always be careful of hymns that only speak about "me and Jesus against the world." Inheriting the promises made to Israel and seeing them as intended for all God's children, we believe we are saved as a people. For us, it is "we and Jesus for the world."

If we have no interest in justice, development, and peace for our world, if we don't care to know our fellow parishioners or if all we want is to be left alone to come to Mass, say our prayers, and save our souls, then we need to hear the story of Christmas all over again.

May this Advent, then, see John the Baptist do what he does best: comfort the afflicted and afflict the comfortable.

THIRD SUNDAY OF ADVENT

 ISAIAH 35:1–6a, 10
JAMES 5:7–10
MATTHEW 11:2–11

Have you ever been on a farm during summer? If you have, you will know how precious water is. When I was a boy, I spent several holidays on an uncle's ranch. There were often six or seven city-based cousins there for the long summer break. It was great fun, but the one thing of which we needed a daily reminder was to be careful with how much water we used. We seemed to luxuriate in the shower for twice as long as our country cousins!

I can remember that, when we arrived for one holiday, it had not rained in the area for nearly nine months. A few days later, just at dusk, the thunder rumbled, the storm clouds gathered, and the heavens burst open. The rain poured down. As in the movies, everyone inside the house just stood up and walked out into the rain. No one said a word. We stood in the rain and soaked it in. The earth was not the only thing in need of a drenching.

In the letter from St. James, the metaphor of waiting for rain is given to us as a way of understanding what it was like to wait for Christ. It is a potent image for Advent. In this season each year, we remember that humanity waited through a long, dry, and exhausting period for the sign of new life in Jesus. For generations people looked to the heavens every day for a sign that today would be the day when God's salvation would come. Then, one night, in a way no one could have ever imagined, with no fanfare, a child burst forth into the world and established the final reign of God's love.

Advent is not the time when we pretend that Jesus hasn't come into our world and that we are the first to anticipate his coming at Christmas. It's a richer season than that. It is the time when we recall what it was like before he came and how much we need him to keep coming again and again in our daily lives.

The first reading and the Gospel make it very clear that farmers never put down tools just because the rain comes. We're told that as a result of being soaked in the love of God we are called to do all we can for those in our world who are lame, blind, deaf, lepers, poor, and anyone left for dead.

This is a vital message for us to hear today because there are some who tell us that all we have to do is look after "our own backyard." Advent reminds us that by welcoming Christ we have an obligation to care for all his children. Everywhere is our backyard because that's where our brothers and sisters live. May we gain from Christ this Christmas the generosity to see that the desert is meant to bloom for all people, not just a few of us lucky to live in an oasis.

We are ridiculously generous to others because God in Jesus has been lavishly good to us, and our goodness remains a most powerful sign of God's salvation that is seen more so in deeds than in words.

FOURTH SUNDAY OF ADVENT

ISAIAH 7:10–14
ROMANS 1:1–7
MATTHEW 1:18–24

This Sunday's Gospel announces that "God is with us." In this final week of Advent, the following story by V. A. Bailey reminds us that God comes to us in unpredictable ways, often with unsettling messages.

> I hurried into the shop to grab some last minute Christmas gifts. I looked at all the people and grumbled to myself. I would be in here forever. I hurried to the toy department and wondered if the grandkids would even play with my gifts.
>
> My eye caught a little boy holding a doll. He kept touching her hair and he held her so gently. I watched him turn and ask, "Aunty Jane, are you sure I don't have enough money?" Gently, the woman replied, "Emily doesn't need a doll, David." The woman went to another aisle. The boy continued to hold the doll. David looked so sad that I couldn't resist asking who the doll was for. "My sister wanted it so badly for Christmas." I told him that maybe Santa was going to bring it. He said "No, Santa can't go where my sister is… I have to give the doll to Mummy to take to her." I asked him where his sister was. He looked at me with the tear-filled eyes, "She has gone to be with Jesus. Daddy says that Mummy is going to have to go be with both of them soon too." My heart nearly stopped beating.
>
> David went on, "I told Daddy to make sure Mummy goes nowhere until I got back from the store. I want Mum to take this doll to Emily."
>
> While he wasn't looking I reached into my purse and pulled out some cash. "David, how about we count that money again?" He grew excited, "I asked Jesus to give me enough money. I just know I have enough." I slipped my money in with his and we began to count it. He looked up from the count and exclaimed, "Jesus has given me enough money for Emily's doll."

In a few minutes his aunty came back and I wheeled my cart away. I could not keep from thinking about the little boy as I finished my shopping in a totally different spirit than when I had started.

On the way home I remembered a story in the newspaper several days earlier about a drunk driver hitting a car and killing a little girl and that the Mother was left on life support. Two days before Christmas I read in the paper where the family had turned the machine off. The day before Christmas there was a funeral notice saying that a Requiem Mass would be celebrated on St. Stephen's Day for Julia Norris and her daughter Emily. Michael was their husband and father, and their son and brother was David.

As I gathered with my family in front of an overblown meal which none of us could finish, holding expensive gifts we didn't need and drinking more alcohol than was necessary, I thought, "We've lost the plot with Christmas." God-with-us arrives as a simple child in need of love; and in the honor of that day we spend money, eat too much, and get drunk.

I left the table, went to my desk, and wrote a card for each member of my family. I told them what I'd never been able to say: "I want you to know I love you."

When they read those cards, my family thought I was losing it, but through David and that doll, God visited me in the last week of Advent, and Christmas will never be the same again.

CHRISTMAS

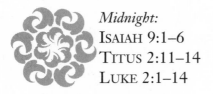 *Midnight:*
Isaiah 9:1–6
Titus 2:11–14
Luke 2:1–14

The worst Christmas I ever celebrated was in Manger Square at Bethlehem. It should have been the best Christmas experience, but after I negotiated the traffic jam, the eight security checks, the guards on patrol, a cast of thousands, and being jam-packed into the church for hours, it lost some of its Christmas appeal!

In all the accounts of Christmas we have in the New Testament, we hear the angel begin her announcement of Jesus' birth with the words, "Be not afraid." Given the world events over recent years, this greeting is just what we need to hear this Christmas as well. "Be not afraid."

Fear is a terrible thing. It cripples us into passivity. It ruins our memories of the past or the present, and it undermines dignified, trusting, and respectful relationships.

In recent years we have seen how these fearful traits can be identified in groups, as well as individuals. We have seen people become anxious, change their lifestyle and travel plans, and worry for their future and that of their children. In a sense, the terrorists win when we change our lives for fear of them.

But we don't need to look to international terror to explore the nature of our fear. Broadly speaking, we fear four things: God, nature, other people, or something in ourselves. For some people, it can be a combination of these things, or, tragically, it can be all of them.

To any degree that fear rules our lives, let's hear God's greeting this Christmas: "Be not afraid."

St. Paul tells us that love drives out all fear. That's who we celebrate this Christmas: love taken human form in Jesus Christ the Lord. Thus today we remember the birthday of a man whose life, death, and resurrection showed us the way out of our fears, revealed the truth that sets us free, and gave us the life that we can live to the full in this world, and in the next.

Christmas is the feast when God calls us to be as active as we can in bringing Christ's kingdom to bear in our world.

Christmas is the feast when our memories are joined to God's, who has remembered us in our fear.

Christmas is the feast when all Christian relationships are defined by the dignity, trust, and respect they bestow on us and on those we relate to.

As a result of the babe of Bethlehem, God has shown us that fear is not our calling, and that the saving love of Jesus impels us to take risks in how we live out our faith, hope, and love.

On any day, then, in the coming year, when we face down our fears and live our Christian life to the full, we'll discover that Christmas is a moveable feast.

"Do not be...afraid, I am bringing you good news of great joy...to you is born this day...a Savior, who is the Messiah, the Lord." Merry Christmas!

HOLY FAMILY

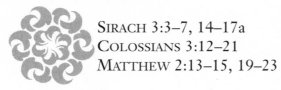 SIRACH 3:3–7, 14–17a
COLOSSIANS 3:12–21
MATTHEW 2:13–15, 19–23

For some years now, family therapists have used an exercise called the genogram to help families understand their internal dynamics.

Each spouse sits down and writes out his or her family tree. Usually it stretches back at least three generations. Next to each name they write a letter indicating any "careers" this relative may have picked up in his or her lifetime. It is not just the person's occupation that interests a family therapist, though it's interesting to see how doctors, farmers, musicians, and civil servants keep popping up in some families.

A career in the genogram has more to do with personal or social dispositions like using alcohol, drugs, work, and gambling in a destructive way; like having a propensity to violence or holding a criminal record; like "having to get married" or whether one's relatives are hetero- or homosexual. When people start to dig, they find all sorts of family secrets, especially in older generations. Most families have an "Aunty Lizzie" who, sixty years on, is still spoken of in hushed tones. They eventually discover she had an abortion. Sometimes there is an "Uncle James" who never married.

What family therapists notice is that certain careers are passed down through the generations. This exercise can be very helpful when families are struggling to understand why a child is an early victim of alcoholism or gambling addiction, is gay, or given to violence. While behavior can be thought to "come out of nowhere," this exercise shows that, whether by nature or nurture, destructive behavior has been on one or both sides of a family system for generations.

The point of the genogram is that knowing our pedigree for good or for ill enables us to build on our strengths while breaking the cycle of our families' negative careers.

The feast of the Holy Family tells us that Jesus, Mary, and Joseph had a career in holiness. I suspect there are not many of us who would write "Savior" or "Saint" on the people in our family trees! But there is every reason to believe that holiness is handed down from one generation to the next.

The problem with holiness is that we often equate it with perfection. To be a holy person does not mean one is perfect. Perfection rests only in God. Jesus enjoyed perfection in his humanity, but we must allow Mary and Joseph to be less than perfect, or else we make them truly divine as well. As a family, they were not perfect, they were holy. They struggled together to understand the best way they could bring God's reign to bear in our world. Their destinies were vastly different, but intimately connected. They needed each other.

And so to us! If we allow the Holy Family to be too removed from our experience, they have little to say to the fights, misunderstandings, and problems that can sometimes characterize our families. If on the other hand we concede that Jesus, Mary, and Joseph, as a family, were not perfect, they can be a model of the very thing we want in our own homes: a love, justice, fidelity, and kindness that reveal a life of holiness. They can show us a mutual respect that allows each family member to find his or her own path to revealing God's creative and saving love for our world. And they can provide us with the assurance of knowing that as a result of their holiness we have all been welcomed into the family of God.

When any of us do the genogram we can rightly and proudly put Jesus, Mary, and Joseph at the top of our tree and mark them as Savior and first among the saints.

EPIPHANY OF THE LORD

 Isaiah 60:1–6
Ephesians 3:2–3a, 5–6
Matthew 2:1–12

In heaven one year it was decided that on the feast of the Epiphany they would have a liturgy that recreated the visit of the three stargazers from the East. The job of the stargazers was given to the founders of three great religious orders in the church.

Everyone gathered to see St. Francis of Assisi come forward at the appropriate time and lay clay doves before the crib of Jesus. As one, the heavenly host all went, "Ahhhh."

St. Benedict was next and he processed beautifully to the crib holding a magnificent bejeweled Bible. On the front of it were the words, "This is your life." Everyone in heaven called out, "Ohhh."

Finally, St. Ignatius Loyola limped forward not carrying a gift. He walked straight past the crib and then past Mary. Everyone in heaven was aghast and thought this is so typical of Jesuits: He doesn't know where he's going at liturgy and turns up empty-handed! They watched as he went over and put his arm around Jesus' foster father, "So, tell me, St. Joseph, have you decided where you're sending the kid to school? Hang with me and I'll get you a special rate."

When we go to the movies, we have to suspend our critical sensibilities to enter into the full power of the story. A similar concession is necessary to reap the full benefit of the story of the first Epiphany. Have you ever wondered, for example, why the wise men, who have been guided from the East to Jerusalem, stop there and ask directions from Herod? Surely the star could have kept doing its job and taken them all the way! And why didn't Herod follow the wise men, or at least send a spy behind them? Furthermore, whatever happened to these wise guys? They're the first in Matthew's Gospel to recognize who Jesus is, and yet they vanish from Jesus' life as quickly as they came into it.

Like many screenwriters Matthew plays with history for another purpose. Like moviegoers, we're happy to suspend our questions and look beyond the story's details so we can enjoy the profound picture that is being painted for us.

Throughout his Gospel, Matthew is at pains to show how the Jews missed out on recognizing Jesus because they were locked in their fears. King Herod is the first public official to be portrayed in such a way, but he is by no means the last or the least. Pilate suffers a similar fate at the end of this Gospel. Matthew links these two rulers. The result of being threatened by who Jesus is, or how he lives his life, results in death—Herod's slaughter of the innocents in the first case, and later Pilate's murder of Jesus.

It is this link between Jesus' birth and death that Matthew is painting today. In the midst of the extraordinary scene of visiting stargazers, their gifts tell us that the richness and power of this Child's reign will be revealed through his death and resurrection.

So often our reactions to Jesus can be like Herod's. We can be threatened and frightened. We want to eliminate the voices that call us to live out the reign of God, and that remind us of the costs involved. Matthew tells us that the enemy of the Christian life is fear. It entraps us and infects those around us. And we are often most fearful when we risk loosing power, so we lie, are deceitful, and cheat to maintain our position at all costs. As with Herod and Pilate, it all ends in death.

But when we face down our fears and name the real threats in our life, we know the overwhelming joy of finding the "Morning Star who came back from the dead and shed his peaceful light on all humanity."

So this story is far more than a travelogue of exotic Persian kings. It's the story of the choices that lie before all Christians everywhere: Do we want to live out of wonder or fear?

To follow Jesus' rule is to keep our eyes on that Star that lights the path to having the courage to live out his gospel, to carry our crosses, whatever they be, and to trust that God will remain faithful to *us* through death, into eternal life—where threats and fears will be no more.

To the degree that we live beyond our fears right here and now, we enjoy our very own Epiphany, wonder-filled as it is!

BAPTISM OF THE LORD

ISAIAH 42:1–4, 6–7
ACTS 10:34–38
MATTHEW 3:13–17

These days there are some young Catholic parents who wonder whether baptism is the proper thing for them to do for their children. One argument they sometimes offer is that it would be better to defer baptism until their child reaches adulthood, when he or she has the opportunity to choose it. As appealing as this argument might seem on the surface, the problem is that the reasoning behind it is so inconsistently applied.

Young Catholic parents do not give their children any choice about eating vegetables, learning to read or write, and living out a moral code. They enforce these things because they know nutrition, literacy, and ethics are *essential* for adulthood. If we recognize that, from birth, a child has spiritual as well as educational, moral, and physical needs, it strikes me as inconsistent to relegate this constitutively otherworldly element of a child's character to a "must be decided on later" category.

Baptism is not brainwashing. Adults can come and go from the practice of their faith as they feel drawn. Sadly for us, they can even choose against belief. To grow up, however, with no religious foundation or no basis on which to make spiritual choices seems to limit freedom rather than promote it. In our culture baptism of infants by their parents is an entirely proper thing to do.

In the Gospel we hear that Jesus got baptized by John in the Jordan because it was "the proper thing to do."

This can seem all quaintly odd to us today because we seem to accept that our only convention is to flout convention. The done thing today is to undo what we've done before.

We hold very strongly, however, to the idea that God always does the "proper thing." It's called "appropriateness" in theology. We believe, for example, that God decided it was proper to become incarnate when he did, how he did, and where he did. Over the centuries there's been endless debate about what would've happened if the Word had come to us as a woman, in another era, on another continent. While these are interesting matters upon which to speculate, they are not what God thought proper—what, in fact, happened.

In line with the right action of God, Jesus does the proper thing in being baptized by John's baptism of repentance, even though he had nothing of which to repent. Jesus is not simply baptized because it was expected of him. Jesus' experience of baptism starts with John's baptism as an admission of guilt and then reveals that baptism is primarily about the Father's love. To this day our baptismal ritual holds these two realities in a healthy tension. When we are baptized in Christ, we acknowledge both original sin and original grace. God's love comes alive in us even though we are aware of how far from that love we stray.

The baptism of Jesus, and every baptism done in his name ever since, is the moment when we hold together the greatness of God's love, which calls each of us by name to be his son or daughter, with the reality of our human frailty. What more appropriate way of welcoming anyone into the world than having a community of frail, human believers initiate its members by reminding them that original sin does not have the last word. For those of us baptized in Christ, the Father's love always and everywhere has the final, appropriate say on every matter.

May this feast make us worthy of the love lavished on us in our baptisms and give us the courage to keep doing the appropriate things for the coming generations.

SECOND SUNDAY IN ORDINARY TIME

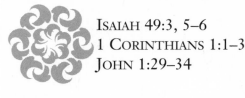 Isaiah 49:3, 5–6
1 Corinthians 1:1–3
John 1:29–34

Some of us remember the provocative and frightening 1991 film, *Silence of the Lambs.*

The image in the title refers to a childhood memory of CIA agent, Clarice Starling. In her interviews with the psychopath, Dr. Lector, he gets her to talk about how she still wakes at night hearing the cry of the lambs as they were led to slaughter on her uncle's farm. This is a pivotal moment in Thomas Harris's book and the film. It is the leverage Dr. Lector needs to unsettle and unravel Clarice's well-formed defenses. Clarice is revealed as vulnerable because of the grief she carries from the violent deaths she has seen.

I remember empathizing with Clarice's memory of the lambs. When I was a child I saw many sheep slaughtered on my family's ranches. I can still see my uncle selecting one of them, holding it in the pen before its execution, and then doing the deed. The scene should have been enough to turn me into a vegetarian! Alas, I got over my pity for the animal and enjoyed roast lamb a few nights later.

John's use of the metaphor of the sacrificial lamb in reference to Jesus in today's Gospel is meant to engender in us a similar empathy to that of the childhood memories of Clarice Starling. While there are many jokes about the stupidity of sheep, lambs still claim a spot in the hardest heart. They are pure, white, fluffy, and defenseless. They demand nurture. And like their parents, they don't seem to be able to smell danger very easily. They follow where they're led, even to execution.

For the agrarian Jews of Jesus' time the sacrifice of a lamb demonstrated how serious they were about atoning for their sins. Jewish law dictated that a lamb had to be killed at least once a year, at Passover. Such a sacrifice cost the shepherd big time. Lambs were currency. This was tithing writ large.

Saying Jesus is the Lamb of God is a shorthand way of telling us two things. The first is that Jesus is God's most precious gift: God's own self, given to the world that we might know how serious God is about us. God can give us nothing more than Jesus. As a result of Jesus' innocent suffering and death there is no need for any lambs to be religiously slaughtered ever again. We need to keep hearing this message because some Christians get caught into glorifying Jesus' suffering so much they get trapped in their own world of pain and go looking for more. Jesus never sought out suffering. He bore what came his way. And the same must be true for us. Christians are not meant to be smiling masochists. Most of us don't need to look for more suffering in our lives because we share in the Lamb of God's sacrifice in the ordinary down times of our own lives.

Secondly, John knew that *talya*, the Aramaic word for sheep, is the same word used for servant. The first hearers of this Gospel knew it too. Jesus, then, is the servant who brings us the truth we need for life, who answers our deepest desires to know that our existence has meaning and purpose, and he opens up for us the life beyond this one, where there will be no more weeping or sadness.

Jesus shows us that when we are baptized into his death and enter his service we also share in his resurrection and glory because he bears, and bears away, the sins of the world.

THIRD SUNDAY IN ORDINARY TIME

Isaiah 8:23b– 9:3
1 Corinthians 1:10–13, 17
Matthew 4:12–23

Recently I was shocked by a Catholic woman who told me she didn't care very much for her local bishop. She enumerated the many faults and failings of her diocese and its leader and then highly praised the pope.

It's hard to argue with her admiration of the pope, but unknowingly, she was falling into the same trap to which the community at Corinth was prey. Unfortunately, my acquaintance thought that her Catholic identity primarily came from her communion with the bishop of Rome. She felt she could bypass her local bishop, "because he's too trendy," and "deal directly" with the pope. She told me she saw the pope as her bishop. The problem with her position is that it is not as Catholic as she thinks it is!

All of us in the church are called to pray for, support, and follow the lead of the Holy Father. But our Catholic identity comes from our communion with our local church, in and through its bishop, who is in turn in communion with the bishop of Rome. This is what the five-yearly *ad limina* visits are all about: a brother bishop sharing with the pope the graces and challenges in his local church and reaffirming the Catholic faith that unites all of us as members of the same universal church.

Soon after Jesus called the apostles, disputes broke out among them. We know from famous parts of the New Testament that there were serious disagreements between the earliest leaders in the church. Their different temperaments and missions led to several misunderstandings. What St. Paul found in Corinth, however, was a fractured church, pleading allegiances to different leaders over and against Jesus. He teaches the Corinthians a critical lesson in being church: We are all one under Jesus' leadership. Christ is the head of the church.

Within ancient and clear limits, the church has a wonderful diversity, a plurality of expression, emphasis, and culture. It's always been like this. It means the church is taking seriously its role of finding Christ in every place and every community in the world. The moment we pit one local church against the other ("I prefer the pope to my bishop") we lose the Catholic communion in Christ Jesus that holds us together.

Paul tells us that preaching the cross of Jesus is the mission of the church. Jesus shows us in the Gospel that teaching, preaching, and healing are the hallmarks of his ministry. And the same should hold for us. No matter how differently any local church might develop, the bishop of Rome confirms in the faith bishops who continue to preach Christ crucified, teach in Christ's name, heal the sick, and reconcile the estranged.

That's what makes us Catholic and why today we need to listen again, and very carefully, to Paul's admonition, "I appeal to you, brothers and sisters, by the name of our Lord Jesus Christ, that all of you be in agreement and that there be no divisions among you, but that you be united in the same mind and the same purpose" (1 Cor 1:10).

To the degree to which we live this out in our communion with our local successor to the apostles, the more chance all members of the church have to use the energy and gifts given at baptism to do what Christ wants of the church: to change the world for good and be a beacon of Christ's saving gifts—faith, hope, and charity.

FOURTH SUNDAY IN ORDINARY TIME

 ZEPHANIAH 2:3; 3:12–13
1 CORINTHIANS 1:26–31
MATTHEW 5:1–12a

In any walk of life there are stories that circulate about an important facet of the job. For priests these stories often focus on sermons.

Like the young priest who was having trouble with his sermons, so he asked the bishop for help. "Well," said the bishop, "you might start with something to get the congregation's attention, such as, 'Last night I was in the warm embrace of a good woman.' I've always found that sparks their interest and then you can go on to talk about how warm and accepting she was and at the end reveal she was your mother. It's great for sermons about family love."

The young priest decided to take the advice the following Sunday, but he was so nervous, something got lost in the translation. He started, "Last night I was in the arms of a hot woman." As the congregation audibly gasped the young priest paused and realized he had forgotten how the bishop's story ended, so he said, "I don't remember who she was but the bishop recommended her."

The Sermon on the Mount is one of the greatest sermons ever given. What makes it great is not just the beauty of its language or the hope of its theology. It is truly great because Jesus was preaching to the reality in front of him. The Jews listening that day were poor, in grief, meek, and hungry for justice. Some were trying to be merciful to their enemies, struggling to find God in the midst of persecution, and attempting to make peace while their family and friends were being falsely accused and condemned.

As true as this was for the Jews of Jesus' day it was even more so for the earliest Christian community for whom this Gospel was written.

Sometimes when we hear a sermon our reaction can be, "What would he know? If only he knew the complexities of my life, he would soon change his tune!" It's true that some preachers have not been sensitive to the human frailties of the congregation in front of them and we have not been able to communicate our own frailties in the words we deliver.

The Sermon on the Mount is a model for all of us in every way. When Jesus says, "Blessed are you" he is not being patronizing, glossing over all sorts of tough human realities with "Well done, keep it up, be happy and we'll fix it all up in heaven."

In the Hebrew scriptures, a blessing is the discovery that God is present and active in one's experience, right here and right now. So the Beatitudes are saying that you do not need to go past your own daily struggles to find the presence of God. Jesus tells us that if we are poor, compassionate, mournful, campaigning for a just society and suffering because of it, gentle, innocent, a peacemaker or a martyr, we are encountering, in a special way, the presence of God.

The God of the Beatitudes is a companion with us in every experience we go through. He is our best friend walking beside us as we get out of bed and meet the days we would rather not face.

Sadly, God-as-friend is a rich image not used as much as it should be. We choose our friends, we like to spend time with them, and we tell our intimate friends things we tell few others. Sometimes, when we are on top of the world or in a crisis, we call our best friends ahead of our family. And we know our friends like us because they seek us out and want to share our life.

Jesus is the best friend we could ever have, interested in every daily event, and he's there for us at every moment in life. Yet he doesn't barge in. He waits patiently for an invitation to enter our lives at whatever level we want.

Jesus-as-friend doesn't give us old-fashioned sermons, but rather meets us where we are, embraces us and holds us close when the going gets tough and helps us find the way forward. Jesus-as-friend is the greatest Beatitude of all.

FIFTH SUNDAY IN ORDINARY TIME

ISAIAH 58:7–10
1 CORINTHIANS 2:1–5
MATTHEW 5:13–16

I imagine doctors and dietitians have some difficulty with the first part of this week's Gospel. Jesus does not seem to know that salt is bad for hypertension and cholesterol! Just as health professionals are encouraging us to be careful in using salt, Jesus is telling us to go for it. Salt in Jesus' day, and for centuries before and after, was the primary preserving substance for food. That day-to-day usage gives us a clue as to the challenge being laid before us.

We are told that if salt has lost its taste it's good for nothing. So the challenge is to keep it fresh so it can keep doing its job. Jesus suggests that, in the same way, we have to be on guard to make sure that our faith remains fresh so it's able to do its job as well.

The fifth and sixth chapters of Matthew's Gospel are devoted to describing the elements of Christian faith. At the start of the fifth chapter we have the Beatitudes that tell us that the presence of God can be discovered in all of life's situations. It reminds us that as Christians we can find God wherever we want to. The rest of these two chapters go on to give us specific directions about the dangers and aids to faith.

Jesus tells us that a hollow attachment to the letter of the law, unbridled anger, an inability to forgive, being unfaithful in marriage, seeking revenge on our enemies, not being true to our word, and being enslaved by money are all examples of bad faith. Think for a moment of people you know who are trapped by any of these vicious forces. It's sad to see the energy it takes them to remain angry, greedy, legalistic, fraudulent, and unforgiving.

More positively, Jesus tells us in these chapters that prayer, being generous to the poor, being discerning about whom we spend time with, what we see and hear, and going without things we often consider essential are helpful to living a faith-filled life. Think for a moment of people you know who live lives like this.

Their detachment, sense of generosity, and ease with others stand out in our stress-ridden world.

My professor of liturgy used to say that, "Good liturgy enlivens faith and bad liturgy deadens it." This is the same message Jesus gives us today about faith in general. It's crazy for us to keep spending time with people and doing things that deaden our faith. We know the impact of these people or activities by the bad taste they leave in our mouths. After an encounter with them, or it, we usually tell ourselves that we must not go back for more, but the bad spirit seduces us into repeating the entire episode with frightening frequency. St. Ignatius Loyola tells us that in these situations we have to deal with the bad spirit quickly and consistently and learn a new pattern of behavior that will lead us away from darkness into the light.

The job of faith is to enable us to live out and build Christ's reign of justice and love in this world as a foretaste of what awaits us in heaven. May the Eucharist enable us to seek out the people and places that will see the saltiness of our faith remain fresh and interesting so that we will have every chance of preserving our faith in the dryer times, confident that our faith in Jesus will preserve us in the face of the trials and tests that come our way.

SIXTH SUNDAY IN ORDINARY TIME

SIRACH 15:16–21
1 CORINTHIANS 2:6–10
MATTHEW 5:17–37

After some famous people die, a book of their favorite or most important sayings is sometimes published. We only have to think of various writings of saints and religious founders or Mao's *Little Red Book* to see the influence for good or ill these books can have. Most times these sayings don't have much in common save for their origin.

The second part of the fifth chapter of Matthew's Gospel is a little like these books of sayings. It groups together in one place several things that the earliest Christians recall hearing from Jesus. Although they are all placed in one chapter, they are not meant to be read as a carefully developed argument on one theme. Some of the sayings are direct and clear, like the one about being reconciled with our brothers and sisters before approaching the altar. Others use highly inflated language, like cutting off our hands or gouging out our eyes if they cause us to sin. We are not meant to take this literally. Jesus is not advocating self-mutilation as reparation for sin. As was the custom in his day, and remains so with some great teachers, he overstates the case to drive the point home, and to help his students commit the principle to memory.

These various sayings stand up on their own, but Matthew collects them under the theme of his community's approach to the law. This was one of the big issues in the earliest church—what laws should Christians keep and what laws should they throw out. This Sunday's Gospel can, on first reading, seem to have a bet both ways, having Jesus advocate the fulfillment of the letter of the law, and then having him go on to reinterpret many of the Mosaic laws in very different ways. But this reading would be a mistake. It is a richer text than that.

Attacking the legal scrupulosity of the scribes and Pharisees, these collected sayings of Jesus outline seven characteristics of the way Christians deal with one another and the world. We seek opportunities to forgive those who have hurt us. We consider reconciliation with those we can see a prerequisite activity before we worship the God we cannot see. We are slow to sue anyone, preferring personal negotiation to litigation. We keep our desires in check and don't objectify other human beings. We look at the causes of our sin and change the circumstances that give rise to our destructive behavior. We remain faithful to those we love. And we mean what we say when we make serious, mature, and adult promises.

The greatest aid to living this challenging life is Christ. He is the letter, the stroke of the letter, and the accomplishment of the law. Having a transparent relationship with Christ, and the community who follows his way, enables us to fulfill the greatest law of all: the law of love, from which all other laws are judged.

So with our eyes on Christ, and supporting, enabling and challenging each other, we go from here as followers of Jesus, at home and in society, known by name and nature to be forgiving, reconciling, faithful, discerning, true to our word, shunning the courts, and giving dignity and respect to everyone we meet.

SEVENTH SUNDAY IN ORDINARY TIME

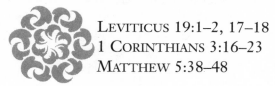 LEVITICUS 19:1–2, 17–18
1 CORINTHIANS 3:16–23
MATTHEW 5:38–48

It came as a shock to me the other day to discover that there are several Web sites dedicated to revenge. The two most popular sites carry the names revengeunlimited.com and thepayback.com.

No doubt the creators of these sites constructed them as a joke. They are not meant to be taken seriously. The promotion line for one of them says, "Have you been wronged, mistreated, annoyed or ignored? Are you ready for some payback?… Explore our site and find piles of good ideas and novelties. Revenge Unlimited believes that there are people in desperate need of a good dose of humility.…"

And while both sites go on to "recommend good natured pranks and non-aggressive expressions of distaste," it is curious that that they link revenge with having a laugh. I only wish we could.

Ask the police about how revenge drives so much domestic violence. Talk to social workers about changing the culture of revenge in gang conflict. Discuss revenge as a trigger for war with those campaigning for peace, and we soon discover that it has nothing to do with fun. Revenge continues to wreak havoc on our world at every level.

And that's why this week's Gospel is so challenging and important.

First-century Palestine was a violent place. The Romans were a brutal occupying force. The nation's neighbors had unjustly invaded Israel several times, and even within Israel it seems that revenge was an acceptable way of reestablishing one's honor.

In the Gospel, Jesus quotes Exodus 21:23–24, which started this ball rolling: that the law required there be a "life for life, eye for eye, tooth for tooth, hand for hand, foot for foot." It is also repeated in the books of Leviticus and Deuteronomy. It has come to be called the Law of Retribution. And as barbaric as this law sounds to us today, in its time it was a moderating influence in society.

It's fairly clear now that in ancient Israel, before any courts were set up, personal justice could entail taking several lives for one life, and the torching of a house for the stealing of a sheep. Curiously we have little evidence of the latter part of the law regarding eyes, teeth, and hands ever being enforced. The Israelites knew that these were figures of speech used to amplify the point. The Law of Retribution established the rights of courts to moderate an overly revengeful response to crime.

Jesus inherits and understands this tradition, but clearly makes a break with it, and that's where we stand.

This is a tough Gospel, maybe as tough as it gets, because it asks us to go against the most seductive part of our human nature: getting even. It applies to the relative we won't speak to, the former spouse against whom we poison our children, the neighbor we delight in annoying, and the work colleague we bad-mouth because he or she got the promotion we were after. That's on the domestic front.

But Jesus' words equally apply to those who commit criminal acts against us or others, and the enemies of our state. This is why the church takes a stand against the death penalty and unjust wars. And the amazing thing is that revenge and retribution has a similar effect on the domestic, national, and international scene—it solves nothing. It just eats us up.

For the fleeting satisfying moment revenge might bring us, it usually continues the conflict, inflames the anger, and distorts us into something much less than God intended.

By contrast, Jesus says that his law is to forgive, love, and pray. This principle is neatly summed up in Al-Anon's advice to screaming spouses as they deal with drunken partners, as described in *Courage to Change: One Day at a Time in Al-Anon II:* You might not be able to change the other person, but you can change yourself. Stop screaming, reclaim your own dignity, and greet your partner as civilly as possible. What often happens is the change in you leads to change in those around you.

And for very different reasons, and only on this score, do the Gospel and those revenge Web sites agree about what is really at stake in retribution: Humility is everything.

Let's pray then for the Holy Spirit to help us conquer our pride, so that we can live more peacefully with ourselves, and then watch how the gift of forgiveness is much more caught than taught.

EIGHTH SUNDAY IN ORDINARY TIME

 Isaiah 49:14–15
1 Corinthians 4:1–5
Matthew 6:24–34

A farmer named Muldoon lived alone in the Irish countryside except for a pet dog he doted on. The dog finally died, and Muldoon went to the parish priest, saying, "Father, the dog is dead. Could you possibly be saying a Mass for the poor creature?" Father Patrick told the farmer, "No, we can't have services for an animal in the church, but I'll tell you what, there's a new denomination down the road and no telling what they believe in, but maybe they'll do something for the animal." Muldoon said, "I'll go right now. By the way, do you think 50,000 pounds is enough to donate for the service?" Father Patrick replied, "Why didn't you tell me the dog was Catholic?"

Father Patrick was a man who could easily serve two masters: God and wealth. For the rest of us, God and wealth can get in the way of one another. The problem is not being wealthy. We all know, and even more especially still we often don't know, generous people whose goodness will leave the world a better place. The issue is what wealth does to us, how it changes us and can distort our priorities. In the Catholic tradition we have a name for the two obstacles that seduce away from a godly use of wealth. They're two of the seven deadly sins: pride and greed. And if ever we wanted to see a portrayal of what pride and greed look like writ large, see the documentary *Enron: The Smartest Guys in the Room*.

Founded in 1985 by the charismatic Ken Lay in Omaha, Nebraska, Enron was a natural gas company. Very successful and aggressive from the start, it expanded quickly. Enron had accountability problems early on, from which, to its eternal shame, it never learned. In 1990 Jeff Skilling joined the company and soon became the Chief Operating Officer to Lay's Chief Executive Officer. In 1991 Enron asked the government watchdog to approve "mark-to-market" accounting, where they could hedge profits on projections rather than actual income. It was approved. Throughout the 1990s Enron grew into one of the largest and most competitive energy companies in the United States, acquiring businesses all over the world, with tens of thousands of employees, posting huge profits and a soaring stock price.

Enron so fulfilled the so-called great American dream that it successfully fended off all internal, shareholder, press, and government investigations and disquiet into its actual financial state and irregular accounting.

On February 19, 2001, *Fortune* magazine journalist Bethany McLean, who could not reconcile the company's performance claims with their balance sheet, wrote a piece entitled, "Is Enron Overpriced?" It was the beginning of the end. Within ten months Enron filed for bankruptcy. Several of Enron's executives have been convicted and sentenced by the courts for the fraud and conspiracy, which led to the largest corporate collapse in world history.

Enron: The Smartest Guys in the Room is a real-life Wall Street, playing out like a Greek tragedy where twenty thousand employees lost $2 billion in pensions, retirement benefits, and health insurance. This film rightly asks how this corporation could get away with its activities for so long. Merchant bankers, stock analysts, the now-discredited and defunct accounting firm Arthur Andersen, government departments, a ruthless internal competitive culture, and all but a few brave business journalists, executives, and market advisers come in for criticism. In Enron's world, pride and greed were endemic.

It would be a mistake to hear Jesus' words this week as only applying to our personal wealth. It does that all right, but in a world where economics and business faculties are the fastest growing schools on campus, where "mom and dad stockholders," mostly through ignorance, sacrifice conscience for profits, and where, in our nation and in the world, the rich are getting richer while the poor are dying, the social gospel also asks us what sort of ethical business culture we want.

We can keep saying all we like that we want to smell the flowers and live the simple life. If we are serious about it we better start working on the pride and greed that can corrupt us personally, corporately, and as a nation. For what will it profit us to gain the entire world, and lose our very souls?

ASH WEDNESDAY

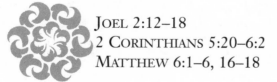

JOEL 2:12–18
2 CORINTHIANS 5:20–6:2
MATTHEW 6:1–6, 16–18

Sometimes you can be half-listening to a poor speaker and then something they say hits you right between the eyes. I had this experience a while back. The overall lecture was OK, but then the professor said, "We are as sick as our secrets." Maybe it was the truth of its sentiment, or the elegance of the phrase or even its alliteration, but it hit me like a bolt. It made the entire lecture worthwhile.

"We are as sick as our secrets."

In Lent I think we could undertake no better work of charity and penance than face up to the secrets that make us sick. And there are usually many of them. In the sacrament of penance I have heard the phrase repeatedly, "Father, I have never told anyone this before." And, rather than tense up at what is about to come, I relax because I know that if God's grace has brought the penitent to this point, the Divine Physician is also attending at that moment with gifts of healing and peace.

Where we come unstuck is that the Christian tradition has not tended to make much of a distinction between privacy and secrecy. But they are very different realities and exercise diverse powers in our lives. Privacy is something we are all entitled to, both in the personal and social sphere. It is now enshrined in canon and civil law. It says that those who have access to our personal information should only be entitled to it for a necessary greater good, and that even then, it should be accessed with our permission. Privacy protects our rights and dignity.

Secrecy is where information is concealed out of fear of detection. Think for a moment of the number of animals who conceal their den or nest from predators. And families who have a family secret that can never be spoken. We are shocked when we find out the secrets governments and corporations sit on, and as bad as the clergy-abuse allegations were for the church, for some Catholics the way in which some church officials covered it up was nearly as bad. Secrets are not about confidentiality, they are about control.

Many of us sit on secrets for the whole of our lives. It takes huge amounts of energy to keep them hidden. And just when we think we have forgotten all about them, in a flush of shame something can cause us to remember what they are, and where we buried them. But it does not have to be like this.

If Ash Wednesday means anything, it begins the annual season in our lives when we can believe again that there is nothing that God's love cannot forgive and heal. Lent is the season that puts an end to all secrets, for at Easter we will remember that God held no secrets in regard to us, but sent his Son so that all the secrets of the world might be laid bare. This is a new way of understanding that "by his wounds we are healed."

In this week's Gospel it can seem that Jesus is contradicting this and promoting a world of secrecy. He was, of course, railing against the Pharisees who loved to parade their good works and fasting before all of the Jews. They were the media junkies of their day. So Jesus tells his disciples that rather than go public with acts of penance and goodness, go about these things privately and quietly.

In Lent this year we could do no better than privately and quietly go over our life and see where the bad spirit has us in his grip. What are things of which we are ashamed? What parts of our life do we work hard to cover up? What are the secrets upon which we are sitting? These are the hiding places where the Divine Physician wants to make a house call this Lent. He knows where to go; all we have do is let him in.

We don't have to think of this challenge exclusively in personal terms either. If we do nothing about helping our families, religious communities, workplaces, cities, or nation face up to being as transparent as possible, then we are complicit in its secrecy.

Confronting personal and social sin is never easy, but what a resurrection we could enjoy at the other end of Lent if in some way we know that we are spiritually healthier for shedding our secrets. There is no point putting it off anymore, because "now is the acceptable time; see, now is the day of salvation!" (2 Cor 6:2). Let's grab it.

FIRST SUNDAY OF LENT

 GENESIS 2:7–9; 3:1–7
ROMANS 5:12–19
MATTHEW 4:1–11

Hearing the story of Adam and Eve in this week's first reading reminds me of the little boy who opened the large family Bible with fascination and looked at the old pages as he turned them.

Suddenly, something fell out of the Bible, and he picked it up and looked at it closely. It was an old leaf from a tree that had been pressed in between the pages. "Mummy, look what I found," the little boy called out. "What have you got there, dear?" his mother asked. With astonishment in the young boy's voice, he answered, "I think it's Adam's suit!"

The Genesis story about the origins of sin in the world rewards very careful reading. The serpent promises Eve two things: that her eyes will be opened to know good from evil and that this will make her like God. Such a temptation was irresistible, and nothing has changed.

Knowledge is a gift given us by God. I am always grateful for being a Catholic because, along with other long-standing Christian denominations, we highly value scholarship, rational thought, and inquiry. As anxious as the church has sometimes been about scientific investigations, our best traditions see God revealed in human thoughts and scientific achievements that ennoble our human family. It is the application of knowledge, or the way it is abused, that is harmful.

On the domestic front, many families have a resident know-it-all, the relative who has an extraordinary ability to retain facts and figures and who seems to gain a sense of self-worth by correcting us midsentence when we get a number, place, or fact wrong. He or she can be very irritating. On the world stage we have seen how scientific knowledge can seduce us into believing that all scientific achievements are good no matter how unknown the consequences of these choices might be for future generations. Every new piece of knowledge brings with it wonderful potentialities and serious responsibilities.

As this story demonstrates, the temptation to know as much as God has never been more real than it is right now.

One day a group of scientists got together and decided that man had come a long way and no longer needed God. The scientists walk up to God and say, "God, we've decided that we no longer need you. We're to the point that we can clone people and do many miraculous things, so why don't you just go on and get lost."

God listened patiently and, after the scientists were finished, said, "Very well! How about this? Let's have a woman-and-man-making contest." To which they agreed. However, God added, "How about we do this just as I did back in the old days with Adam." The scientists said, "Sure, no problem," and bent down and grabbed some dirt. God just looked at them and said, "No, no, no. You go get your own dirt!"

This week's Gospel is about knowledge too. Satan knows who Jesus is. His temptations are an attempt to get Jesus to betray his humanity and not endure the limitations of his daily life. Jesus knows that the only way to be true to his divinity is to allow us to see it shine in and through his human life. The rejection of the temptation to compromise his frail human frame gives us the hope that we, too, can glimpse the power of God's greatness in every moment we reject the desire to be directors of our own destiny and to see good triumph over evil in the choices we make.

It's a relief to know we don't have to be God!

May this Lent see us do what we are created for: to use all our knowledge to praise, reverence, and serve the Loving One who willed us into being.

SECOND SUNDAY OF LENT

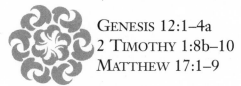 GENESIS 12:1–4a
2 TIMOTHY 1:8b–10
MATTHEW 17:1–9

Three of the stars of the Old Testament are given to us in this week's readings: Abram, Moses, and Elijah. Unfortunately, most of what we know about these men is fairly sketchy. Who can blame the young children, then, who recently wrote down the following answers in an exam on the Old Testament?

> "The first five books of the Bible are: Guinness, Exodus, Laxatives, Deuteronomy, and Numbers."

"In Guinness God gets bored of creating the world so after six days he takes the Sabbath off."

"Moses led the Hebrews to the Red Sea, where they made unleavened bread, which is bread made without any ingredients. The Egyptians were all drowned in the dessert. Afterwards, Moses went up Mount Cyanide to get the Ten Amendments. The First was when Eve told Adam to eat the apple. The Fifth was to always humor thy father and mother. The Seventh was thou shalt not admit adultery."

The Jews of Matthew's community, however, would have been able to remember by heart every detail about Abram, Moses, and Elijah. These men remain the Jews' greatest heroes. The first hearers of the transfiguration story would have immediately made all the connections between Jesus' story and Abram, Moses, and Elijah's experience of God on a mountaintop, where each has a life-changing encounter with the presence of God and is illuminated in every way. Each of them is called by God to fulfill a special task and so descend from the mountain with the strength to see it through.

Matthew is especially interested in the story of Moses. One of the refrains of the entire Gospel is that Jesus is the new Moses, the fulfillment of the Law and the light that illuminates the darkest night. As interesting as the similarities are between Moses on Sinai and Jesus on Tabor, the differences are even more revealing for us on our Lenten journey.

Moses goes up the mountain alone, Jesus takes companions with him who share in the experience and witness to it. The face of God is hidden from Moses, whereas on Tabor Jesus is given to us as the face of God for the world. On Sinai, Moses receives a code of law and is told to make sure the people obey it. On Tabor, Jesus receives a proclamation of God's love and we're told to listen to him. While Moses' face shines, Jesus' whole body is transfigured with light. Moses descends to enforce the law; Jesus comes down to die that we might live.

Just when some of us think Lent is a grim season of self-denial, the church gives us the story of Jesus' transfiguration to put our sacrifices in context. The only reason we deny ourselves anything or commit ourselves to actions of service for these forty days is to grow more deeply in love with the God who loves us into life. Penance is not meant to attack our self-esteem; it's intended to help us sort out what really matters, to cast some light in the darkness of our lives, and to focus on the relationship that gives meaning and purpose for this world and the next.

The God of Mount Tabor is not interested in each of us feeling isolated as we fulfill the letter of a legal code. He wants all of us to have hearts that listen to the gospel of love so that we can gain the power to transform the world through the sacrifices of our daily lives.

On a much gentler scale, Sunday Mass is meant to be a weekly mountaintop experience for us where we hear God call us by name and confess his love for us, where we feel reenergized for the commission we have to bear his light to the world. In this context, anything we can do this Lent that helps remove the blocks in our full response to his love must be worth the effort.

THIRD SUNDAY OF LENT

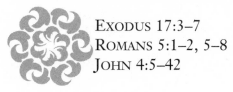

EXODUS 17:3–7
ROMANS 5:1–2, 5–8
JOHN 4:5–42

Father Jim was invited by Caritas, the Catholic Development Agency, to travel to the Philippines and see the excellent work they were doing with the monies collected in their Lenten appeal.

When he arrived in Manila, he was asked if he would like to have some exposure to the real lives of the people Caritas was helping. It was decided that for two days he would live with a family on Smoky Mountain. Smoky Mountain no longer exists, but for over thirty years it was home to nearly ten thousand people. Smoky Mountain was the refuse dump for metro-Manila. It got its name from the smoldering fire that was at the core of the mountain of rubbish. People lived on three sides of this mountain of waste and made their homes and livelihood from the city's refuse.

Jim had heard of Smoky Mountain, but nothing prepared him for the reality. He smelled it before he saw it, and when he saw it he couldn't believe it. The crest of the hill was indeed billowing smoke, and canals of water surrounded it. Running water was only available at public pumps. Over the canals were semi-public cubicles where people showered and used open toilets. As the bulldozers shoveled the day's deposit into the mountainside, the residents picked through the collection to see what could be salvaged. Homes were made of every weather-resistant material imaginable.

Jim met the Jesuits who looked after the Smoky Mountain parish. They were campaigning to have it shut down. The parish priest took him to meet the family with whom he would be staying. On a hot, humid afternoon he started the climb to Bing's home. There were children everywhere—dirty, energetic, scavenging children. His heart was close to breaking; his stomach was dry-retching.

When he arrived at Bing's neatly kept home he was given a warm welcome. Bing saw that Jim was hot and bothered by his new surroundings and offered him a drink of water. Nothing prepared Jim for this dilemma: How far was he prepared to share in the life of the poor? All Jim could think of were the diseases he could catch from drinking water from the pump. As thirsty as he was he declined the offer, knowing that later he would privately gulp down one of the bottles of water in his backpack. Jim watched as the glasses of water were served on a tray. As he chatted with the family about Smoky Mountain he felt a fraud. Bing's daughter emerged with a sealed bottle of water and proceeded to fill up all the glasses. On seeing the bottle, Jim had a change of mind and accepted the water. Bing then produced a plastic glass in a sealed package for Jim's use. Flushed with embarrassment, all he could think of was Jesus and the woman at the well.

At that famous well, Jesus enters the world of a poor Samaritan woman who has been dumped five times by the men who married her. By asking for a drink, by engaging her in conversation, by understanding her situation, and offering her a way out of the cycle of emotional abuse in which she was caught, Jesus gives her the greatest gift of all: personal dignity. This changes her life and turns her into one of the earliest missionaries in John's Gospel.

Although separated by time and space, a drink of water helped a Samaritan woman and Father Jim confront the embarrassment of their worlds, their quick and inaccurate judgments, and reassess the choices that could lead them to life. Both of them recognized that no matter how good the gift of water was that day, the unknown and unexpected Giver of the gift was so much greater.

May the season of Lent help us do the same.

FOURTH SUNDAY OF LENT

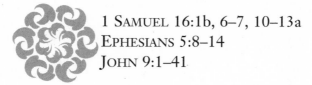

1 Samuel 16:1b, 6–7, 10–13a
Ephesians 5:8–14
John 9:1–41

I have never been able to reconcile the long faces some of us put on in Lent with the prayers of the church that describe this as "a joyful season." The following story takes seriously that laughter is an essential element of our Lenten observance.

> Once upon a time in a nice little forest, there lived an orphaned bunny and an orphaned snake. By surprising coincidence, both were blind from birth.
>
> One day, the bunny was hopping through the forest while the snake was slithering along the same path. The bunny tripped over the snake and fell down. "Oh, my," said the bunny, "I'm terribly sorry. I didn't mean to hurt you. I've been blind since birth, so I can't see where I'm going. In fact, I'm also an orphan, so I don't even know what I am." "It's quite OK," replied the snake, "my story is much the same as yours. I've been blind since birth and never knew my mother. Tell you what, I could slither over you, and figure out what you are."

"Oh, that would be wonderful," replied the bunny. So the snake slithered all over the bunny, and said, "Well, you're covered with soft fur, you have really long ears, your nose twitches, and you have a soft cottony tail. I'd say that you must be a bunny."

"Oh, thank you! Thank you," cried the bunny in obvious excitement. The bunny then suggested to the snake, "Maybe I could feel you with my paw, and help you in the same way you've helped me." So the bunny felt the snake all over, and remarked, "Well, you're scaly and smooth, you have a forked tongue, you're impossible to pin down, and you have no backbone at all. I'd say you must be a contractor, a consultant, or possibly someone in senior management."

On reflection, the Gospel of the man born blind is a joyful one too. Imagine this man's elation at having his sight restored. As the story develops, the all-seeing Pharisees move to spiritual blindness by putting on the blinkers of the law. They cannot recognize Jesus or his works of mercy because of their tunnel vision. Jesus doesn't fit their worldview. Meanwhile, the blind beggar, who has sight restored, goes on to gain insight about who Jesus is and the way that God works in the world; he begins to see how shallow and pathetic the Pharisees really are.

This Gospel also contains a critical theological lesson: Disability and illness do not come from personal sinfulness. It's surprising that we need to keep saying this, but too readily we hear otherwise intelligent and good Christians, for example, telling us that some illnesses have been "sent" by God as punishment for sins, or they wonder what their families have "done" to deserve disabled children. It's true that God permits us to live in an imperfect world where we are prone to illness and disability. But that same world gives us the freedom to be creative in the face of adversity, to be compassionate with those who are sick or disabled, and to be free to believe that there is a purpose for each human life. God, the source of all life, does not actively send bad things to us, instead, he is our constant companion in dealing with them, giving us the courage and strength to cope with, and sometimes overcome, them.

The task of this joyful season is to bring our good humor and compassion to bear on the blind spots in our own lives and be on our guard for the times when we are too confident about who God is, how he works, or what he can or cannot do. May it never be said of us that we were so consumed by our own religious vision that we missed God's woods for the trees.

FIFTH SUNDAY OF LENT

 EZEKIEL 37:12–14
ROMANS 8:8–11
JOHN 11:1–45

The plunging of an adult or an infant into the baptismal font three times is the most important moment in the baptismal ceremony, and meant to be the most moving one as well. Most of us understand that this action is associated with the Trinity. It is. But the more ancient association is with the three days Jesus lay in the tomb. This is one reason why the church now encourages candidates for baptism to be fully immersed wherever practicable. The sprinkling of water over a catechumen's head just doesn't capture the drama which the ritual intends. But when we see a person take a breath, plunge under the water, and come up for air three times, we can powerfully see the identification between Jesus' time in the tomb and the person rising to new life in Christ.

The season of Lent has its origins in third-century Egypt, where there was a commemoration of Jesus' forty days in the desert. In the fourth century, these forty days were moved to their present location in the church's calendar as the final preparation time for baptismal candidates at Easter, and by the fifth century these penitential and baptismal focuses came together as one season for all believers to observe. Even the word *Lent*, from the old English word *lencten*, meaning spring, alerted Christians in the northern hemisphere that this season was linked to the waking of nature after the long sleep of winter. Lent is about waking up to see that light and life have come in Christ.

Over the centuries, the church has tended to place more emphasis on penance than baptism in the Lenten season. The Second Vatican Council, however, went back to the most ancient sources of this season, reestablished the Rite of Christian Initiation of Adults, and encouraged us to see the link between our acts of penance and our ongoing conversion to Christ expressed in the baptismal promises made for us many years before.

On this last Sunday in Lent, Lazarus is given to us to help us think about the tombs in which we lie hidden and the life to which we are called. The bad spirit seduces most of us into having some form of secretive life. It might be a secret we can't tell, a sin we can't confess, or a memory we want to bury. At its worst, it can be a lifestyle or a pattern of unethical behavior we have divorced from the rest of our lives. We may even con ourselves into believing that all of this is normal and "not so bad."

These tombs often look similar. They seem small on the surface, but as we get away with our secrets we bury ourselves in them more deeply. We jealously guard the entrance, displacing energy to defend our tombs, and we're ashamed if anyone rolls away the stone and sees the mess inside.

But this Sunday Jesus stands at the entrance of our tombs and calls us out of them. We're asked to face down the bad spirit that keeps us locked in secrecy, to move away from shame, embrace repentance, recognize the price to be paid for being true to what's best in ourselves, and we're invited to know the light and life of Christ's healing and forgiveness.

No one can pretend that this journey is easy, but it's what Lent is all about: the journey from the tomb of our own particular deaths, through penance, to the new life of Easter. May the Eucharist allow us to see the Lord stand at our tomb and gently call us by name, "Come forth." And at his word may we be unbound and let free.

PASSION SUNDAY (PALM SUNDAY)

Procession: MATTHEW 21:1–11
ISAIAH 50:4–7
PHILIPPIANS 2:6–11
MATTHEW 26:14—27:66

As a child, I can remember our diocese having large processions for the feasts of Corpus Christi, Christ the King, and one of the Marian feast days. They were called "public demonstrations of Catholic faith." For children, they were often long and boring, but it did give us a sense that we belonged to something big, and someone bigger, and that our faith had a "stand up and be counted" dimension to it. For many Catholics today, large-scale religious processions are quickly becoming a thing of the past. That's a pity.

The point of religious processions is not just to get us from one location to the next. It is also to mark a rite of passage. Think of the smaller processions most Christians undertake in their lives: to the baptismal font, down the aisle to take their marriage vows, to graduate from a school or college, and to be bid farewell. In each case, we recess out of the church differently from how we entered it: as a newly initiated member of the Christian community; as a husband or wife; as a graduate; and to be buried.

The Palm Sunday procession is the last congregational procession mandated by the missal to be observed throughout the entire church. Recalling Jesus' procession into Jerusalem, this procession is not meant to be an historical pageant. Like all liturgical moments, it's meant to intersect with our own lives and speak to our journey of faith. What makes this procession so powerful is that it starts with hysteria and ends in death. And that tells us something we need to hear.

Matthew's account of the Passion is very tough on the Jewish leaders. His entire Gospel has been preparing the hearer for this. Matthew shows that even though the Jews had the New Moses right in front of them, they were unable to recognize him because he didn't fit their expectations of the Messiah. The crowd in Jerusalem receives him like a pop star, acclaiming him as their own. By week's end, the Chief Priests and elders manipulate the crowd's enthusiasm to force Pilate to execute Jesus. And throughout it all—during the adulation of the crowd, their change of allegiance to Barabbas, and at his trial—Jesus hardly says a word. In Matthew's Gospel, Jesus' silence is deafening.

In the journey of faith we should always be on our guard against being part of a manipulated crowd. The unchecked enthusiasms of a crowd can carry us away to places, people, or things we would not ordinarily choose and should not embrace. If we are vulnerable, then a gifted guru, through his or her version of eternal life, can whip us into a frenzy. We only have to look at the power of the media and advertising to see how susceptible we are to becoming a slave to fashionable ideologies, dress codes, and what and who is in or out. Every time we buy something because someone else has it or because we convince ourselves that our wants are really our needs, the crowd has won. The story of Passion Sunday is that manipulation of a crowd, even by legitimate authorities, can be the beginning of spiritual death. Hype often distorts priorities, blurs good judgment, and can choose expediency over integrity.

So what's the remedy to being manipulated, to regaining a sense of what really matters, to standing up against the crowd for the values we know are right? Jesus shows us in Matthew's Gospel. It starts with silence. It's being a contemplative in a manic world and praying for the courage to dissent from the crowd's hyped-up madness.

As we process into Holy Week, this annual rite of passage for our faith, may we model our lives on Jesus in every way by creating the silence we need in our lives to sort out our priorities, by using silence powerfully in a world that loves words, but has very little to say about our meaning and destiny, and allowing our sacrificial love, even to the point of death, to do all the talking.

HOLY THURSDAY

EXODUS 12:1–8, 11–14
1 CORINTHIANS 11:23–26
JOHN 13:1–15

The verses of a well know African American soul song runs, "Let us break bread…drink wine…love one another…(and) praise God together on our knees." These verses finish, "When I fall on my knees with my face to the rising Son, O Lord, have mercy on me."

The earliest name the Christians gave to the Eucharist was "the breaking of the bread." In the most ancient description of the Eucharist in the New Testament, St. Paul says in the First Letter to the Corinthians that he is handing on what he received: that to share in the Lord's supper we must break the bread and drink the cup. In the story of the disciples on the road to Emmaus, they only recognize Jesus when, at journey's end, while at table, the bread is broken. And in the Acts of the Apostles we're told several times how the earliest Christians gathered in one another's homes for the breaking of the bread.

Whatever else the Eucharist meant to the early church, the action of breaking apart and pouring out captured how they wanted to remember Jesus and the meal he gave them. Although these days other terms like *Mass* and *Eucharist* are much more frequently used for our ritual of word and sacrament, to this day the liturgy maintains a connection with this legacy in the *fractio panis*, the breaking of the bread, during which we sing the Lamb of God.

If Easter is to come alive for us, then, we too have to be prepared to be broken and poured out in love for our world. No wonder St. Augustine encourages Christians taking communion in the fifth century to "become what you eat." It's not just the static presence of Christ we're asked to imitate, but the challenge to enter into his activity of sacrificial love. Every time we come forward and receive communion we say "Amen" to Jesus Christ as body broken and blood poured out. In doing so, we reaffirm that this is how far God went to show his love for us. This is also the intimate moment where God meets us in the most broken parts of our lives and in the times we feel completely poured out. God is a companion in our suffering and sacrifices. In turn, it shows us how we should live. Everyone who receives Christ in communion says they are prepared to pay the price of being one with him in being broken and poured out in love for the world.

Breaking and pouring, however, are but two of the four actions given to us by Jesus. The other two are washing and sending. More than anyone else, St. John in his Gospel knew how interconnected all these are. These last two actions alert us to the fact that what we do away from the Eucharist indicates how seriously we take what we do here. At the end of every Mass we are told to go out and "love and serve the Lord." Even the term *Mass* comes the Latin word *missa*—"to be sent."

By taking up Jesus' commission to serve, we show how his life, death, and resurrection continue to "Easter in us" and change the world for good. As a result of that first Holy Thursday there is no service too small, no act of kindness too insignificant, and no moment of love too inconsequential in our service of Christ's kingdom. We are people who look for opportunities to take up the commission to serve all those who feel spent with the brokenness of their lives.

And when we do this, we discover it has an extraordinary effect on us. With our brothers and sisters whom we serve, we can recognize the face of the Rising Son and praise God together on our knees.

GOOD FRIDAY

 Isaiah 52:13—53:12
Hebrews 4:14–16; 5:7–9
John 18:1—19:42

Given that on Good Friday we hear the greatest story ever told, let us simply think about the three great questions in John's Passion:

"Who are you looking for?"
"What charge do you bring against this man?"
"Aren't you another of that man's disciples?"

In the Passion the answers run:

"Jesus of Nazareth."
"King of the Jews."
"I am not."

We would not be here today if our answer to the first question was not the same as the soldiers. For vastly different reasons, we also seek Jesus of Nazareth. Rather than arrest him, however, we're here because his love has arrested us. Rather than mock the kingdom he proclaimed, we are heirs to it, servants of his reign. Rather than condemn him to be crucified, we see in his death our path to freedom. "Who are we looking for?" Jesus of Nazareth is the one we seek.

The second question belongs to Pilate. On the basis of the charge that Jesus is a rival king to Caesar, he is condemned to death. All these years later we know Jesus still presides over a kingdom of justice and peace. He remains a threat to anyone in our world, anyone here today, who stands against faith, hope, and love. "What charge do you bring against this man?" We stand accused of claiming his reign in our lives.

The third question is to Peter. Although Peter wanted to remain faithful to Jesus, fear got the better of him. Most of us can be empathetic to his plight. Faced with a choice between Jesus and death, how many of us would choose death? And because actions always speak louder than words, every time we compromise the goodness of God within us or work to undermine another person's rights to dignity and life, we join Peter around that fire denying that we are a disciple of Jesus. "Aren't you another of that man's disciples?" If only we were more so.

The good news today is that apprehension, accusation, and denial were not the last words in Jesus' life. And because of him, they're not the last words in our lives either.

No matter what we've done or what we're doing, nothing can separate us from the love of God poured out in Jesus Christ the Lord. No matter what particular crosses we carried to Good Friday, we believe that God's commitment to us was such that he even went to suffering and death to reveal his saving love.

If we feel apprehensive, allow Christ to arrest us with his peace. If we stand accused of destructive behavior, allow Christ to convert our hearts and change our lives. If we deny Christ by what we say or how we live, let's decide today to be as faithful to him as he is to us.

I promise you that by doing this a surprising thing will happen. Even in the midst of carrying our own particular crosses, we will feel the weight lifted as the one who loves us helps shoulder our burdens as well.

No wonder we call this solemn feast "Good Friday." What greater goodness could we know than that the cross of Jesus reveals that our God, whether named or not, is our companion at every step of life's journey?

EASTER VIGIL

Genesis 1:1—2:2; 22:1–18
Exodus 14:15—15:1
Isaiah 54:5–14; 55:1–11
Baruch 3:9–15, 32—4:4
Ezekiel 36:16–17a, 18–28
Romans 6:3–11
Matthew 28:1–10

At the Easter Vigil we enjoy listening to one of the most ancient and important hymns in the Church's tradition: the Exsultet, literarily, Rejoice! In the early church, the deacon would have known the Exsultet by heart. The honor of singing it was handed down from one generation to the next.

There are several images in the Exsultet that help us name our joy: freedom from slavery; an end to fear; the triumph of life over death; and God's utter fidelity to his Son, Jesus. The Exsultet sings that God has not done this because we have earned or deserved it, but simply because he loves us. This is the holiest of nights because it seals the family covenant between God and us. We are coheirs with Jesus, sons and daughters of God. Is it any wonder, then, that heaven and earth are called to explode with joy?

As Christians, Easter joy is meant to mark our lives—though if some of us are truly joyful we should start by telling our faces about it! Not that we can, or should, walk around perpetually smiling. Christian joy is more profound than that. It's about facing up to the most difficult and tragic moments in our lives knowing that we don't have to be afraid, that God's faithful love will see life win out over death.

We all know this is easier said than done. Take the Gospel for example. The women are told twice to tell the disciples to go to Galilee where they will meet Jesus for themselves. I've always wondered about Galilee. What a desolate trip that must have been for the disciples. Believing the extraordinary story of Mary Magdalene and her companions, the disciples set out in fear of their lives, and in the hope of seeing Jesus raised from the dead. There were no reassurances from anyone's previous experience. No guidebooks to say what to look for at the end. Not even a promise from Jesus himself. Just an instruction, "Go quickly and tell his disciples, 'He has been raised from the dead, and indeed he is going ahead of you to Galilee; there you will see him.'"

Galilee does not have to be a place for us. It's a situation, a frame of mind, or a choice we make. Our particular Galilee could be the desolate journey of physical, emotional, or spiritual pain. It could be dashed promises, broken relationships, or unrealized hopes. Whatever it is, this night promises us that Christ is not only there when we arrive, he has gone ahead of us, to that desolate place, so that we might have loving arms in which to fall at journey's end.

The reason we are so exultant is that the first Jerusalem did not have the last word in Jesus' life. God did. So, all our deaths in Jerusalem and all our fearful, anxious trips to Galilee can end in new life and fresh starts.

With the whole church we can make Mary Magdalene's invitation to the disciples our own. This Easter let's go to Galilee, wherever and whatever it might be, and find the Lord there. Then, we can explode with joy and sing Christ Risen.

EASTER SUNDAY

ACTS 10:34a, 37–43
COLOSSIANS 3:1–4 *or* 1 CORINTHIANS 5:6b–8
JOHN 20:1–9 *or* MATTHEW 28:1–10
EVENING: LUKE 24:13–35

If we did a survey today of what words we associate with the name Mary Magdalene, chances are *prostitute* would be at the top of the list. The Christian tradition has not been very kind to Mary or her memory. There is nothing in the New Testament about her being a woman in prostitution. Unfortunately, there are other women in the gospels who have "a bad reputation in the town" or weep at Jesus' feet and wipe their tears away with their hair, or are caught in the "very act of adultery," or pour oil over Jesus' head. These women are not Mary of Magdala. The first we hear of Mary Magdalene is that she has seven demons cast out of her by Jesus. We're not told what these demons are, but given what people wrongly thought at the time, they could have been a tummy complaint, acne, and a twitch! There is nothing in the text to suggest that they were sexual demons.

Jesus Christ Superstar didn't do Mary Magdalene's saucy notoriety any favors by giving her character the song of the show, "I don't know how to love him." Curiously, some brides have wanted this song sung at their weddings, to which I reply when they ask if it's OK with me, "If you don't know how to love him, you shouldn't be here!"

The most important thing we know about Mary Magdalene is that she is the first to experience the Risen Christ and is the first Christian missionary, the apostle to the apostles. One detail is especially poignant in the week's Gospel. We're told that Mary encountered the Risen Christ while weeping outside Jesus' tomb. She felt a double loss on that first Easter Sunday. Not only was she grieving for the loss of the One whom she had seen tortured to death, but she also wept for what she thought was the ultimate insult inflicted on Him—the desecration of his grave and the stealing of his corpse.

Mary Magdalene is the patron saint of those of us who have ever stood at tombs and wept. And she shows us that in the midst of any grief Christ comes to us and calls by name.

Because of Mary's tears and even more because of her evangelization, we believe that there is not a human being who has died in the last year, or any year, who is not known to God by name. God makes no distinction between the rich or poor, whether we are from a developing or developed country, whether we are Christian, Muslim, or atheist; we are all called by name to share in his life according to the grace which has enabled us to do so. God knows not only our name; he knows our heart, our history, and our selves.

What the first Easter tells us is that we are sent out armed with the knowledge of Christ's sacrificial love to live it out in the world. There is not a person in the Gospel for whom the encounter with the Risen Christ doesn't turn around his or her life. And the same must be true for us. Easter only means something for the world if we live it out each day this year, in the joyful times ahead, and when even we weep in the dark.

How do we do that?

Jesus tells Mary Magdalene that there is no longer an exclusive God, but his God and Father is now Mary's God and Father. And maybe that's a good place to start. All people of faith and goodwill, whether they realize it or not, and some in vastly different cultural ways, seek and serve the same God.

As a result of that first Easter, God is not a great "other" unknown to us, or distant from our experience. Our God is a loving Father, a saving Son, and a comforting Holy Spirit. Easter also means that there is not another person on this earth who can be "other" to us, unworthy of our care. Jesus was not raised from the dead for us alone, but for all people, so that we might know that the best way to be worthy of him calling us by name is in living lives of faith, hope, and love. Along with Christ, may these gifts rise in us this joyous Easter Day.

SECOND SUNDAY OF EASTER

 ACTS 2:42–47
1 PETER 1:3–9
JOHN 20:19–31

The Gospel story about doubting Thomas has to be one of the most misunderstood episodes in the New Testament. If you're like me, for years we have been consoled by Thomas doubting that Jesus had been raised from the dead. Thomas's doubts were in Jesus, we have been led to believe. But let's read the story very carefully. It's not Jesus Thomas doubts, it's the disciples. In fact, when Jesus appears to them seven days later, Thomas has the opportunity to share in the experience of the Risen Lord and like the others he immediately confesses Easter faith.

There are three elements in this story that should give us great comfort. The first is that Thomas doubts the early church, and not just in regard to a minor issue of discipline or procedure. He doubts the central Christian message: that God raised Jesus from the dead. Some of us, too, at various times in our lives, can have doubts about all sorts of things in our faith.

There are very few Catholics who get through life without asking some serious questions of God, about Jesus, the Spirit, and the church. These questions are good in themselves. They are necessary for a mature, adult faith. What we need to ensure is that we sincerely want answers to the questions we ask and not just use them to justify our wandering away from our faith. Thomas is the patron saint of all of us who sometimes struggle to believe what everyone else in the church seems to accept. And he is also the patron saint of those of us who seek the courage and patience to wait for the answers.

The second consoling fact to this story concerns the earliest church. Even though they are filled with the presence of the Risen Lord and though Thomas refuses to believe their witness, they remain faithful to him in his doubts. We know this because he is still with them a week later. They didn't expel him from the group or excommunicate him; they held on to him in the hope that he would experience the Lord for himself.

Sadly for us today, there are some who argue that Catholics who struggle with their faith should "shape up or ship out." While every group has its boundaries and there are limits to what people can dissent from, we could take the earliest church as our model and stay faithful to our doubters and help them come to see the transforming truth that has changed our lives.

The final element in this extraordinary story that can help us in our Easter faith concerns the significance of the time between the first and second appearances of Jesus. We're told it was seven days, and the parallel to the story of creation would not have been lost on the first hearers of John's Gospel. And even though the earliest disciples experience the Risen Lord on Easter Sunday, they are still locked in their fears one week later. The creation of the early church, the movement of its earliest leaders from timidity to boldness, took time, and having a doubter in their midst ends up a great blessing for them all, for Christ is present at every step of the church's creation and re-creation as well.

This story was written for people like us who do not have access to the historical Jesus. The birth of the church is an ongoing act of God's creation in every generation. It takes time, and people will be at different stages at different moments. Our fidelity to one another on the long journey of faith is only surpassed by our crucified God who does not give up on us, no matter how many questions we ask or how much we doubt.

May the Eucharist give us confidence enough to hold on to each other in good times and bad so that we can all continue to experience his presence and have life in his name.

THIRD SUNDAY OF EASTER

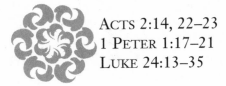

ACTS 2:14, 22–23
1 PETER 1:17–21
LUKE 24:13–35

With very good reason, the story of the road to Emmaus is thought to be the best parallel we have in the New Testament to our weekly celebration of the Eucharist. This idea could be a little surprising for some who might think the Last Supper would hold more similarities. Luke, however, reminds his community, who are like us, that even though they are prevented from seeing Jesus, they can still have a life-changing experience of his presence.

The disciples are on a journey of faith and Jesus meets them where they are, as they are. This is a critical detail in the story. Jesus listens to their expectations, hopes, and disappointments, and only after they have expressed the reality of their situation does Christ open the scriptures to them. In doing so he takes their disillusionment and enables them to see the connections with the story of salvation. This leads them to hope. Even then, they do not recognize who Jesus is until he breaks the bread, and in that action he is revealed as the one in whom they had been hoping. This experience drives them back to Jerusalem to witness to the power of Christ's resurrection.

Every Sunday, as part of our journey of faith, we embark on our road to Emmaus. There is never any point in us coming here pretending to be different from how we actually feel and who we are. God sees our heart and mind and wants to meet us in the midst of our life, whatever it may be like. The Emmaus story teaches us that Jesus first wants to listen to us before he wants us to listen to him.

Emmaus, however, was not just about the disciples and their lives, in the same way that the Eucharist is not just about our lives either. Christ opens the scriptures to us each week so that we can make sense of our experience, see the ways in which God is present and absent, and recognize our own foolishness. As with the Emmaus disciples, we are welcomed to the table of the Lord where we recognize Christ in the breaking of the bread and the pouring of the cup. This meal enables us to go out from here and proclaim to all we meet that Christ is risen.

One of the things the church values most deeply is its connection to the experience of the earliest church. And rightly so! It's a great privilege for us to recall that what we do here each Sunday is built upon the faith and weekly celebration of countless generations.

And though, appropriately, many things can be different in various cultural settings for the Eucharist throughout the world, several elements always stay the same. It is the Risen Christ who accompanies us, listens to us, opens our minds to the scriptures, hosts us at his table, and sends us out to tell the world that he has been raised from the dead.

This is the best way to understand ourselves as "traditional Catholics." We share with thousands of generations the same fire of God's faithful love burning in our hearts as we are welcomed here each week, are listened to, taught, nourished, and sent out to do our bit for the coming of Christ's kingdom.

FOURTH SUNDAY OF EASTER

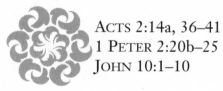

ACTS 2:14a, 36–41
1 PETER 2:20b–25
JOHN 10:1–10

I have a friend who is a great lover of classical music. His knowledge of it is vast. He only needs to hear a few bars of most musical works and he confidently declares, "Mozart's Piano Concerto in A" or "Stravinsky's *Rite of Spring*." He's always right.

Another of his superfluous, but amusing gifts is to pick the singer. He can hear a soprano and declare it to be Callas, Te Kanawa, or Sutherland. He knows which of the three tenors is belting out that particular top C. Again, he's almost always right. What intrigues me about this gift is that he remembers the timbres of each voice, not just the famous ones, but some rather obscure soloists as well. It helps that he has listened to the sound of these voices for years. It's the same with recognizing the voice of Christ—it comes with practice and exposure to it.

In our world there are a multitude of voices clamoring for attention. The loudest voices we hear are not always the wisest ones. Jesus invites us to attune our listening to the sound of his voice so that even if it is faintly heard amidst the noise, we can lift our heads, turn our gaze, and walk toward it.

More than ever, there are some voices that entice us away from the gospel. We are told that it is impossible to be happy unless we are wealthy. Impossible to be fulfilled unless we are sexually active with several partners. Impossible to be free unless we answer to no one.

And in this crowded marketplace the voice of Jesus keeps saying the same thing it's been saying for two thousand years. Happiness is found in sharing what we can with the poor, in being faithful and loving in all our relationships, and in surrendering our freedom to the service of his kingdom of justice and peace.

The problem is not that Jesus should yell more loudly, it is that, at crucial moments in our lives when we have to make important decisions, we often close our ears. We refuse to listen to any other voice except the one that reinforces the destructive decision we want to make. Jesus reminds us in the week's Gospel that this choice can be a moment of death. What his call offers is life, and life abundantly. But at various times we blot it out and tune our hearing elsewhere.

There are, however, at least two times in our lives when we respond immediately to the sound of a loving voice: as a baby and in old age. A parent's voice soothes and reassures a baby as no other. Look at how a screaming child calms down as a mother nurses it. Look at how a loved one's voice comforts and gives confidence to an older person when they are distressed or disoriented.

What wonderful images these very human moments provide in terms of hearing the voice of the Good Shepherd. At the moment of our death, in the midst of all the other sounds we hear as we leave this world, we will hear Christ's voice—soothing, reassuring, comforting, and confident. And it's our prayer that at that moment we will do what we have tried to do throughout our lives—we will walk straight toward it.

Now that will be life, and life abundantly.

FIFTH SUNDAY OF EASTER

ACTS 6:1–7
1 PETER 2:4–9
JOHN 14:1–12

For many people, "going home" means a return to comfort and security.

In the best homes, children are unafraid, they know that their home is a buffer against some harsh realities beyond the door. As adults, we carry that desire for security into all the various homes in which we live.

When we reflect on our childhood homes, many of us can say of it what Jesus says of himself. It was the first place almost all of us learned about "The Way." The earliest Christians were called people of the Way. It's a rich image denoting that Christianity is not an idea; it's a way of living, a path to follow.

For better or worse, one of the distinctive features of most of our homes is that it's also where we are told "the truth." Sometimes that deflates our egos or means we hear things we would rather not listen to. But hopefully the comfort and love that accompany this truth telling come from the ease and care in the relationships at home. Most families don't pull any punches with the truth because they know us too well and love us too much.

Most adults also remember their childhood houses as lively. "The life" in our homes was about the buzz of children going to and from school, various friends calling, the reign of organized chaos where space was claimed and a position defended. Minor dramas were never far away and life was lived to the full.

It's not by accident that the image of Jesus preparing us a house and being the Way, the Truth, and the Life are put together in the week's Gospel. In another part of John's Gospel, Jesus goes further in describing himself as our master builder, as our home and even our lodger. We are told to make a home in him as he makes a home in us. What a terrific image of the intimacy Christ wants to share with us, and we with him!

The best homes, however, do not just protect and keep their occupants safe for eternity. A home is a means to an end, which is to give us the stability and sanity we need to keep going out to the world beyond it. In the same way, our home of faith with Jesus enables us to keep going out to a sometimes hostile world and share with others the Way, the Truth, and the Life that sustains us. In a world where 70 percent of all people have substandard housing and millions of displaced people have to create homes wherever they are, we have our work cut out for us.

The Way we follow is about justice, development, and peace for all people everywhere and not just the select few who can build the biggest mansions on earth. We are invited to keep speaking the Truth even if that makes us unpopular or different or at odds with the majority. And we have to keep living the Life that sees that our greatest joy comes from human dignity being celebrated everywhere.

If all Christians lived out this Way, Truth, and Life, we would, by his grace, fulfill Jesus' extraordinary prophecy that we could do greater works than he did. Now that's a challenge to take with us into the coming week!

SIXTH SUNDAY OF EASTER

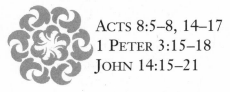

Acts 8:5–8, 14–17
1 Peter 3:15–18
John 14:15–21

There are two strong images in this week's Gospel: the law and love. In a few verses Jesus keeps moving between the two ideas because he knows how closely related they are.

This can seem curious to modern ears because we have been duped into thinking that the law is the enemy of love, and that only freedom and joy are love's fruits. But think for a moment of people or projects we love, ones to which we are committed. We don't need a rule book to call us to the most generous and sacrificial behavior in their regard. We respond "above and beyond the call of duty" not because of the law, but because of love. Jesus teaches us today that obedience to his commandments is a subset of our loving relationship with him.

The word *obedience* comes from the Latin word *oboedire*, meaning "to listen carefully." That's a gentler way of understanding Jesus' call. The more obedient we are to Christ's commandments, the more we are listening to his Spirit's call in our lives. And what are these commandments to which we have to listen? Jesus said the whole law and the prophets could be summarized as "You shall love the Lord your God with all your heart, and with all your soul, and with all your mind.... You shall love your neighbor as yourself" (Matt 22: 37, 39). If this seems too general a statement, then Paul helps us fill out the details. Like Jesus, St. Paul tells us the law of love is not primarily revealed in what we say, or how we feel, but in what we do. Christian love is an intensely practical affair. When we are patient, kind, and gentle with each other, we are obeying the law of love. So too when we forgive each other, tell the truth, and remain faithful, we are listening most carefully to Christ's commandments.

St. Paul also tells us that another of the fruits of Christian love is self-control. Sacrifice and self-control are really where the law of love comes into its own. The secular world keeps peddling the myth that self-expression is the only way to happiness. Most of us can see how irrational this position is and how unlivable the world would be if everyone expressed all their feelings and desires as they wished. Sometimes the most loving thing is to do nothing. If we are very angry with friends, for example, abusing them physically or verbally won't help. If we are sexually attracted to our best friend's spouse, having an affair will end in tears. On a more positive note, if we are alert to the poverty in which others live in our world, making sacrifices so that they might have something will not take away from us at all. Self-control is the ally of love and it helps us sort out the appropriate time to undertake the appropriate action.

The path to true happiness is found in being self-controlled. The problem is that self-control doesn't come easily. We need to train ourselves in its art and practice it regularly and consistently so that we can enjoy seeing the benefits of winning smaller battles before we venture out on larger campaigns. If we cultivate an attitude of self-control we can be sure that when we most need to exercise it we are in charge of our emotional life rather than it being in charge of us.

May the Eucharist effect a change of heart in us. May we embrace sacrifice and self-control as the doors to an even greater practical experience of the Risen Christ's law of love.

SEVENTH SUNDAY OF EASTER

ACTS 1:12–14
1 PETER 4:13–16
JOHN 17:1–11A

These days we have all learned to live with "call options" when we telephone a variety of places. I look back with nostalgia on the old days of speaking with a human being as soon as the phone was answered. The other day on the phone, while waiting for my option to be opted for, I wondered what would happen if God decided to install voice mail?

Imagine praying and hearing this:

>Thank you for calling heaven. Please select one of the following options:
>Press 1 for Requests;
>Press 2 for Thanksgiving;
>Press 3 for Complaints;
>Press 4 for All Other Personal Inquiries;

Press 5 for Information on the Whereabouts of Deceased Family and Friends;

Press 6 for Your Heavenly Reservation.

Heaven is closed for the Jewish, Christian, and Muslim holy days; please pray again on Monday morning at 8.30 a.m. If you need emergency assistance when this office is closed, contact your local priest, rabbi or imam.

Then, while waiting, we would hear, on a never-ending loop, King David sing a psalm, Mary sing the Magnificat, or Miriam belt out her Red Sea hit with the original tambourine accompaniment. Every twenty seconds a familiar voice would cut back in, "I'm sorry, heaven is busy helping other sinners right now. However, your prayer is important to us and will be answered in the order it was received, so please stay on the line."

After fifteen minutes the voice would say, "Our computers show that you have already prayed *three* times today. Please hang up and try again tomorrow."

In the Acts of the Apostles we are told that the earliest church was constantly devoting themselves to prayer, and John's Gospel has Jesus praying for himself and his followers. One of the unexpected gifts of Easter is the ease with which we should be able to pray. Our God cannot do more to show us how real and powerful his love for us is than in the life, death, and resurrection of Jesus. Through Jesus we have been brought into the family of God and our prayer is like dinnertime conversation, catching up on how the day is going and alerting our father and brother to what's in store in the coming days.

Jesuit priest Frank Wallace wrote a book on prayer that I've never read. I am sure it's a fine book, but I've never got past the front cover. It's called *Encounter, Not Performance.* That about says it all. Most of us who find prayer difficult think that prayer is about a performance that will change God. We turn up and put on a show that we hope God will find pleasing. This is similar to pressing the right "call option."

Frank Wallace, however, says prayer is an encounter. We do not have to *do* anything in prayer. God does not need a show from us, in fact the more we pretend before God, the more God must wonder why we are going through this routine. Following the witness of Jesus and the leaders of the early church, we just have to be available to God and experience his loving presence in any way that helps us draw closer to the one who created, loves, sustains, and saves us. What helps one person in prayer may not help someone else, and so the rich diversity in the church's tradition in prayer reflects the variety of ways we can encounter God. The best rule of thumb I know for prayer is "if it helps, do it; if it doesn't, don't."

That said, my favorite prayer at the moment is called The Senility Prayer: "God grant me the senility to forget the people I never liked anyway, the good fortune to run into the ones I do, and the eyesight to tell the difference."

Amen.

ASCENSION OF THE LORD

ACTS 1:1–11
EPHESIANS 1:17–23
MATTHEW 28:16–20

As a boy, Sir Edmund Hillary came to speak at my school. I can remember the fuss surrounding the visit of the first person to scale Mount Everest. And though there is now a school of thought that holds that he was beaten to the summit by Tenzing Norgay, his Nepalese colleague, there was an aura around this New Zealander who had been to the top of the world.

Some of my usually dour teachers were in awe of Sir Edmund. There was more than a little hero worship going on that day. Rather surprisingly, in his address Sir Edmund did not say very much about his adventure to the peak. He was much more interested in what we do to each other on the plains than what he did on the mountaintop. He spoke about justice, peace, and the dignity of humanity. I can vividly remember him sending us out at the end of his speech to create a better world for all people everywhere. When questions came, there were several about whether he felt closer to God at the top of Mount Everest, and although he said he did, he mentioned there were life and death moments on the way up and down, where God's presence and companionship were much more real to him.

Hillary's visit to my school is not far from what happened to the disciples in this week's Gospel. Matthew tells us that the eleven men worshipped Jesus, were commissioned by him to go out to the world, and were promised that he would stay with them until the end of time.

Worship is a word Catholics don't use all that often. While other denominations describe their liturgy as "worship," we tend to use it only in a more secular way as in "hero worship" or "not an altar at which I worship." The concept behind this word, however, is an important one. To worship God is to admit that we are not God. We are creatures and our worship is directed toward our Creator, Savior, and Sustainer.

Whether we realize it or not, we are commissioned to go out to the world at the end of every liturgy: "Go in peace to love and serve the Lord." This changes our worship. We are not here just for ourselves. Mass, which comes from a word meaning "to be sent," indicates that our liturgy is about celebrating what God has done in the world in and through us, and is a preparation for what God still wants to accomplish.

Finally, we continue to experience the abiding presence of Christ in our daily lives or else we wouldn't be here. God, as revealed in Jesus Christ, is not distant to our lives or impervious to our needs; we believe in a companion-God who seeks our company as much as we need his.

In this Mass, then, let's thank God for the mountaintop of Christ's ascension that lifts us up out of our everyday life to celebrate that we are creatures, not the Creator. Let us hear again Christ's call to each of us to move away from the complacency of a spiritual cafeteria to a church moving out to change the world. And let's rejoice in Christ's presence that abides before us, behind us, over and in us, within and without, now and forever. Amen.

PENTECOST

ACTS 2:1–11
1 CORINTHIANS 12:3b–7, 12–13
JOHN 20:19–23

Have you noticed how, these days when we meet someone and ask how they are, they reply, "busy" or "frantic" or "as busy as ever"? I wonder what would happen if we replied, "Relaxed and laid back" or "taking time to smell the roses." I don't think we would be believed, or we might get a lecture from our friends on how lucky we are not to be busy!

As Christians we have to be careful about this busy-ness competition. Being active in our lives and engaged with the world around us is a gift, but if we are honest about our busy-ness, some of it is not virtuous. It's about denial, avoidance, or trying to stay up with our peer group.

In John's account of the first Pentecost, the primary gift Jesus' Spirit bestows on the disciples is peace. It's curious, isn't it, that just as we all compete with each other to be the busiest person we know, we also complain that what we really want is "some peace and quiet." We can't have it both ways. Compulsive, frantic activity is the enemy of peace.

Sometimes we can think that peace and quiet is sitting in the lotus position in a darkened room. Christ's gift of peace is more robust than that. Peace is like all the best things in life: an attitude of mind and a habit born of consistently making good choices. Some people can do a large amount of work and be quite serene about it. Peace, for them, is an affair of the mind and a way of life.

Seneca, a second-century philosopher, noticed even in his day how most of his friends and acquaintances were lacking peace. He wrote a famous book on anger and how to deal with it. He especially noticed that his richest friends were the angriest of all. Seneca came to believe that the reason so many people were agitated was that they had an unreasonable expectation about how smoothly their day would go. Those who were rich thought their money would buy them an easier life in every way, and so when it didn't, they got the angriest of all.

If Seneca is right and we want more peace and quiet, we have to have realistic expectations of each day and factor in the things that might go wrong.

Seneca's secular wisdom holds that the more aware we are of the frailties in us, others, and life, the less fights we would have. In turn this would lead to fewer occasions when we would need to ask or give forgiveness. In the week's Pentecost Gospel, forgiveness is the second gift Jesus bequeaths the disciples.

If we really want to cultivate peace and quiet in our lives, we have to confront the things we are trying to avoid or deny. Often these things hinge on painful memories or events where we were destructive toward others or they were so toward us. Unless we forgive ourselves or forgive them, our busy-ness will ensure that we have enough clamor and activity to stay away from ugly memories. Unfortunately, it usually follows that when we are so busy not dealing with the sins of our past, peace and quiet stay well away from us as well.

Let's pray that while the Spirit might allow us to retain any sins, we choose Jesus' first option this Pentecost and forgive as generously as we can those who have tried to crucify us. We might have to forgive ourselves as well. And then, like Jesus, with old wounds exposed, we can rejoice that the Spirit has breathed into us the greatest gift of all: the peace and quiet we most crave and need.

MOST HOLY TRINITY

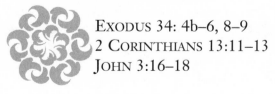

Exodus 34: 4b–6, 8–9
2 Corinthians 13:11–13
John 3:16–18

Years ago I was asked to take a CCD class for children from an inner-city school. I started by trying to work out how much the children knew about the basics. I asked, "When we make the sign of the cross, what do we say?" "Father, Son, and Holy Spirit" came the firm reply. So far so good! I tried upping the bar. "What do we call the Father, Son, and Holy Spirit?" There was complete silence. I tried another track. "What do you think of when you make the sign of the cross?" There was an awkward silence and then a bright little boy cheerily said, "The old man, the young guy, and the bird!"

No one can blame those children for the poverty of their images of the Trinity. Many older Catholics have similar images from paintings and holy pictures. The mystery of the Trinity means that in whatever way we portray God as Father, Son, and Spirit it will always be inadequate and incomplete. No one has ever seen God or the Holy Spirit. No one has a portrait of Jesus. All the images and words we use for the Trinity are more a reflection of our faith than the final word about God. God is always more than any name we use or any concept we have. But the special insight into God we celebrate today is that relationships are at the very center of who God is.

It took the early Christians four hundred years to fully grasp what Jesus was talking about when he spoke of his relationship to the Father and Spirit. They struggled to understand how and why God would have three faces and yet exist as One Being—love as One, act as One. They settled the "how" of the Trinity's nature by teaching us that the Persons of the Trinity are coequal, cosubstantial, and coeternal. They settled the "why" of the Trinity by reflecting that their experience of the Father, Son, and Holy Spirit was an encounter of love. They knew the core of God was not an idea or a principle, but was a loving relationship. Furthermore, the early Christians knew that they were invited into this relationship.

What was true for them is true for us. Think about this for a minute: We believe that the God who creates, redeems, and sustains the world seeks us out and invites us into a loving relationship. This is what gives us our greatest dignity and urges us on to share this message with everyone we meet. What a privilege! What an invitation! What a God!

It also follows that if relationships are at the core of God, then, for those of us who accept the invitation into the Trinity's embrace, relationships are meant to be our core business too. We are not to be isolated believers or private disciples. The degree to which we understand the feast of the Trinity will be shown in the care we take in our many and varied relationships, be they social, intimate, professional, civic, or international.

Every time we do anything to form new and good relationships, mend those that are broken, help other relationships to be deeper and richer, or just enjoy the ones we have, we discover one thing: Trinity Sunday is a moveable feast.

BODY AND BLOOD OF CHRIST (CORPUS CHRISTI)

 DEUTERONOMY 8:2–3, 14b–16a
1 CORINTHIANS 10:16–17
JOHN 6:51–58

Some years ago, Pope John Paul II went to Lima, Peru. There he was met by a massive crowd of two million people. Instead of the usual greetings from the president and the cardinal, two people from a shantytown stepped forward to the microphone. Their names were Irene and Viktor Charo. As the huge crowd went quiet, they begin to speak to the pope.

"Holy Father, we are hungry, we are sick, we lack work, our children die before their time. Yet we believe, Holy Father, we believe in the God of life. And we hunger for bread." Before a hushed crowd, the pope replied in his best Spanish. "You tell me you hunger for bread." "Yes, yes," the millions yelled in reply. "You tell me you hunger for God," said the pope, and again the crowd swelled with an emphatic "Yes! Yes!" "I want this hunger for God to remain; I want your hunger for bread to be satisfied."

The pope then turned to the generals and the wealthy politicians gathered there—many of them devout Catholics—and said very starkly, "I won't simply say share what you have. I will say give it back. Give it back—it belongs to the poor."

As extraordinary as the pope's words were that day, Jesus words about the Eucharist in the week's Gospel are even more so. In the sixth chapter of John's Gospel many people were so horrified by the claims Jesus makes for the reality of his presence in the Eucharist that they stopped following him. John clearly links Jesus giving himself for the sake of God's kingdom and our redemption with the communion we share with him in every Mass.

When we receive the Risen Christ in communion, we do not say "Amen" to a symbol of his presence or a sign of his life. It is Christ who hosts us, who gives us himself so that we might be transformed into his image and likeness. In modern language, Christ says to us at every Mass, "Here I am, broken and poured out in love for you. Take me. I'm here for you."

The danger with all gifts, and most especially with this gift, is that we can think it's just for us, an intimate moment between each of us and Christ. It is that, but it's also much more. St. Augustine in a sermon on the Eucharist on August 9, 413, wrote that the Mass was about three things: goodness, unity, and charity. Augustine taught that if we were not better people, working for unity and loving each other away from the Eucharist, it fails to achieve its purpose. Hence, like the pope in Peru, many people have linked the reception of the Bread of Life here with the giving of bread that sustains life away from here. On average in our world, more than thirty thousand people still die everyday of starvation. John F. Kennedy observed in his address to the UN General Assembly on September 20, 1963, "Never before has man had such capacity to control his own environment, to end thirst and hunger, to conquer poverty and disease, to banish illiteracy and massive human misery. We have the power to make this the best generation of mankind in the history of the world— or to make it the last." We could feed the world's poor. We choose not to.

In an address given before the 1976 International Eucharistic Congress in Philadelphia, the former Jesuit General, Father Pedro Arrupe, once said, "If there is hunger anywhere in the world then our celebration of Eucharist is somehow incomplete in the world." By this he didn't mean that when we gather for Mass anything is wrong in the act itself. Rather he meant that when we gather around Christ's holy table for this sacred meal while people still starve in the world, then something vital is lacking about how we gather and what we do away from Christ's table. There's an emptiness in us.

Yet it's an emptiness that invites us in. The God who comes to us at every Eucharist as real food is the same God who asks, "When I was hungry did you feed me?" This question says that just as God feeds us, so we too should and can feed each other.

May this feast of the Body and Blood of Christ give us the strength of our convictions. May the real food and drink we provide away from this sacred table prove to the world the power of the Eucharist to change us into a people that are good, unifying, and loving. And may we not just share with the poor from our excesses, but give them back the food that is rightly theirs.

NINTH SUNDAY IN ORDINARY TIME

 DEUTERONOMY 11:18, 26–28, 32
ROMANS 3:21–25a, 28
MATTHEW 7:21–27

You might remember the 2003 hit film, *Lost in Translation*. The title is pregnant with meaning as the characters deal with being translated into a world in which they can discover what they've lost, and how to get it back. In this film we meet Bob and Charlotte, two U.S. citizens visiting Tokyo.

Bob is a fading movie star in town to shoot a whiskey commercial, while Charlotte is a young woman tagging along with her workaholic photographer husband, John. Unable to sleep, Bob and Charlotte cross paths one night in the bar of their luxury hotel. The chance meeting between people who have thirty years between them soon becomes a surprising friendship. Bob is falling out of love with his controlling wife. Charlotte wonders why she recently married her inattentive husband. Both console each other in their depression, but not via the usual sexual clichés and adultery to which many other films resort.

Charlotte and Bob venture through Tokyo, having often incredible encounters with its citizens. In the end they discover that what they want is to live their present lives with their present spouses with a greater level of integrity and respect.

On several levels I think that this film casts a contemporary light on this week's readings.

In Deuteronomy we hear about blessings and curses. When I was a child, I was frightened of God's curses. When I was a child, I was frightened of God's curses. And given the way some people spoke about God, that's a reasonable conclusion at which to arrive. In the name of our fear of the Lord, we were petrified of sinning, breaking the rules, ruining our fast, and forgetting about abstaining from meat on Fridays. We thought that if we broke the rules God would curse us. Our fear of the Lord was about anxiety at being condemned.

Something got lost in translation. The Hebrew word for fear of the Lord is *yare*, and rather than meaning to be terrified of God, it is better translated as "reverence," which puts an altogether different complexion on what sort of believer the Bible is calling us to be.

A friend of mine once told me that such was the loving respect and admiration he had for his father, the most cutting thing his dad ever said to him was "I am disappointed in you." That comes close to helping us translate into our vernacular what fear of the Lord is all about.

When we admire and respect someone, we don't want to let them down; we want to emulate their achievements and grow in their esteem. Their love of us doesn't put us down, it builds us up, and it helps us love ourselves. It changes us for the better. This is what our reverence for God is all about.

And one of the ways we show we "get it" in relation to our veneration of God is that we are true to our word, which is what Jesus speaks of in the week's Gospel. In the earliest church there were some people who were saying one thing and doing another. Such a betrayal at that time cost lives, and in some parts of the world it still does. They were "good-time Christians"—all glory but no guts.

For most of us the stakes are not nearly as high or dramatic, but the challenge remains. A simple test would be: If I were the only Christian another non-Christian met, would they be able to tell by how I live that I was a follower of Jesus Christ?

The problem is that we can often be like Bob and Charlotte in Tokyo, not knowing who we really are, or what we want until we are about to lose it all. Everything about our faith can be going along well, until we are thrown into a world for which we have never prepared, nor could have imagined. At that point all of our commitments to faith, hope, and love could be up for grabs.

If we have a genuine and real reverence for the Lord, if we have built our house of faith on rock, then we will never want to let God down, not because God will curse us if we do, but because we have been given the gifts at baptism to be "guts-and-glory believers."

And that is the will of the Father—that we be people of integrity who mean what we say and practice what we preach, at home and on the days when we are translated to other places where life takes us.

TENTH SUNDAY IN ORDINARY TIME

 HOSEA 6:3–6
ROMANS 4:18–25
MATTHEW 9:9–13

I like Ordinary Time. It's the moment in the church's year, coming as it does out of the northern hemisphere's summer season, when we change gears and take life more gently. As the northern part of the world goes on summer holidays, the southern hemisphere, literally, cools its heels in winter.

What I like best about Ordinary Time is that it values the everyday, predictable routine that makes up most of our lives. If we had no Ordinary Time we would not be able to celebrate extraordinary feasts; we would be at fever pitch all the time. This would be unsustainable and unhelpful. It would be a bit like singing happy birthday every day. If we did, after a while it would lose its shine. So the church now asks us to we settle into weeks of celebrating the quiet processes of our lives.

Every Sunday, however, we also celebrate the Lord's resurrection, even in Ordinary Time. I like this even more. We often think Christ's resurrection should be marked with great pomp or hallelujah choruses, and yet on the Sundays in Ordinary Time we indicate that the Risen Christ can be found in moments we might think of as tedious, uneventful, and humdrum.

This Sunday we are told that Christ came to call sinners, not the virtuous. Sin has many definitions: One I find helpful is that sin is the behavior we do that is most destructive, leading us away from God, alienating us from others, and disabling us from reaching our full potential. Seen in this light there is no such thing as a private sin without any consequences, because even if I am the only one who knows of my destructive behavior then it changes me and alienates me from God and others. Every sin—personal, communal, and social—has implications for us all.

One destructive behavior that we don't hear much about is the devaluing of the ordinary events of our lives. We can be so busy planning and looking for spectacular occasions we do not pay sufficient attention to the seemingly banal details of each day and to the relationships that form the foundations of our happiness. Turning the phrase, "the devil is in the details," on its head, this week's Gospel indicates that Christ is in the details, calling us to pay attention to the here and now.

The Gospel indicates that Jesus calls us as we are—sinners— and where we are—in the normal world in which we live. But his call offers a promise: We don't have to be trapped in the destructive behavior that can mark our lives. We can, if we really want to, start again and reconstruct a better life transformed by his love.

May Christ give us a quiet, gentle reminder that new life can be celebrated in the everyday routine of our hectic existence—that every day provides us with a choice to be converted by his love and live our ordinary lives to the full.

ELEVENTH SUNDAY IN ORDINARY TIME

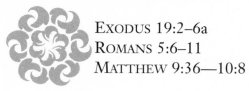 EXODUS 19:2–6a
ROMANS 5:6–11
MATTHEW 9:36—10:8

Damian told me that his life changed when his sister was involved in a car accident that left her with brain injuries. As tragic as this terrible event was for his sister, Damian told me that it was a defining moment for him as well because it enabled him to work out what truly matters, what he took for granted, what he hoped for, and if he could hold on to faith in the face of tragedy.

Damian said that one of the things he learned in the experience was what not to say to people in grief and shock. He reported that the nicest people said some of the worst things to him and his family. "It's all God's will and now you just have to accept it." "God only gives the biggest crosses to those who can bear it." "God was clearly trying to teach you all a lesson and we'll only find out in heaven what she did to deserve this." He said he wanted to scream. Some of his family have not been back to church since the accident.

The most helpful comment, however, the one that gave Damian and his family the greatest consolation, was "I can only imagine what it would be like if it were my sister." The people who made this comment weren't trying to find an answer for him in his shock and grief; they were trying to struggle with him in his pain and questioning and understand what it might be like.

This response has a name. It's called compassion, and it is what the week's readings are all about. The Lord claims the Israelites as his treasured possession out of compassion. St. Paul reminds us that God sent his Son to save us from our own destructiveness because he had compassion on us in our sinfulness. And when Jesus saw the crowds, he had compassion for their diseases, sufferings, and lack of leadership, and he did something about it.

We are called to see the crowds of our own day and be moved with compassion. Coming from the Latin words *co* meaning "with," and *pati* meaning "to suffer," compassion asks us to imagine what it's like to be a refugee, homeless, a victim of domestic violence, HIV positive, substance addicted, a person of color, or unemployed.

We may not be able to answer these people's suffering or perhaps for some reason we should not be the ones to respond to their suffering. In either event, what we should do is secondary to how we feel with them.

And often the people we find it hardest to be compassionate toward are the ones to whom we are closest. We often expect so much of our wife or husband, children, friends, and parents that we allow the poor to lay a greater claim on our compassion.

We don't have to be stingy with compassion; there will always be enough to go around. By virtue of our baptism and our coming to this Mass, however, we should be well known for being very compassionate, even foolishly so.

For Jesus doesn't teach us today to solve all the world's problems, just that we have to have the right attitude toward our brothers and sisters, imagining what it's like for them and treating them in the way we would want to be treated.

In the ministry of compassion we are all laborers sent out to harvest love in Christ's name; all of us are commissioned to confront evil and offer goodness in its place. And all of us are called, like the apostles, to go to every lost sheep, especially the one who may be under our own roof, and offer healing and peace.

Following Jesus in this way is not easy. Nearly every name read out in today's Gospel died a martyr for our faith. May the way we live be worthy of their example.

So this week when we catch ourselves jumping to an immediate condemnation of someone, let's stop and pray for the gift of compassion, that we might ask, "What must life be like for you?" At that point, our understanding will be touching the Divine.

TWELFTH SUNDAY IN ORDINARY TIME

JEREMIAH 20:10–13
ROMANS 5:12–15
MATTHEW 10:26–33

A few years ago there was an English film entitled *Secrets and Lies*. It charted the story of a dysfunctional family who sat on terrible secrets and told many lies for decades.

Like many successful dramatic films, audiences flocked to see it, not only because of its compelling story, but also because it tapped into an important truth about family life as many of us live it.

When I was a boy I was often told that "what's said and done in the home, stays in the home." And to a degree, this is a good and loyal principle. There are, however, family secrets and lies that cause untold damage for generations because no one is allowed to speak about them. Sexual abuse, domestic violence, suicide, incest, drug taking, alcoholism, theft, adoption, and abortion are only some of the secrets and lies that many families sit on.

Jesus, however, tells us in today's Gospel that what you "say…in the dark, tell in the light…what you hear whispered, proclaim from the housetops."

This doesn't mean that Christians tell everyone their personal business, but it does cut to the heart of what stunts spiritual and personal growth.

To the degree that something shameful remains buried, hidden, and unhealed, its power over us is increased. It remains the thing about which we can never speak. The bad spirit has a field day with this sort of stuff, feeding our fears and lowering our self-esteem.

In this regard, some Christians make a false distinction between their spiritual and psychological lives. They hold that the exploration of one's personal history or emotional problems is self-indulgent or unimportant for how we live.

We all know people who, in the pursuit of emotional health, become obsessed by their own story, feelings, reactions, and psychology. We also know others who never deal with the heavy hurts they seem to carry through the years, even though the pain of them seems to be as powerfully felt now as they were when they were inflicted upon them. Today's Gospel reminds us that there is a middle road between denying what should be acknowledged and dealt with, and being absorbed by it.

The church rightly holds that the best psychological tools can bring out into the open memories and experiences that can be seen for what they are and dealt with. We just have to be sure that we don't get conned into believing that psychology and therapy are anything but pit stops in life, so that we can attend to the working order of our mental machinery and, importantly, get back on the road with everyone else. We can call in later for another pit stop, if need be.

Long before the therapist's office Christ enabled the church to develop the sacrament of penance, where we admit our most destructive behavior and hear that we are forgiven and healed. At that moment, the love of God is active in us drawing out what Christ wants in the light, spoken of, and healed.

Jesus invites all of us to find a person we respect and trust, and to end the tyranny of the power of secrets and lies. I promise you when you take this risk with the appropriate person, the presence of God won't be very far away either.

THIRTEENTH SUNDAY IN ORDINARY TIME

2 KINGS 4:8–11, 14–16a
ROMANS 6:3–4, 8–11
MATTHEW 10:37–42

For all the great things the church of yesteryear achieved, it also did some terrible things. One of the worst demands it made was that a Catholic who marries a person who is not a Catholic do so at a side altar, oratory, or in the sacristy of the church. How humiliating this directive was. For how long were we going to punish the Protestant reformers and young Catholic woman or man who fell in love with someone from these denominations? In these ecumenical days, it's hard for us to understand these actions.

Today, especially at weddings, I hear older Catholics talk about this experience more than anything else. It's often given as the reason why the person or their family stopped practicing their Catholic faith. Recently an older wedding guest told me that her wedding at the side altar of the church was the last day she came near us of her own free will. She never had her children baptized, and her painful experience was still palpable forty years on as she compared and contrasted her wedding day with the Catholic marriage ceremony of a couple in a similar religious circumstance to her own that we had just celebrated. All I can do in such circumstances is apologize for the hurt our shortsightedness caused and be full of admiration for those who were subjected to similar treatment but have remained constant to our Catholic community.

These days, interdenominational marriages are rarely the reasons over which a family will divide. But we know that other religious issues can still break up a family. It's always a tragedy when this happens. For example, maybe you've had a son, daughter, or a grandchild join a religious sect or cult. It's heartbreaking stuff for parents who wonder what their child sees in the sect and where it will all end.

The church has sometimes let families down in this regard. Appearing to prefer dogma to the complexities of people's lives, formal liturgy to creating communities of hospitality, care, and justice, the church can appear to be out of touch, especially with our young. I know that every person in authority in the church today knows that Catholic Church needs to listen to our young people, hear about the issues that concern them, and present our faith in a way they find accessible and engaging. Very often it's not what we say about our rich faith; it's how we say it. Many people don't leave the mainstream churches because they are attracted by another group's doctrine, though some do want the world to be very black and white. Many leave for smaller groups offering a tightly knit community.

From today's Gospel we know that the same family heartbreak occurred in the early church. At this time, however, Christianity was the small sect drawing believers away from Judaism, to acknowledge Jesus as the Messiah. It ripped families apart. The early church became the new family of many followers who were disowned. They lost their old life and found a new one in Christ.

There can be moments when a family's lifestyle, beliefs, behavior, or values are such that one member feels that, in conscience, or by conviction, he or she does not belong anymore.

When this happens we can listen carefully to reasons the family member gives. Maybe we *have* lost something essential in our life together that needs challenging and change. And maybe it's the family member who is in the wrong.

Keeping the lines of communication open, speaking the truth with calmness and love, and remaining as compassionate as possible are the best Christian responses.

I can't pretend that any of this is easy, but when I have seen families do it, the prophetic, truthful, and charitable reward Jesus offers in today's Gospel is powerfully in evidence.

FOURTEENTH SUNDAY IN ORDINARY TIME

ZECHARIAH 9:9–10
ROMANS 8:9, 11–13
MATTHEW 11:25–30

Before I said my first Mass, an old priest gave me two great pieces of advice.

"You know when the congregation is filled with optimists. After you have given a long series of announcements at the end of Mass and then you say, 'and finally'—people take out their car keys!"

The second was "Never underestimate the burdens people bring with them into the church. Often we have little idea of the difficulties and pain our parishioners will be carrying."

I can only imagine the anxiety and burden some people carry to the Eucharist. Whatever it is, Jesus invites us to let go of it, if only for a while, and be at peace.

Now all this "come and rest a while" talk can be very pious and not sound all that in touch with reality.

The Gospel, however, came from the community of the apostle Matthew and was probably written in Jerusalem about forty-five years after Jesus' death. We know that this community experienced intense suffering and heavy burdens. They had been expelled from the synagogue and were being martyred for their faith in Jesus Christ.

No wonder they held so strongly to the words, "Come to me, all you that are weary and are carrying heavy burdens, and I will give you rest." And they found consolation in Jesus' example, "Take my yoke upon you, and learn from me; for I am gentle and humble in heart."

There have been times, however, when Christianity has been guilty of trying to spiritually wallpaper over some tough realities rather than preaching that God is our companion in facing up to whatever our reality is and dealing with it.

Our faith is not about praying away our problems or fears and wishing it were otherwise. Our faith means we have experienced the love of God in Jesus Christ so that we never carry our burdens alone. God is our companion and guide, and, as with every Christian community, we are called to be the sort of place wherein we carry each other's burdens and rest with each other awhile.

What we celebrate here each Sunday is that God will have the last word, a just, joyous, loving, and peaceful word, in this world and when we enter our final rest.

Jesus didn't come to us as a divine magician, waving a wand over our problems to wipe away all our tears. Rather, he accompanies us so he can show us that the gift of peace and a release from our life's burdens are often found in having the perspective to exercise the gift of right judgment. Making the best possible choices lead to the alleviation of our pain and difficulties.

This type of spiritual sanity reminds me of the story of the nun who was trying to be a trendy catechist with the communion class by drawing an analogy about how food is essential to life:

"What's small and furry and eats nuts?" she asked the class.
To which there was bemused silence.
So Sister tried again.
"What's small and furry and eats nuts?"
There was now stony silence. Sister then picked out Billy and asked him for the answer. After several awkward moments, Billy tentatively replied, "Sister, I know the answer is supposed to be Jesus, because the answer to all your questions is always Jesus but, I got to tell you, it sounds like a bloody squirrel to me."

Sometimes the answer is not simply "Jesus." As we all know, for some of our difficulties, there is no spiritual quick fix. There is no cheap grace. The answer is not simply Jesus.

In confronting issues, however, it is necessary for spiritual and mental health to take time out, to be as gentle with ourselves as possible, and to know that the burden of life is best shared with others.

We often never know the burdens others are carrying. Our prayer is that all of them might know a moment's rest, the companionship of fellow travelers, and the gift of Christ's peace.

FIFTEENTH SUNDAY IN ORDINARY TIME

ISAIAH 55:10–11
ROMANS 8:18–23
MATTHEW 13:1–23

A newcomer to a city known for its wind and rain arrives on a rainy day. She gets up the next day and it's raining. It also rains the day after that, and the day after that. She goes out to lunch and sees a young child and, out of despair, asks, "Hey, kid, does it ever stop raining around here?" To which the child replies, "How should I know? I'm only six."

With the three readings this Sunday, we could easily cele- brate Environment Sunday today. Rain, snow, seeds, sowers, fer- tile soil, and a laboring creation giving birth to the fruits of the Spirit are all rich ground upon which we can reflect on the impor- tance of our earth's ecology.

In recent years the church has regularly reminded us that the issue of caring for the environment is an important part of our Christian commitment for justice, part of the seamless garment in our ethic of life. We have been reminded that while the earth has been entrusted to us as stewards, to be preserved, it is also given into our hands to be developed in such a way that there will be a productive earth for future generations to inherit.

If this means we must limit our consumption, change our priorities in regard to energy and trade, and show the third world the way in developing eco-friendly industries, then all the better for us. Most of us know that we cannot keep going as we are, with ever increasing unsustainable demands on our planet. There is no point in any of us crying over the demise of our environment in the future if we are doing nothing to help it now.

Every small thing we do—from being conscious of the issues, to recycling and using our cars less—is not unimportant. Some of us are in positions to do a lot more than these things as well and we should take our Christian responsibilities in this regard very seriously.

One creative reading of today's Gospel is that it parallels how we can react to the news of the degradation of the environment.

For some of us the facts and figures about the planet's ecosystem fall on rocky ground. We are not receptive to hearing anything that might demand a change in our lifestyle or a lessen- ing of our comfort.

For others of us, recent debates fall among the thorns. Competing with other issues for our attention and action, the plight of the earth is not able to take root in our consciousness or sympathies. We think it can all wait for another generation who will have the ability to fix the problems then.

For some of us, however, recent surveys and our own sense of environmental changes mean that what experts are saying falls on fertile soil. We want to do whatever we can to see that the earth continues to bear fruit for as many generations as God intends.

The Old and New Testaments are filled with the importance of our relationships to the earth. In the Book of Genesis humanity is told to care for and subdue the earth, not wreck it. We cannot be irresponsible about the world's finite resources in the hope that we will find solutions in the future. Avarice is not one of the seven deadly sins for nothing.

We believe the bread and wine of the Eucharist, which we say are "the fruit of the earth and the work of human hands," are changed into Christ present among us. May these Eucharistic gifts rooted in our soil effect in us a change that might enable us to have ears to hear the groan of creation as it calls for us to be careful sowers and responsible reapers. May our stand for justice always take into account the care our earth requires so that we have a productive planet to hand on to our children.

By how we choose to live now may we hand it on to them in better shape than we found it.

SIXTEENTH SUNDAY IN ORDINARY TIME

WISDOM 12:13, 16–19
ROMANS 8:26–27
MATTHEW 13:24–43

Today's Gospel gives us both a parable and then an interpretation of that parable. I'm very grateful for this pattern in the thirteenth chapter of Matthew's Gospel. It indicates to us that not everything that Jesus says should be taken literally. Clearly the disciples were sometimes confused and needed some private coaching to bring them up to speed with what Jesus was talking about.

As much as I respect the faith of our fundamentalist Christian brothers and sisters, it is at this point, on the way we interpret the scriptures, that we cannot agree. The Catholic community has always taken the process outlined in Matthew's Gospel very seriously. We have always held that the full richness of the scriptures needs careful study and tested interpretations.

Unfortunately, in previous generations, the anxiety over people's private interpretations of the scriptures led Catholics to be suspicious of the Bible and the private reading of it. To read the Bible was often seen as a "very Protestant thing to do." Given that Jesus, Mary, the apostles, and the disciples are all recorded in the New Testament as reading, meditating on, or hearing the scriptures, nothing could be further from the truth. To be a Christian is to ponder the word of God.

That's why the Second Vatican Council encouraged us all to return to regular private reflection on the Bible. Along with this encouragement the council also reminded us, however, that as strong as the feelings and revelations we experience in our private scriptural prayer may be, these may have little or no consequence for the wider community of faith. We believe that the whole church has the task to discern where the word of God is leading us.

To help this discernment, our scholars, who pay great attention to the history and the literary, textual, and cultural issues in and around the Bible, have always aided the Catholic community. They look at how various interpretations and approaches of the scriptures have helped or hindered the church over the centuries. We place great weight on the "here and now" of the faith community who listens to the word of God and lives it out.

Our approach is a long way from those who hold that the entire truth of the scriptures is found in the text itself. Fundamentalist interpretations of the Scriptures dismiss the importance of studying the scriptures by reducing it to a book of facts. In doing so, they tie themselves up in all sorts of textual knots whenever the scriptures seem to contradict themselves.

We hold, however, that the scriptures are not books of facts, though they contain historical information. We believe we have seventy-three sacred books that cannot err in leading us to the saving truth about God. The word of God is for us the pathway to faith, a series of revealed and inspired portraits of God and a distillation of God's saving love for us and our response to him.

When there are inconsistencies or differences in any two scriptural texts, rather than unsettle us, we see these differences as examples of the various rich approaches to the truth of our salvation in and through Christ. This is nicely summed up in Dana Livesay's, "The Bible in 50 words":

God made
Adam bit
Noah arked
Abraham split

Joseph ruled
Jacob fooled
Bush talked
Moses balked

Pharaoh plagued
People walked
Sea divided
Tablets guided

Promise landed
Saul freaked
David peeked
Prophets warned

Jesus born
God walked
Love talked
Anger crucified

Hope died
Love rose
Spirit flamed
Word spread

God remained.
(from Dana Livesay, "The Bible in 50 words," in *Top of the Morning Book of Incredibly Short Stories*, ed. Brian Edwards, Auckland, New Zealand: Tandem Press, 1997.)

Let's give thanks that Jesus often used stories to communicate his truth and that he explained their meaning to those with ears to hear. Let's be grateful that we are inheritors of this intelligent legacy.

SEVENTEENTH SUNDAY IN ORDINARY TIME

 1 Kings 3:5, 7–12
Romans 8:28–30
Matthew 13:44–52

After being nearly snowbound for two weeks last winter, a Seattle man departed for his vacation in Miami Beach, where he was to meet his wife the next day at the conclusion of her business trip to Minneapolis. They were looking forward to pleasant weather and a nice time together. Unfortunately, there was some sort of mix-up at the boarding gate, and the man was told he would have to wait for a later flight. He tried to appeal to a supervisor but was told the airline was not responsible for the problem and it would do no good to complain.

Upon arrival at the hotel the next day, he discovered that Miami Beach was having a heat wave, and its weather was almost as uncomfortably hot as Seattle's was cold. The desk clerk gave him a message that his wife would arrive as planned. He could hardly wait to get to the pool area to cool off, and quickly sent his wife an e-mail, but due to his haste, he made an error in the e-mail address.

His message therefore arrived at the home of an elderly preacher's wife whose even older husband had died only the day before. When the grieving widow opened her e-mail, she took one look at the monitor, let out an anguished scream, and fell to the floor dead. Her family rushed to her room where they saw this message on the screen:

> Dearest wife,
> Departed yesterday as you know.
> Just now got checked in.
> Some confusion at the gate.
> Appeal was denied.
> Received confirmation of your arrival tomorrow.
> Your loving husband.
>   P.S. Things are not as we thought. You're going to be surprised at how hot it is down here.

Old-time missioners used to have a field day with today's Gospel, or at least with part of it. While they may have liked the passages that suggested that heaven was *like* a treasure in a field or *like* a pearl of great price, they told us that hell *was* a furnace of fire where there was weeping and gnashing of teeth.

Some of those preachers seemed to know an awful lot about hell! It's as though they were travel writers who had visited the place several times just to warn us about what to expect when we got there. And do you remember how easy it was to get in? Many of us thought we had a first-class ticket in our pocket most of the time.

If we believe in heaven and free will, it has to be logically true that hell exists and that, consistent with some people's free, knowing, and serious rejection of God and of love all their lives, these choices will destine decisions made for, and by, them in the next world as well.

There are two major differences, however, between how we used to speak about heaven and hell and what we say now. Just as we know the treasure hidden in the field or the pearl of great price are metaphors for heaven, rich and wonderful ones at that, they remain images that enable us to grasp an unimaginable concept. So it is with hell. How can we imagine life without love and God? We have learned that our guidebook regarding hell needs to be more circumscribed about what that destination or state of being holds. All we can confidently say is that hell is non-God.

The second change is that we are more careful about being so confident in regard to who is going there. Jesus tells us that God wants all humanity to be saved. We can't take that seriously and then have people slip into hell for a small infringement of the rules.

If we read today's Gospel in a different way, it can be a commentary on what God has done for us. Humanity can be seen as the treasure in the field that God has sold everything to own. We are the pearl of great price that God has moved heaven and earth to possess and we are the fish caught up in the net of God's love.

Our God is the one who became one like us, in Jesus the Lord, so that we might know, love, and serve him. That's what today's Gospel is all about.

Jesus reminds his disciples that in glimpsing the things of heaven they have to be like the master of a household. That's a rich image. In Jesus' day such a person would have provided protection, love, security, and justice for all.

God has given us free will and treasures, both new and old, to help us protect each other, love each other, feel secure in the truth, and act justly. But we need to know that the choices we make in regard to these things have implications for how we live now and in the life to come.

EIGHTEENTH SUNDAY IN ORDINARY TIME

ISAIAH 55:1–3
ROMANS 8:35, 37–39
MATTHEW 14:13–21

There is an old line that runs, "If you feel distant from God— guess who's moved?" It echoes the verse from Romans, "[Nothing] will be able to separate us from the love of God."

In the midst of persecution and suffering, St. Paul writes to the community at Rome to tell them that even in their fear, desolation, and grief that nothing, and no one, can separate them from God's love. This shows us that when we feel separated from God, it's because we have walked away from him, usually through destructive behaviors that set up and maintain distance between us and the source of our faith, hope, and love.

St. Matthew and Isaiah also knew that nothing can separate us from God's love. Isaiah's river of plenty and Matthew's loaves and fish are all about the plenty of God's kingdom, the abundance of God's goodness.

Too often we focus on the miracle of transformation that occurs in Matthew's Gospel when all he tells us about the actual miracle is that Jesus "breaks and shares." Matthew is more interested in the leftovers than he is in the miracle itself. From five loaves and two fish we are told twelve baskets of scraps are left over.

Numbers are rarely random in the Bible. The echo of the seven days of creation would not have been lost on the first hearers of this story as Jesus takes seven fruits of the earth to feed the crowd. Similarly, the twelve baskets of scraps, the remnants of the meal at which all were filled and satisfied, echo the sign of God through the twelve tribes of Israel in the Old Testament.

For us today this story also has consoling resonances. Matthew is telling us that Jesus sees our need, does not turn us away, comes to where we are, as we are, and re-creates us through the abundance of his love, so we can be signs of his kingdom in the world.

The church has always believed that the feeding of the crowd prefigured the Eucharist, this weekly time where we receive the fullness of God in his word, in the life of the community, in the minister, and through the transformation of the bread and wine.

It's all about abundance. Our God has abundantly provided for us so that we can abundantly provide for the entire world that is given into our care. "From everyone to whom much has been given, much will be required; and from the one to whom much has been entrusted, even more will be demanded" (Luke 12:48).

The problem is that when we look around we see that while some of us have so much, others have nothing at all.

If this reality doesn't move us to a change of heart and right action, then we have not understood the story of the loaves and the fish, that God's goodness is never intended for a select few.

Sometimes people look at the poverty in the world and think, "How could God allow that?" This question can cause us to feel distant from God, but given all God has given us and our ability to share from the abundance we have, the right question to ask is "Guess who's moved away from whom?"

NINETEENTH SUNDAY IN ORDINARY TIME

1 KINGS 19:9a, 11–13a
ROMANS 9:1–5
MATTHEW 14:22–33

A conservative Protestant church in a sleepy fishing village had to find a new minister. Over the protests of Jimmy, the senior elder, a woman was hired as the new pastor.

After the Reverend Gayle had been there a few weeks, Tom, a member of the congregation, offered to take her out fishing. Jimmy reluctantly agreed to allow them to use his boat for the day's outing, but insisted that he lead the expedition.

The trio got into the boat and motored out on the lake. When they got ready to fish, they realized that all their tackle had been left on the dock. Tom concluded that they would just have to go back and get it. The Reverend Gayle said that wouldn't be necessary, and she got out of the boat and started walking across the water toward the dock.

Jimmy, who refused to be impressed by Gayle's miraculous abilities, observed, "See, I told you we never should have hired that woman. She can't even swim."

The hit animation film *Shrek* was praised by critics for many things but most especially for the clever way it quoted from several other much-loved animation films. When writers do this it's called "intertextuality," where one text uses another text to tell the story. Some of the references in *Shrek* were obvious; others took a little longer to reveal themselves. Some were used in a new way that turned the original story upside down. Whether any of us got all or none of the references didn't affect the enjoyment we derived from the film; it only added to what was already a great tale.

The story of Jesus walking on the water is in a similar vein to *Shrek*. In eleven verses Matthew quotes several other stories in the Old Testament, uses them in his own way, and reinterprets all of them in reference to Jesus. It might be lost on some of us who just enjoy the power of the story, but none of this intertextuality would have been lost on Matthew's first hearers.

Poor old Job found God in the midst of a storm, and winds and waves is a common Old Testament shorthand for the perils of life. The image of the boat was an early symbol for the church, and Matthew has all Jesus' disciples in it. Jesus hovering over the waters has echoes of the action of the Spirit in the first account of creation in Genesis. Even Jesus restoring calm to the sea follows from what the prophet Jonah had done before. For the keen student there is much more besides.

Matthew's account is magnificent on its own terms, but with these details we can begin to see his theological message. Jesus, the Son of God and Lord of creation, remains faithful to the disciples, no matter how treacherous the seas or how great their fear. He comes to them so that they may be saved and re-created as the church who recognizes that he is the fulfillment of creation, the one whom Israel has been longing to see and embrace.

And what does this all mean for us?

We are inheritors of Matthew's faith. We're here because we believe that Jesus is the Son of God who has saved us from ourselves and from destruction. But it also means that in every storm that threatens our lifeboat Jesus comes to call us to faith, to catch us when we think we're drowning, to accompany us back to safety, and to bring calm to the troubled seas of our life.

Aren't we lucky Jesus never learned to swim?

TWENTIETH SUNDAY IN ORDINARY TIME

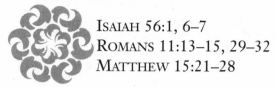

Isaiah 56:1, 6–7
Romans 11:13–15, 29–32
Matthew 15:21–28

One bright Sunday morning, everyone in the town got up early and went to the local church. Before Mass started, the townspeople were sitting in their pews and talking about their lives, their families.

Suddenly, Satan appeared at the front of the church. Everyone started screaming and running for the front entrance, trampling each other in a frantic effort to get away from the devil incarnate. Soon everyone was evacuated from the church, except for one elderly lady who sat calmly in her pew, not moving, seemingly oblivious to the fact that Satan was in her presence.

Now this confused Satan a bit, so he walked up to the older lady and said, "Don't you know who I am?"

The woman replied, "I sure do."

Satan asked, "Aren't you afraid of me?"

"No, certainly not," said the woman.

Satan was a little perturbed at this and queried, "Why aren't you afraid of me?"

The woman calmly replied, "Because I've been married to your brother for forty-eight years."

Until quite recently in many cultures around the world, events or experiences that had no ready explanation were put down to evil forces. This was certainly true in Jesus' day. Diseases, physical deformities, mental illnesses, accidents, bad weather patterns, and defeats in battle were attributed either to God's vengeance or the work of a demon. Although we no longer hold this to be true, we still hear this line from some people today.

The Syro-Phoenician woman considers herself cursed for having a daughter who is tormented by a demon. It is very unlikely that her daughter is possessed by the devil. She probably had a chronic illness that could not be cured. Furthermore, the woman is also considered cursed by others because she is a Gentile, a non-Jew. In fact this story is unsettling and rather unflattering to Jesus on several levels.

Because of her ethnicity and religion, the disciples do not think she should ask for anything from Jesus. He seems to concur with them. If it wasn't for the woman's courage and persistence, she would never have got what she wanted. And by Jesus referring to them as dogs, he seems to agree with the contempt with which the Jews held the Gentiles.

Again it is the woman's quick wit and faith that turn the situation around. She domesticates the racial slur and argues that if she is to be considered a dog she is not a wild one, but of the house variety where she should be able to enjoy the leftovers. The power of her insight and the rightness of her cause catches Jesus off guard, her daughter is healed, and everyone is taught a lesson about how the kingdom of God breaks through in the most extraordinary ways.

This story also tells us of the power of intercessory prayer. The woman goes through her ordeal not for herself but for her daughter. Her faith in Jesus is the vehicle by which someone else's life is enriched. So too for us. As Christians, many of us regularly tell others, whom we know are in need, that we will pray for them. Often these people, some who do not share our faith, are touched by this kindness.

When we make our prayer intercessory, either at home or in the Prayers of the Faithful at Mass, it can be our finest hour. We can learn a lot about a parish from its intercessions. It can be the time when we forget about ourselves and our needs for a while and ask for the needs of someone else, even if we don't know them. This type of prayer has the possibility of helping us place our lives in context and reminding us that while we have a seat at the world's table others are at our feet scavenging for scraps.

The best prayer reminds us that we have to get down and get dirty and work to raise up all of God's children to the places of honor that everyone deserves.

TWENTY-FIRST SUNDAY IN ORDINARY TIME

ISAIAH 22:19–23
ROMANS 11:33–36
MATTHEW 16:13–20

A furor broke out in a rural diocese some years ago about the retreat style of priest who was taking Catholic students in their last year of high school, or who were attending university, away for weekend retreats. On the Friday night of the retreat this priest would tell the young people that by the end of the weekend they should make a decision about their Christian faith.

Some parents were shocked that their young people were given an ultimatum that included the possibility of rejecting their faith. The priest replied that Catholic youth have to make all sorts of decisions in regard to career, lifestyle, residence, studies, and relationships. Religion, he contended, often fell by the wayside, either not important enough on which to make a decision, or relegated to the personal shelf of neglect to be possibly taken down and dusted off years later for a hatching, matching, or dispatching.

The priest argued that this wasn't good enough. After years of Catholic education or many years of CCD, the church had to take the risk of calling for a personal decision for faith. Some of the young people consciously chose membership in the church. In making such a profession of faith many young people reported having a deep encounter with God and an experience of their faith in Christ. Other students made the decision, which, of course, is never irrevocable, against belonging to the church.

The entire retreat process was based on the question in today's Gospel: "Who do you say that I am?"

The disciples, reflecting on their experiences with Jesus, offer various possibilities, but it is Peter who says that Jesus is the revelation of God for the world. This is the great profession of faith and the basis on which the church comes into being.

And what was true then is true now. At some point, if we want our faith to move from being a code of law, a concept, or some excellent ideas, toward something we can experience, we must take the faith of the church, which has nurtured us up to now, and make it our own. In doing so, when we encounter Christ, we contribute to the refounding of the church in our generation.

Just being part of the "Catholic crowd" is hardly the challenge Jesus presents to the disciples in today's Gospel. We are commissioned like the disciples to bear witness to Christ's personal love in the workplace, with our friends, and in our families.

It's always helpful to be reminded that we might be the only face of Catholicism, or even Christianity, that another person may encounter. The way in which we bind them up or set them free might be the measure by which they judge if the church is the face of Christ in today's world, and whether they could find a home with us.

And it all hinges on that great question that is asked of each of us today: "Who do you say that I am?" How we answer this question reveals so much, including whether Christ is an idea we like or the object of our passion.

TWENTY-SECOND SUNDAY IN ORDINARY TIME

JEREMIAH 20:7–9
ROMANS 12:1–2
MATTHEW 16:21–27

At the morning parade in Dachau on July 22, 1943, six prisoners were found to have escaped. Retribution was swift and brutal. Randomly selected, twelve people were hanged. As the other prisoners watched their twelve fellow inmates gasp for breath, someone in the crowd cried out, "Where is God?" Silence descended on the yard. The twelve bodies were now in spasm, jerking and struggling for breath. As everyone watched, the voice came again, this time more urgently, "Where is God now?" "My God," another voice yelled back, "my God is hanging there."

This sort of faith is what today's Gospel is all about. Christianity holds that God took our flesh, suffered, died, and was raised to life.

It is certainly true that we have domesticated the scandal of the cross, even to the point that, these days, it dangles from various parts of people's anatomies. I often wonder, had Jesus been electrocuted, whether we would have little golden chairs around our necks? But while we have tried to tame the reality of Jesus' torturous hours in Jerusalem, the reality of the cross in each of our lives cannot be so commercially soothed.

Christians are not meant to be smiling masochists. We are not meant to be lovers of pain—just bearers of it.

We are invited, by Jesus, to see the burden of suffering in our lives as an opportunity to be faithful to his example. It also gives us an opportunity to be in solidarity with all those who suffer in our world. This is easier said than done. When we suffer in our daily lives, thoughts of others rarely come to mind easily, but it can be consoling to keep our suffering in context and know that we are not facing it alone.

We are encouraged to see that suffering can be an opportunity to grow in love. If we understand our crosses as our particular schools of love, then we learn more about ourselves and God and are able to help others carry their crosses as well.

Carrying our cross, however, is not just about bearing physical, personal, sexual, spiritual, or emotional pain; it can also be about the sharing of our gifts and talents, our love and compassion. In every gift there is a burden. Following Christ's example, we are called to share our gifts heroically, with anyone in need, even to the end.

Some people complain these days that God is often presented as a big marshmallow, all sweet and soft. Today's Gospel shows the edge involved in being a follower of Christ. I don't know of a more demanding vocation in our world than that of taking up the cross of being faithful, loving, and selfless.

And while we are invited to take up our cross and follow Jesus, we never do it alone. If we have the eyes to see it and the humility to accept it, Christ, literally, hangs in there with us every step of the way.

So let's recall the first cross from which we take comfort as we bear our own crosses, "In the name of the Father, the Son, and the Holy Spirit. Amen."

TWENTY-THIRD SUNDAY IN ORDINARY TIME

 EZEKIEL 33:7–9
ROMANS 13:8–10
MATTHEW 18:15–20

When couples who are going to be married in the church come to see me for the first time, I get them to fill out a brief questionnaire. The last two questions on the form ask:

> "What do you like best about your partner?"
> "What do you like best about yourself?"

The first question usually presents no problems, although it can hold a few surprises and sometimes a playful push if the right answer is not forthcoming! The second question seems to present all sorts of difficulties, especially for prospective grooms. Some of us find it hard to name the God-given qualities we value most in our character. Some couples try to pass it off: "That's for others to say" or "I don't want to blow my own trumpet." Others try to dismiss the question as being new age or trendy.

But the question does, in fact, cut to the heart of both today's second reading and Gospel. "You must love your neighbor as you love yourself." We cannot say in the same breath, "I hate myself, but I am a good Christian." For St. Paul, love of self was not indulgent, but the cornerstone of our mission to love as Jesus loves us.

Paul knew the difference between self-love and self-adoration. Our love of God is expressed in the healthy and appropriate esteem we have for ourselves. Put another way, we cannot love anyone else if we don't love ourselves. If we have poor self-esteem then often we need others to fill up this gap in our self-love. Most relationships cannot sustain such a demand.

The church has to take some responsibility for this state of affairs. We used to be taught that mortification and self-denial were good Christian virtues, and indeed they can be. When properly understood they are never opportunities for self-hatred. The sanest spiritual writers in our tradition saw these virtues as paths of closeness with God and service of our neighbor.

One such writer was St. Ignatius Loyola who in his *Spiritual Exercises* saw that it was precisely as sinners that God loves us. He saw that one of the greatest gifts the Lord can give us is when we see our sinfulness for what it is, but are not overwhelmed by it, and that we experience the power of God's love for us who calls us to walk as children of the light.

Jesus in today's Gospel attends to this destructive side of our human nature. Jesus teaches us that those who do not love their neighbor as they should are to be treated with dignity and respect and offered every opportunity to seek forgiveness until it is clear they can no longer be a part of the Christian family.

The challenge and hallmark of the Christian life is the way in which we live out God's love and forgiveness. And, although the Christian community should be the last group to exclude anyone, even we have to have our boundaries. Sometimes this involves holding others to account for what they say and do. The love and forgiveness of God does not mean that "anything goes." It is a love that calls for constant conversion. We can witness to it only to the degree that we have experienced it, from God, from others, and in the way we love and forgive ourselves.

And we know when these qualities are taking deep root in us because answering a question like "What do you really like about yourself?" is a piece of cake!

TWENTY-FOURTH SUNDAY IN ORDINARY TIME

SIRACH 27:30—28:7
ROMANS 14:7–9
MATTHEW 18:21–35

Charged with the rape and murder of a young woman, it only took the jury minutes to return a guilty verdict for the three men in the dock. The courtroom erupted in cheers as the verdict was read out.

As the men were being led away from the courtroom, the mother of two of them ran toward the dock yelling, "I think what you've done is despicable, but I want you to know that I love you."

Outside the courthouse, the media were expecting the parents of the victim to advocate capital punishment for the criminals. Instead, they said they wanted to forgive the perpetrators of this vicious crime. Everyone looked on in disbelief.

No one at that courthouse was running away from the heinous nature of the crimes, nor from the life sentences the men deserved, but the parents involved chose to focus on either love or forgiveness.

In today's Gospel, Jesus tells us we should forgive each other seventy-seven times. In the Bible the numbers 1, 3, 7, 12, 40, and 50 all have specific meanings. To number something as seven is to describe it as being perfect. When we hear Jesus use this phrase we recall the story of the seven days of creation in the Book of Genesis where, on the seventh day, God looks at the result of his creative love and sees that it is very good. Jesus, using some shorthand, says that not only is forgiveness "good," but that it is a creative act that gives life to the world and gives glory to those who exercise it.

In the fifth century, St. Augustine said that forgiveness was like a mother who has two wonderful daughters named Justice and Compassion. In using such a metaphor Augustine knew that forgiveness was not a one-time event; it was a process that involved other virtues as well. Jesus teaches a similar lesson in today's Gospel, where he uses the image of the king settling his debts. Because the king is just, compassionate, and forgiving, he rightly expects that, in turn, his steward will be so as well.

It's easy to be forgiving in the big picture. We can talk strongly about war, peace, and reconciliation. It's quite another to forgive those closest to us. Sometimes the hardest place to be compassionate and just is in our own home. If we are not speaking with a husband, wife, child, parent, sibling, friend, or member of our community, then today's Gospel has a strong challenge right where we live.

Part of the problem is that we might have accepted the film *Love Story*'s motto, "Love means never having to say you're sorry." The problem for us is that this film's tagline is not Christian. For followers of Jesus the exact opposite is true. We seek opportunities to forgive and we look to those who we have offended to ask for their forgiveness.

Jesus doesn't tell us that forgiveness is easy, just necessary. To forgive someone in our family, workplace, our circle of friends, or in our church is not to pretend that a sinful situation did not occur, but to face it head-on and demand justice with compassion.

For when we stand before God with the weakness and sinfulness of our own life, God will not settle old scores, take revenge, and exact retribution. Rather, God will be perfectly just and completely compassionate. When we choose forgiveness over revenge, and love over hate, we begin to glimpse God's creative goodness coming to perfection in us, because forgiveness is a participation in the very heart of God.

TWENTY-FIFTH SUNDAY IN ORDINARY TIME

 ISAIAH 55:6–9
PHILIPPIANS 1:20c–24, 27a
MATTHEW 20:1–16a

The film *Forrest Gump* was once described as the "battler's triumph." On one level it was about how the last will be first. This story picks up where the film left off.

Forrest Gump dies and goes to heaven. On arrival, St. Peter informs him that there are three questions he has to answer before he can enter.

1. What days of the week begin with the letter *T*?
2. How many seconds are there in a year?
3. What is God's first name?

Forrest answers right away, "Shucks, there are two days in the week beginning with the letter *T* - Today and Tomorrow." St. Peter replies, "That's not what I was thinking, but you have a point. How about the next one?" "I think the only answer can be twelve." "Twelve?" St. Peter asked. "Shucks, there's gotta be twelve: January 2nd, February 2nd, March 2nd...." "Hold it," interrupts St. Peter. "I see where you're going with this. Let's go to the final question." "Sure," said Forrest. "It's Andy!" "Andy?" exclaimed an exasperated St. Peter. "OK, I can understand how you came up with your answers to my first two questions, but just how in the world did you come up with Andy as God's first name?" "Shucks, that was the easiest one of all," Forrest replied. "I learned it from the hymn...Andy walks with me, Andy talks with me, Andy tells me I am his own." St. Peter opened the pearly gates and yelled, "Run, Forrest, run!"

In today's Gospel, in which the first laborers are paid the same wage as the afternoon workers, what the early birds didn't reckon on was that they could have come much later and got the same deal.

We would cynically call the afternoon workers, "Johnny-come-latelies" and chances are if we were confronted with the same situation we would be with the complainers.

This story was important to the early church because generations of Jews waited and longed for the Messiah and, like the first workers, they were the first to respond to the call of Jesus and to work in the field of his kingdom. For some of the early Jewish-Christians, including St. Peter, it came as a surprise that the Lord was calling Gentiles to the life and work of Jesus' kingdom as well.

We can imagine that it rankled with some of the early birds to see these Johnny-come-latelies taking charge of the Christian mission. This wasn't how it was supposed to be!

This story, then, is a wonderful commentary on how fickle we are and, luckily for us, how extraordinarily generous God is. What we see in ourselves and others is only a glimpse of what God is like. God is so much more: more loving, more forgiving, more compassionate, and more just.

And because God is so much greater than anything we could ask or imagine, we are constantly surprised at how he overturns our expectations. We look for God in the big and spectacular and he comes to us poor, naked, sick, in prison, and hungry. God speaks through the most surprising people at the most surprising times.

That's why those people who have decided that God can only work in certain ways, places, people, institutions, and times so often end up at the end of the line when it comes to religious wisdom. Michael McGirr in his book, *Things You Get for Free*, argues that there is a crisis of belief today, but not the way we often think. In a brilliant turning of the tables, McGirr says that the crisis of belief is that people inside the church sometimes cannot believe that people outside its traditional structures can experience the love of Jesus. God loves and guides the church, but is not bound by it. God is busy about making sure those who might be last have a chance to become first.

Rather than resent this, however, let's thank God for being bigger than we are and for being just to all of us, no matter when, or how, we get the word.

TWENTY-SIXTH SUNDAY IN ORDINARY TIME

EZEKIEL 18:25–28
PHILIPPIANS 2:1–11
MATTHEW 21:28–32

A young priest was sent by his bishop to a parish that had a red-light district within its boundaries. On his first day in the parish a nun, who had worked in the area for many years, took him on a tour of her beat, the area where all the prostitutes were plying their trade. As they went along, Sister introduced the priest to her friends Bubbles, Ginger, and Calamity Jane. "Sister, it's fantastic that you know these women so well," he said. "Don't worry," replied the nun, "you'll know them in no time as well, and they'll know you by name too."

Seized by panic, the young priest had visions of the bishop, the parish priest, or worse still, his mother coming to visit and walking with him down the street as Bubbles, Ginger, and Calamity Jane all wave and call out across the road, "Hello, Father." Who would ever believe he only knew them pastorally?

"Truly I tell you, the tax collectors and the prostitutes are going into the kingdom of god ahead of you."

The preaching of Jesus attracted all sorts of people who lived at the fringes of, or were oppressed by, Palestinian society. Jesus' message was especially attractive to them. Tensions among the huge variety of Jesus' disciples, between the rich and the poor, men and women, the Jews and Gentiles, the socially respectable and those with outrageous backgrounds, continued after his death throughout the next decades, during which the Gospels were written.

It's hard for us to imagine what a diverse and scandalous group in many respects the first fathers and mothers of our faith were seen to be. Imagine, if you will, the fuss that would still be created if the local bishop was seen constantly dining with women in prostitution, drug dealers, or known terrorists. People would be outraged, but the bishop would be doing nothing short of following Jesus' example. This situation gives us a little insight into how affronted the Chief Priests and Pharisees were by Jesus and, in turn, by his disciples' behavior.

For Jesus there was never a lost case, or a person beyond help. He didn't just spend time with the poor and broken of his society, but offered them a new way of life, an opportunity to start again, and redemption from their destructive behavior. He went to where they were, as they were. And we do the same because this is precisely what God has done for us. God didn't wait for us to "talk the talk" before we could "walk his walk." Jesus came to us when we were religiously dumb and immobile and showed us how to speak, what to say, and where to walk.

The Christian walk and talk is meant to have a profound impact on our daily lives, our concerns, our priorities and compassion. So much so that if, over a period of time, what we celebrate here each Sunday makes no inroads into our family life and workplace, our professional life, our business practices, and our relationships, then we should ask ourselves: What are we doing here?

And, what's worse, we could even miss the ongoing revelation of Christ's presence in the poor, weak, and vulnerable of our own society. We constantly look for Christ in the spectacular and the wonderful and he comes to us in the least of our brothers and sisters.

May we gain the strength to not only "look good," but to "be good," to start over if we need to, and do our best to live out the faith we profess. May we be strong enough to find the Lord where he is, and not keep looking in the places where we would prefer him to be.

TWENTY-SEVENTH SUNDAY IN ORDINARY TIME

Isaiah 5:1–7
Philippians 4:6–9
Matthew 21:33–43

Jesuit priest Bernard Lonergan was a Canadian theologian who had a major impact on philosophy and theology last century. Sometimes his language was so complex we had to buy a companion book to help us read the original work. Surprisingly, however, his most important insights were very simple and expressed in everyday language. One of them was that we regularly have "ah-ha" moments, where we get an insight into God, the world, or ourselves. Lonergan argued that these moments make sense of things we have previously only seen as problems.

Matthew's Gospel is filled with "ah-ha" moments. Written for a generally Jewish audience, it reflects on Jesus in light of the history of Israel, the Hebrew scriptures, and the expectations of the Messiah. Jesus was for Matthew's community, and is for us, the "ah ha" in world history. By Matthew reflecting on his life, death, and resurrection, things he had previously only wondered about now made sense.

The phrase, "the stone rejected by the builders," originally referred to Israel. In Psalm 118 and, more generally, in the Book of Psalms, the trials and defeats of Israel are seen to be tests of strength, love, and endurance. Despite everything they have gone through, the people of Israel continue to sing of God's fidelity to them and what marvels God has done before their eyes, making them into a more faith-filled people.

Matthew, however, reflects on what happened to Jesus at the hands of the Chief Priests, scribes, and Romans. In a great "ah-ha" moment he sees that it is Jesus, not only Israel, who is the stone rejected by the builders that has now become the key building block of a new edifice.

Doing exactly the same as Matthew does with this passage, we can apply it to our own lives as well. There are often facets of our personality or character of which we are ashamed or about which we despair. From gossip to greed, past hurts to anger, sexuality to broken relationships, we can often get discouraged at how un-together our Christian life is.

Even though we have worked hard to overcome our worst traits, we often think nothing good will ever come of them. In such a context we need to hear today's Gospel, "The stone that the builders rejected has become the cornerstone; this was the Lord's doing, and it is amazing in our eyes."

The parts of our character we most despise could be the most marvelous moments of amazing grace. Nothing is irredeemable to God; nothing has gone too far or become too entrenched. In the Christian life there is no room for shame, only for repentance and starting over. Looking at things we have thought of as only being problems provides us with the greatest potential for "ah-ha" moments, where the healing and love of Christ enable us to turn our lives around, to demolish all the negative and defeatist self-talk in which we can indulge and rebuild ourselves with Christ, the master builder.

Once we get into the habit of doing this, it's amazing how many "ah-ha" moments we have as our history ceases to be a problem to be overcome but turns into a challenge to be harnessed for the building up of the kingdom of God on earth.

TWENTY-EIGHTH SUNDAY IN ORDINARY TIME

Isaiah 25:6–10a
Philippians 4:12–14, 19–20
Matthew 22:1–14

These days young couples ask for their children to be baptized for a variety of reasons. Initially, it's clear that for some baptism is an elaborate naming ceremony or the ritual preliminaries to hosting a "we've had a baby" party. For others, while they don't quite know why they want baptism, they just know they do. And for some parents, it's clear that they wish to pass on to their children the life of Christ that has nurtured them.

At the baptismal ceremony, I always begin by saying that for the first three centuries of the church's history, this sacrament was celebrated at dawn on the Easter Vigil not only because the rising sun symbolized Christ's light dawning in our lives, but also because baptism was always done in secret. For 300 years Christians who took the waters of baptism at dawn could be dead by lunchtime. For them, baptism was no social day out; it was a life-and-death commitment.

In the parable of the king's banquet, Jesus foreshadows the days when those whom one would expect to be Christian would reject the invitation to faith, and when those thought least likely to respond to God's call would flock into the church.

Since the earliest days of Christianity, the wedding banquet was seen as a metaphor for two things: the Eucharist and eternal life. Curiously, this parable, while using the imagery of the banquet, is less concerned about the meal and more about who's in and who's out, and why!

We can see this through the tenants who turn down the opportunity to go to a royal wedding or a presidential reception—still an almost unimaginable thing to do. It's seen in the poor who recognize the gift and the giver, get dressed up, and have somewhere to go. And it's seen in the impostor who is not correctly dressed for the occasion and is speechless when called to account.

This last character is clearly the one in the earliest Christian community who has taken the waters of baptism, but was betraying St. Matthew's persecuted community. When discovered, people like this guest were thrown out. In Matthew's time, impostors cost lives.

So what does all this have to say to our own time? It's not about how one dresses for Mass, or for eternal life! It's not about the fear of being found wanting in being able to mouth the right words when called to account. It is about being poor enough to recognize the gift of God in the invitation to faith and about being generous enough to respond completely. For taking care about what we say and do, the values by which we live our lives at home, at work, at play, and in the way we relate to each other is how we show that we mean what we profess. It is also how others legitimately judge whether we are really genuine about our faith or just another impostor.

Like the earliest Christians, when we were baptized we were clothed in a white garment—a wedding robe. Like theirs, our baptismal day was no naming ceremony and no social day out. It was the day we were issued with a standing invitation to the feast of life in Christ where people act as they profess, and where frauds are spotted a mile away.

TWENTY-NINTH SUNDAY IN ORDINARY TIME

ISAIAH 45:1, 4–6
1 THESSALONIANS 1:1–5b
MATTHEW 22:15–21

There are people inside and outside the church who think that Christ did not give the church a mandate to speak about political matters. They regularly cite this week's Gospel to support their case. But if one knows and understands the context and meaning within which this text was written, it provides no ammunition for those who want the church to stay indoors, reflect on things "spiritual," preach the eternal verities, and sing hymns more ancient than modern.

In Jesus' day, we know that some people thought he was a Zealot. Zealots were a well-organized group who agitated for the end of the Roman occupation of Israel. One of the things Zealots did was withhold paying the Roman taxes. We can see why some people thought Jesus may have been a Zealot. He took the part of the poor, the sick, women, and those who lived on the fringes of society. He challenged the religious authorities of his day and certainly stirred up trouble in many places he went. On the other hand he rejected violence, taught his followers to pray for their enemies and to return good for evil. Jesus showed us that the justice and equality God longs to see in the world comes from a community that is converted by love, not by weapons, fear, or revenge. Jesus was no Zealot.

Rather than undermine civil authority, however, Jesus, in this passage, supports it. But he does more. "Give therefore to the emperor the things that are the emperor's" is followed by "and to God the things that are God's," which encompasses all the emperors or Caesars of this world, all civil authorities and states. The sense that we as the people of God can split off our obligations to the gospel from the state is as false as it is dangerous.

We only have to think of some of the darkest chapters last century to see what happens when good, churchgoing people like us do not put their Sunday devotion in touch with their Monday politics. Evil can reign.

Christian leaders, who are charged to proclaim and defend the gospel, are obliged to use whatever forum necessary to declare that God's personal love encompasses everyone and everything under heaven. As the prophet Isaiah reminds us, God calls each one of us by name.

At times we may not agree with our religious leaders; we may think them ill informed; we may even think they have overstepped the mark. If this is the case we should write to them, enable them to consider other perspectives and to broaden the basis upon which they make their judgments. But we should never be seduced by those who want the church sidelined from the mainstream of the debates that shape the way we live, the values we share, the laws we draft, and the priorities we draw up for our human community.

If the church shows disinterest in any of this, it is untrue to the very things for which Jesus lived, died, and was raised from the dead. By all means we should give to Caesar all that Caesar is justly entitled to have for the sake of the common good. A higher allegiance, however, goes to God, who will call all Caesars to account for what they have done and what they failed to do. And we might be asked to explain how we let them get away with it in the first place.

THIRTIETH SUNDAY IN ORDINARY TIME

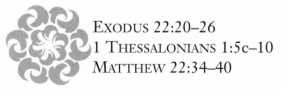

EXODUS 22:20–26
1 THESSALONIANS 1:5c–10
MATTHEW 22:34–40

Nguyen Van Mah is one of eight sons. In 1978 his poor, farming parents had to decide which one of their eight children would be sent on a boat from Vietnam. They knew there was a great risk that they would be sending their son to his death on the South China Sea.

At 4:00 a.m. the knock at the family home came and Mah said his good-byes. He has not seen his parents since. Mah was blindfolded and travelled in the back of a truck for eight hours. He was led through the jungle to a beach where the blindfold was removed. At this moment some people were shot by evil traders who collected money without having any intention of dispatching a boat. That families never hear from their children was no surprise to them. The risk did not pay off.

"We were lucky," Mah said. "We made it off the beach." There were twenty-nine adults in a boat built for ten. Inadequately prepared for the two-week trip, all the boat people were sick, hungry, and exposed. Thai pirates attacked their boat, executed three men, and raped all the women on board. They were to bury another six people at sea who died from the effects of the journey.

On sighting land, the remaining twenty people in Mah's boat thought their hopes had been fulfilled. But the Malaysian navy, under orders to fire on all Vietnamese boats, forced it to return to international waters. Mah told me, "At this point I almost lost my faith in God and human beings. I was going to die."

The boat began to take on water and was noticed by a Dutch trading ship, which rescued them and deposited them in the Philippines. Mah immigrated to Australia twelve months later and is now the local doctor in a rural community that could not get a doctor for two years.

In Exodus, the Lord tells us today, "You shall not wrong or oppress a resident alien, for you were aliens in the land of Egypt." Jesus tells us in the Gospel that the love of God is fulfilled precisely when we love our neighbor.

No pressing issue in the Western world, it seems to me, elicits such hysteria as does immigration. Until recently, most Western countries have been good in offering hospitality to people who have chosen to leave, or have had to flee their country of birth. Given our comparative wealth, this hospitality is entirely appropriate. And it is also appropriate for our countries to have a threshold number for the sake of the common good.

In today's Gospel, however, Jesus does not promise us that the love of God and neighbor is going to cost us nothing. Jesus' law of love involves sacrifice for us individually and as a nation. Through the acceptance of this teaching we are committing ourselves to being our neighbor's keeper. In another part of the same Gospel, Jesus tells us, "From everyone to whom much has been given, much will be required; and from the one to whom much has been entrusted, even more will be demanded." Sadly, many of us want the good life for ourselves, while doing very little to help other countries become more livable, and then we can reject people who want to share in the blessings we have worked for and inherited.

The Gospel of Matthew gives us the story of Mary, Joseph, and Jesus being forced to flee Israel for Egypt as refugees. If the Holy Family was coming our way these days, they might be sent back to King Herod. May the Eucharist see in us a change of heart so our faith enables us to act justly toward everyone. May our goodness and hospitality mirror on earth the welcome we hope to enjoy from Jesus, Mary, and Joseph in the kingdom that is promised to all, irrespective of where any of us has been born.

THIRTY-FIRST SUNDAY IN ORDINARY TIME

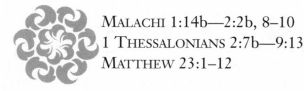

MALACHI 1:14b—2:2b, 8–10
1 THESSALONIANS 2:7b—9:13
MATTHEW 23:1–12

As we come to the end of the church's year, it's good for us to do some soul-searching. Recent years have been tough ones for the church, and today's Gospel sums up what it's been like for many of us to hear about how some priests betrayed our trust, how many victims were disbelieved, and how a few of our bishops have tried to cover up criminal actions. We have seen the exalted being humbled and the humble being exalted.

Jesus tells the crowds to listen to what the Pharisees teach, but not to follow their appalling example. The behavior of the Pharisees has a name, hypocrisy, and it's one of the reasons we have received such a public pasting in recent times. Some of it has been justified. We have been seen to be a community more interested in our good name and public standing than in the damage done to those brothers and sisters of ours who were given into our care and became victims of physical and sexual abuse. We have been exposed as not practicing what we preach.

The church is in a bind here. We are not like other groups who can simply expel their worst members and move on. If we are going to be faithful to all of Jesus' teaching and the entire Christian tradition, then we have to comfort and heal the victims of abuse and call the perpetrators to the demands of the law, treatment, and reconciliation. But we also believe that the only way to healing is through forgiveness. True forgiveness never runs from the truth or minimizes our sinfulness. It confronts the human condition with justice and compassion for all concerned.

The press may not like it, the public may be baying for blood, and we might want an instant fix so we can put tragic chapters behind us quickly, but a forgiveness, which is just and compassionate, is the only way we can practice what we preach. It takes time. True forgiveness never runs from the truth or minimizes our sinfulness. It confronts the human condition with justice and compassion for all concerned.

On the other hand, while some in our Catholic community have been exposed as hypocrites, some other truths remain consoling, or at least provide a context within which we can confront the sins of our fathers and mothers. For example, though there should never have been one case of child abuse in the church, less than 2 percent of all Catholic priests have been convicted of this dreadful crime. An accusation is not a conviction, and even priests and religious deserve the presumption and rights of innocence before they are proven guilty. Even though the public perception may be otherwise, the vast majority of all Catholic priests are faithful servants of the gospel, practicing what they preach.

Against a prevailing misconception, church-run institutions are not the places where children are most at risk. Tragically, it's the family home. Over 80 percent of all child abuse occurs there. This does not excuse one case of abuse in the church, but it does suggest that, if our wider society really wants to tackle this problem, we are all going to have to start by looking in our own backyards.

Furthermore, against those who claim that the church is only hypocritical, they cannot take away from us the fact that our community, in the name of Christ, remains the largest provider of education, health care, and welfare both here and overseas. This often-heroic work will rarely make it to the front pages of newspapers, but it's the backdrop against which we face up to the criminal actions of a few and those who try to protect them from public scrutiny.

Let's pray that, as hard as these times have been for all of us, we are converted again by the forgiving, just, and compassionate example of Jesus, who calls us to leave behind any trace of triumphalism and arrogance and recommit ourselves to what we should do best: the self-sacrificing love of one another and the world.

THIRTY-SECOND SUNDAY IN ORDINARY TIME

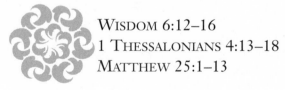

WISDOM 6:12–16
1 THESSALONIANS 4:13–18
MATTHEW 25:1–13

One Sunday a pastor told the congregation that the church needed some extra money and asked the people to prayerfully consider giving a little extra in the offering plate. He said that whoever gave the most would be able to pick out three hymns. After the offering plates were passed, the pastor glanced down and noticed that someone had placed a $1,000 check on the plate.

He was so excited that he immediately shared his joy with his congregation and said he'd like to personally thank the person who placed the money on the plate. A very quiet, elderly, saintly spinster at the back shyly raised her hand. The pastor asked her to come to the front. Slowly she made her way to the altar. He told her how wonderful it was that she gave so much, and in thanksgiving asked her to pick out three hymns.

Her eyes brightened as she looked over the congregation, pointed to the three most handsome men in the congregation and said, "OK, Pastor, I'll take him, him, and him." Now that's a modern take on a wise virgin!

In one sense the parable of the wise and foolish virgins could be considered the first known oil crisis in the East. It is, however, about planning for the future and pacing oneself to see that one has a future to enjoy.

In Christian theology this is called "discernment." St. Ignatius Loyola, the founder of the Jesuits, wrote a lot about discernment, and one of his teachings is that the Holy Spirit allows us to prepare for our future without living it.

Think for a moment of the times when we are going to have a difficult interview or a conversation we would rather not have. We play out in our mind how the interaction will run. It rarely goes how we imagine, and often our anxiety and fear have been misplaced. What is curious is that on the next occasion we go through the same process of trying to live the future all over again. Tragically, some people are so anxious about their future they try and control it and everyone associated with it. It's always a disaster.

St. Ignatius was suspicious of this process. Ignatius seems to have understood today's Gospel very well. The early church thought Jesus would return quickly. There was a crisis of faith when he didn't. Some Christians lived as though this imminent return was a fact. We are still waiting. Matthew tells us, then, that the Christian life is about wisdom, right judgment, and reading the signs of the times.

St. Ignatius tells us the best way to prepare for the future is to let go of the unhealed past, as best as we can, and live in the here and now. The Holy Spirit helps us see what needs to be done today and what preparation is necessary for tomorrow. This is such simple and sound advice and yet many of us don't heed it. It takes nothing for us to feel the hurt and pain of our past or to be consumed by the future.

Alcoholics Anonymous sums it up neatly when it tells us to take life "one day at a time," which is another way of saying what Matthew's community came to see, "Keep awake, therefore, for you know neither the day nor the hour."

THIRTY-THIRD SUNDAY IN ORDINARY TIME

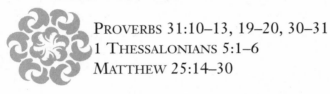 PROVERBS 31:10–13, 19–20, 30–31
1 THESSALONIANS 5:1–6
MATTHEW 25:14–30

As Catholics, we have no problem with the time-bound nature of the Bible. In fact we appreciate it, believing that the scriptures deserve to be read within their context, and also need careful interpretation. And while the Catholic Feminist Association may not choose to have today's first reading as the opening text at their next convention, we would be mistaken to hear it only in terms of our world today.

The Book of Proverbs is a distillation of sayings and teachings that had grown up over hundreds of years, most probably from rabbis and scribes. Its world is a vastly different one from ours. This is clearly seen in the tasks of the "capable wife." She is praised for her work with wool and flax, in the vineyard and in real estate. It's only in the context of an agrarian society that the power of this text makes sense.

Until quite recently, women in Palestinian society, and in wider society for that matter, were considered the "possessions" of their husbands. They could be bought, sold, divorced, or killed without any appeal to the law. Wives in this society had no legally recognized human rights. They expected to serve and shut up.

By contrast, then, this text from the Book of Proverbs, which can seem so old fashioned to us, was a liberating text in its day. A woman's right to work is not only defended, but also extolled. She is praised for her creativity, wisdom, goodness, strength, sense of justice, generosity, joy, and faith. In any age and for either gender this is not a bad list of virtues toward which we should all aspire.

And these days, of course, through the ongoing revelation of the Spirit, we believe that what the Book of Proverbs expects and praises in a capable wife, we should equally look for in a capable husband.

It is almost possible that Jesus had women in mind when he shared the parable of the talents in today's Gospel. What can often get lost in the debates about who should be ordained in today's church is that women have always and still "lead" the church in powerful and long-lasting ways. From the extraordinary abilities of religious and lay women in Catholic welfare, education, health care, overseas missions, and theological institutions to wives and mothers who daily witness to the fidelity and goodness of God, this all reveals in innumerable ways the power of the parable of the talents. The reality is that if it were not for women's leadership, commitment, and faith, it would be hard how to see how the church could survive. We would not be able to continue almost all of our ministries.

None of this minimizes the pain and hurt some women have experienced at the hands of the church. Some feel as though their particular contribution to the life of the church has not been fully realized.

All we can hope and pray for is that we may find ways to use everyone's talents for the building up of the kingdom of God, and that we may see that everyone's contribution, irrespective of gender, is precious and worthy of praise.

FEAST OF CHRIST THE KING

EZEKIEL 34:11–12, 15–17
1 CORINTHIANS 15:20–26, 28
MATTHEW 25:31–46

The Roman emperor Constantine was baptized in 337. He put it off for years. In the early church Christians could only confess their sins once in their lives, so Constantine remained a catechumen until he was nearing the end. Despite what *The Da Vinci Code* says, when he thought his death was imminent, and that he could probably sin no more, he asked for baptism, received holy communion, and later confessed his sins. It was a watershed moment for the church.

In 313, a few years before his death, Constantine had already declared that Christianity was to be the new state religion. No one could hold any other belief. It was meant to unify the empire as trade, law, taxation, and Roman culture had done. I think we should admit that this move has been a mixed blessing for the church ever since.

On the positive side of the ledger, it finally sealed the end of the persecution of the earliest Christians. The blood of the martyrs had been so eloquent that their witness caused even a few emperors to ask what sort of love would see so many followers be prepared to die for their beliefs. It also saw the church become a significant player in shaping the values of society, especially in the West. There is no question that Christianity moderated, cultivated, and humanized some of the worst Roman excesses.

On the cost side, the church became very powerful very quickly. Bishops started to wear the purple robes of the senators. Churches took on the shape of the Roman basilicas, while the government of the church mirrored that of the empire. Our liturgy imported all sorts of practices that were popular in the Roman temples. Tragically, for the next few hundred years, conversions were demanded at the end of a sword. No religious dissent or pluralism was tolerated. It's in this context that Islam arises against imperial Christianity in the sixth century.

It cannot surprise us that after Constantine's conversion the image of Christ the King becomes one of the most popular ones used in religious art. Up to this time the image of Jesus as the Good Shepherd was the most represented. After 313, however, Jesus is dressed in royal robes, with a crown, scepter, and orb. Mary is often presented in similar dress and starts to be called the Queen of Heaven.

The problem with all this is not that worldly imperial language was now being used in reference to Jesus. He described himself as a king. Christianity started to forget that Jesus also pointed out that his kingdom was "not of this world" and that his courtiers could be recognized by how they feed the hungry, water the thirsty, welcome strangers, clothe the naked, care for the sick, and visit prisoners. Jesus' reign and his courtiers are of an altogether different order from that usually prized in worldly kingdoms.

That's why today's feast is so important. On the last day of the church's year we are challenged by Christ our King to give our true allegiance to what really matters. Not ambition, greed, status, and power, but the quiet revolutionary work of making the world a more just and peaceful place for everyone to live in.

To the degree that we do this we are coheirs to the kingdom Jesus lived, died, and was raised for, then we are witnesses to the real meaning of Christ's reign in our lives.

Cycle B

FIRST SUNDAY OF ADVENT

Isaiah 63:16b–17, 19b; 64:2b–7
1 Corinthians 1:3–9
Mark 13:33–37

These days most people keep vigils because they are anxious. We wait in hospital corridors for news of a sick relative. A parent stays up with an infant who may be teething or has a high temperature. We might even sit by the phone waiting to be reassured that a loved one is safe and well, or that we have passed the exam or got the job. Many of these occasions are highly stressed vigils. Some of the younger or more hardy ones among us sometimes keep vigils that are filled with excited anticipation, as when some of us sleep outside to get tickets to a sports game or concert, or when we see the old year out and the new year in.

It was not long ago, however, that vigils were a much more common feature of people's lives. We often kept vigil with the dead. We used to keep all-night vigils of prayer, especially when parishes had perpetual adoration of the Blessed Sacrament. Perhaps before any of us can remember, there were also vigils kept with the bride the night before her wedding, when she waited and watched for the sign of her approaching groom and his attendants. The church has enshrined the experience of keeping vigil through the Vigil Mass on Saturday night, the Vigil Ceremony in the funeral rites, and the most important one, the Easter Vigil.

This tradition starts with today's Gospel where we are exhorted to be alert, keep awake, and wait for the Lord to return. In a sense this is a strange Gospel to have as we prepare for Christmas. It is linked to the first preface of Advent, which reads, "Now we watch for the day, hoping that the salvation promised us will be ours, when Christ our Lord will come in glory." Our attention is, therefore, directed to a great future event, not the future feast we are about to celebrate.

This is unique. All other feasts of the church either remember a past event, like those of Holy Week or Pentecost, or they are "title feasts" that proclaim a truth about God's action among us that the entire church holds to be true, like Trinity Sunday. But not the First Sunday of Advent. Rather than talk about the coming of Jesus at Christmas it helps us reflect on the final coming of the Lord at the end of time. It is the bridge between the "last days" of the church's year, which we have been celebrating over recent weeks, and the first days of the church's New Year.

And how does the church ask us to approach this feast? As on a vigil. Not a vigil of anxiety, where we never want to hear the worst news. Not a vigil of excited anticipation, where we pin our happiness on entry into an event. But a vigil of hope, where we wait and trust in a person who has shared our lot, understands our frailties, and loved us to death. We place our hope in Jesus the Christ, our brother, savior, and friend. This First Sunday of Advent we look beyond Christmas to the final moment when heaven and earth will be united and our vigil will be complete. On that day we believe the Son will have dawned once, and for all, on the world. Now, don't you think that's something worth being awake to see?

The first week of Advent is like the first days of other vigils wherein we pitch out tents and begin the wait to make sure we have front-row seats for what is going to be, when it arrives, the best show in town!

SECOND SUNDAY OF ADVENT

 ISAIAH 40:1–5, 9–11
2 PETER 3: 8–14
MARK 1:1–8

During Advent, Daniel went to his mother demanding a new bicycle for Christmas. "Danny, we can't afford it," she said, "so write a letter to Jesus and pray for one instead." "Dear Jesus," he wrote, "I've been a good boy this year and would appreciate a new bicycle. Your Friend, Daniel." Now Danny guessed that Jesus really knew he was a brat so he tore it up and tried again. "Dear Jesus, I've been an OK boy this year and I want a new bicycle. Yours Truly, Daniel." Danny knew this wasn't true so he tore it up and tried again. "Dear Jesus, I've thought about being a good boy so may I have a new bicycle? Daniel."

Finally, Danny thought better of making these false claims and so ran to the church. He went inside and stole a small statue of Mary and ran out the door. He went home, hid it under his bed, and wrote this letter. "Jesus, let's face it, I've broken most of the Commandments; tore up my sister's doll and lots more, I'm desperate. I've got your mother Mary, if you ever want to see her again, give me a bike for Christmas.—You know who."

There is a little bit of Danny in all of us.

We often think that we can bargain with God to get the best possible deal out of life. The problem with this bargaining image is that it cannot be reconciled with a Christian faith that believes in Advent. The bargaining image of God is the furthest thing from the mind of the writers of today's readings—Isaiah, Psalm 85, St. Peter, and St. Mark.

These scriptures remind us that God has not held back one thing in his love for us. By becoming one with us in our flesh, God has done everything he can to assure us of his saving love. He has shown us all that can be shown about how to live lives of sacrifice, justice, and love and how to transform our world for the better.

The image of us "doing a deal" with God is so prevalent in our theology and prayer that we can find ourselves lapsing into it all the time. "If you make me well, God, I will lead a better life." "I will return to Sunday Mass if I pass my exams." "I will raise my children Catholic if I have a fine day for my wedding." This is all dreadful stuff. And some of our Catholic forebears have to take some responsibility for this.

The scriptures tell us, from the beginning of time to the preaching of John the Baptist to the life, death, resurrection of Jesus Christ and to the ongoing work of the Holy Spirit among us today, that we have a God who risked everything so that we might know love and life in this world and in the next. We hold and proclaim, in season and out of season, a God who emptied himself of power and might and came to us as a baby.

That's not the profile of a deal doer. It's the portrait of a lover.

So this Advent let's not ransom ourselves to a benevolent dictator. Let's ask for anything we need with confidence that God has heard our words and so sent love itself in Jesus Christ our Lord.

THIRD SUNDAY OF ADVENT

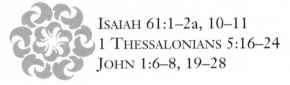

ISAIAH 61:1–2a, 10–11
1 THESSALONIANS 5:16–24
JOHN 1:6–8, 19–28

Today is traditionally called Gaudete Sunday. Over the first millennium of Christianity, Advent was like a late Lent. Both were five weeks long. Both were marked by fasting and penance, and both gave the faithful a day off halfway through.

In Lent, Laetare Sunday is still, roughly, halfway through the five-week season. Advent, however, got shortened to four weeks in the sixth century by Pope St. Gregory the Great, and the fasting and penitential aspects of this season were also eased in time, but the now not-so-halfway Gaudete Sunday has remained with us. It is, literally, the "rejoicing Sunday" when we look more directly at the coming of Jesus at Christmas.

To enable us to look at who Jesus is for us, the church gives us the one who heralded his mission in the world, John the Baptist.

In today's Gospel John the Baptist is the model of humility, opening the way for the kingdom of Jesus to break in upon the world. We should never underestimate how important talent spotters are, for as this story demonstrates, they all have John the Baptist as their patron saint.

Fleming was a poor Scottish farmer in the nineteenth century. One day, while working in his field, he heard a cry for help coming from a nearby bog. He dropped everything and ran to the site. There, mired to his waist in black muck, was a terrified boy, screaming and struggling to free himself. Farmer Fleming saved the lad from what could have been a slow and terrifying death.

The next day, a fancy carriage pulled up to the Scotsman's simple cottage. An elegantly dressed nobleman stepped out and introduced himself as the father of the boy Farmer Fleming had saved. "I want to repay you," said the nobleman. "You saved my son's life." "No, I can't accept payment for what I did," the Scottish farmer replied, waving away the offer.

At that moment, the farmer's own young son came to the door of the family home. "Is that your boy?" the nobleman asked. "Yes," the farmer replied proudly. "I'll make you a deal. Let me give him a good education. If the lad is anything like his father, he'll grow up to be a man you can be proud of." Farmer Fleming agreed.

In time, Farmer Fleming's son graduated from St. Mary's Medical School in London, and went on to become known throughout the world as the noted Sir Alexander Fleming, the discoverer of penicillin. Years later, the son of the nobleman who had paid for Alexander Fleming's education was stricken with pneumonia. What saved his life? Penicillin. The nobleman's name? Randolph Churchill. And who did his sickly son go on to be? Sir Winston Churchill.

Winston's grandfather recognized the greatness in Farmer Fleming, and in turn opened the way for many of us to benefit from the saving intelligence of his son. Even more so, John the Baptist recognized the Son, and through him many have come to know the saving love of the Father.

John is the embodiment of the Old Covenant, who recognizes that Jesus is the new and everlasting covenant. John the Baptist knew that in Jesus Love itself had taken human form. Through his talent spotting, and in his promotion of the kingdom Jesus lived and proclaimed, he enabled the first generation of Christians to see and believe that the promises made to their ancestors had been fulfilled.

No wonder we have him as our focus on Gaudete Sunday. And so may all of us rejoice today, not only because salvation is always close at hand in Christ the Lord, but because we are also called to spot his love in every act of goodness we see, encourage and promote it as best we can, and then watch nature and grace do the rest.

FOURTH SUNDAY OF ADVENT

2 SAMUEL 7:1–5, 8b–12, 14a, 16
ROMANS 16:25–27
LUKE 1:26–38

Jesus and Satan have an argument as to who is the better computer programmer. Eventually they agree to hold a contest with God as the judge. They set themselves before their computers and begin. They type furiously for several hours, lines of code streaming up the screen. Seconds before the end of the competition, a bolt of lightning strikes, taking out the electricity. Moments later, the power is restored, and God announces that the contest is over. He asks Satan to show what he has come up with. Satan is visibly upset, and cries, "I have nothing! I lost it all when the power went out." "Very well, then," says God, "let us see if Jesus fared any better." Jesus enters a command, and the screen comes to life in vivid display, the voices of an angelic choir pouring forth from the speakers. Satan is astonished. He stutters, "But how? I lost everything, how can Jesus' program be intact?" God chuckles and says, "Ah—because Jesus saves."

On this final Sunday of Advent, the church moves our gaze to the annunciation. The whole scene hinges around one word: "Yes." Mary's fiat sets in motion the entire Christian drama. In his film *Jesus of Nazareth*, Franco Zeffirelli pictures the annunciation this way: Mary is asleep at night when a gust of wind opens a high window. Afraid at all the commotion, Mary gets up and starts to pray. As she prays, we see her face change and her body bend over. With tears in her eyes, Mary looks up through the window to the moonlit sky and simply says, "Be it done unto me as you have said." The swirling wind dies down at once.

In recent years, successive popes have reminded us that the best devotion to Mary is one that leads us to do what she did: say yes to accepting Jesus into our lives. Mary is not a stop on our journey of faith; she is a guidepost that always sends us on to Christ. Mary does not save us, for we believe she needed to be saved by Christ as well. That's why she could say yes in the first place. Mary recognized the gift and the giver and became the bearer of God for the world.

In this final week of Advent, let's keep reminding ourselves of this simple but life-changing fact: Jesus saves us. Jesus saves us from death. Jesus saves us from living lives devoid of purpose and meaning, and Jesus saves us from the worst things in ourselves.

We don't save ourselves. We cannot earn salvation by good works or prayers or penance. And, as difficult as it is to hear, we cannot save anyone else. That includes our children, spouse, grandchildren, parents, or friends.

Our prayers, good works, and faith are the responses we make to the salvation of Christ we claim here and now. And how we live is the way by which those we love will find the gift of God's salvation for themselves.

In the midst of this frantic, final week before Christmas, when so many other things can distract us from what this grace-filled feast is really all about, let's take a moment to join Mary in accepting into our lives and hearts the greatest of all gifts—our undeserved salvation, Jesus Christ the Lord.

CHRISTMAS

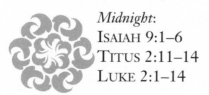

Midnight:
ISAIAH 9:1–6
TITUS 2:11–14
LUKE 2:1–14

A Pentecostal friend of mine tells the story of leaving church one Christmas morning as the preacher was standing at the door, greeting everyone and shaking hands. He grabbed my friend by the hand and pulled him aside. The pastor said to him, "You need to join the army of the Lord!" To which my friend replied, "I'm already in the army of the Lord, pastor." The pastor looked amazed and said, "How come I don't see you here at church then, except at Christmas and Easter?" My friend whispered back, "Because I'm in the secret service."

If you're like my friend and find yourself in the "secret service," you're in good company at Christmastime. The first hearers of the Christmas story were not much into churchgoing either. Shepherds in first-century Palestine had to watch their flocks around the clock for fear of thieves and wolves. This didn't leave much time for Temple attendance. They prayed where they were, as they were. These shepherds, however, were in the right place at the right time to hear the first Christmas message. Maybe they had the right disposition too.

Sometimes, publicly religious people can sound as though they know the mind of God better than God does! It's a trap we need to avoid and Christmas helps us do it. No one predicted the way God would send us a savior. No one knew the day or the hour of his coming. No one foresaw that he would be born a homeless person. No one envisaged that the first witnesses to his birth would be illiterate shepherds from nearby fields. While some waited for a mercenary to overthrow the Romans, others held their breath for the procession of a heavenly king. The love of God, however, took flesh of our flesh, bone of our bone, and came to us as a poor, defenseless baby.

That's our God, not bound by our precepts or expectations, but honoring the promises made to our ancestors, in the most surprising of ways. And Christmas provides us with the most tender images of our God—he who needs to be nurtured, suckled, and held tight.

It's not a bad metaphor for our Christian faith either. If Christmas means anything to us, then it's not an annual religious outing or something to fill in time on a public holiday. We celebrate it every time we do something just, loving, or peaceful. That's why we gather here for the Eucharist each week: to be nurtured, fed, suckled, and held in God's embrace, if only for a while, so that we find the courage and strength to go out from here, confront the wolves and thieves of our own day, and be in the right place at the right time for God to find us.

As a result of that first Christmas, Christ wants to nurture us so that we change the world for the better. So this Christmas cash in your secret service card and, "Go tell it on the mountain, over the hill and everywhere. Go tell it on the mountain, that Jesus Christ is born."

HOLY FAMILY

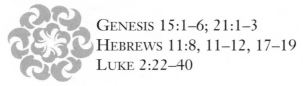 GENESIS 15:1–6; 21:1–3
HEBREWS 11:8, 11–12, 17–19
LUKE 2:22–40

When I was sixteen, I read the works of Jesuit Father John Powell. In one of his books he wrote, "We should never leave this world not having the people that we love know that we love them." Now, I don't come from a particularly demonstrative family. We do not make regular declarations of our love accompanied by long hugs. So I took John Powell's line as a personal challenge.

At the time, my sister was working with Mother Teresa in Calcutta, and my brother was working in another city, so I wrote them both letters and told them I loved them. I never heard a word back.

That left my mother. I stayed in one Saturday night and, with my heart pumping and my tummy churning, I approached my mother after dinner while she was watching the news on the TV. "Mum, I have something very important to tell you." My mother, not taking her eyes from the screen, casually said, "Oh Yes, what's that?" "Mum," I responded, "I've never told you this before and I need to say it tonight." As she slowly turned off the TV and faced me, I could tell there were now two hearts pumping and two tummies churning in that room!

I plucked up all my courage and came straight out with it. "Mum, I just want to tell you that I love you." And such was her relief that my mother replied. "I hope so!" And quickly turned the TV back on. There were no hugs and kisses, no violins playing or statements about how long Mum had been waiting to hear one of us talk of our love for her. As I walked back to my room I thought I would never take John Powell's advice again!

My brother and sister wrote to my mother asking her what was wrong with me. They all concluded it was a phase I was going through. I hope it's a phase I never get over!

Today's feast of the Holy Family is about faithful love that looks after the most important people in our lives. We all know that fights and bitterness can wreck families for generations. If today's feast means anything, it is not about romanticizing how difficult family life can be these days. It is about affirming that forgiveness, compassion, and kindness are the blocks upon which Christian family life is built. Without these virtues family life crumbles.

The best way to honor today's feast is to do something about the faithful love it celebrates. I have often been with people on their deathbed when they speak about things they have left undone and would have liked to have achieved in their life. No one ever says that they wish they had spent more time at work. No one says they wish they had made more money. But many people say that they wish they had told those they love that they loved them. We shouldn't assume that our families know about our love for them if we haven't said it. If we show it, we should be able to say it. So write a letter, make a call, or go and see them, but let's pluck up our courage and tell our families that we love them. It's too late once we're dead.

And the best news is that when we profess our love to our families we get to glimpse the joy holiness can bring.

EPIPHANY OF THE LORD

ISAIAH 60:1–6
EPHESIANS 3:2–3a, 5–6
MATTHEW 2:1–12

Last year some Christian scientists got to work on trying to explain the star that led the wise men to Bethlehem. They came up with a complicated, and no doubt plausible, astronomical theory about how a certain, brilliant star may have appeared around the time of the birth of Jesus. Though I was intrigued by their methods, I wondered why they bothered. Matthew's wandering star is not about astronomy. It's religious shorthand for describing how the heavens preside over and guide the events of the world. The image of a star is used in similar ways in the books of Deuteronomy, Numbers, the prophet Isaiah, and the Psalms. This entire feast is all about symbols, not science. Recorded by Hippolytus as early as the third century, it is celebrated twelve days after Christmas, the number itself echoing what the twelve tribes of Israel longed to see.

The wise men's star is on a par with the other images Matthew uses. At the center of each of the first three chapters of his Gospel, there is an extraordinary event. In chapter one, Joseph hears the message of an angel in a dream. In chapter two, the wise men find Jesus by following a star. And by chapter three, the heavens open and God speaks at the baptism of the Lord. By any standards that's quite an opening to a biography! It's all about the manifestation, or epiphany, of God's glory in the world.

And let's look carefully at where and for whom this glory is revealed. The first instance is to Joseph while he's in bed asleep. The second is to Gentile astrologers who, by reporting their news to Herod, set up an immediate threat to Jesus. The third instance is to all those Jews who were coming to hear John the Baptist. Within three chapters of Matthew's Gospel, the circles of God's glory revealed in Jesus become more public and change lives. The lives of Joseph, the stargazers, John the Baptist, and those who heard Jesus preach will never be the same again.

The feast of the Epiphany is not an ancient version of Halley's comet. It is about how God's glory changes human hearts. And we believe that God's glory was not revealed through the power and might of armies, princes, and priests. It came to us through Mary, a Galilean teenager who said yes to God, through Joseph her husband who refused to see her publicly disgraced, and uniquely in a baby, who changed our world forever.

These days we talk a lot about stars—Hollywood stars, sports stars, and even those who star in our families. At their best they can be role models, giving their all in such extraordinary ways that our ordinary lives are transformed, at least for a while. Jesus is not just stalked by a star in Bethlehem, he is our star. He is the role model once and for all, who shows us that in the Father's eyes we are all stars, and can bask in his reflected glory.

And so may this feast change our hearts and enable us to die to self so as to be born to God's glory that can and does shine through us. And may we remember that this epiphany is not meant for us alone, but that we are called to go public with it and demonstrate our belief in today's feast by the way we live, the world we help create, and the one we strive to re-create.

BAPTISM OF THE LORD

Isaiah 55:1–11
1 John 5:1–9
Mark 1:7–11

A very drunk man stumbles upon the local Baptist minister conducting his Sunday service down by the river. He proceeds to venture into the water and stand next to the minister. The minister turns, notices the man, and says, "Mister, are you ready to find Jesus?" The man looks back and says, "Yes, Reverend, I am." "The minister then dunks the fellow under the water and pulls him right back up. "Have you found Jesus?" the minister asks. "No, I didn't!" says the man. The minister then dunks him under for a quite a bit longer, brings him up, and says, "Now, brother, have you found Jesus?" "No, I did not!" says the drunken man again. Disgusted, the minister holds the man under for at least thirty seconds this time, brings him up, and demands, "For the grace of God, have you found Jesus yet?" The man wipes his eyes and pleads, "Are you sure this is where he fell in?"

One of the actions I find most consoling about the scene into today's Gospel is that John the Baptist immersed Jesus in the waters of the Jordan. Indeed the word *baptism* is derived from the Greek word, *bapto*, or *baptizo*, "to wash" or "to immerse." Most of us were baptized with just a sprinkling of water. These days, however, the church encourages adults and infants, where possible, to follow in the more ancient tradition of full immersion.

We all know the amount of water used in the baptism does not destine the power of this sacrament; that's found in how we live our Christian commitment away from the font. What full immersion does is link the ritual of baptism more directly to the experience of Jesus and enables the symbolism of the water to be more fully realized.

There are no half measures about immersion, we are in there boots and all. In an extraordinary visual metaphor, Mark tells this that is what God does for us in Christ. We don't have a detached God who only presides over us. We don't have a coaching God who sits on the sidelines barking orders at us on the field of life. And we don't have a policeman God who wants to catch us breaking the rules. We have a God who in Jesus the Lord immersed himself in our world, heart and mind, soul and divinity, boots and all.

This is why the earliest association the Christians made with the waters of baptism was that it symbolized Jesus' tomb. We are the only world religion to believe that God took our flesh and died. Because of the three days Jesus spent in the tomb, we plunge our adults and children into the watery tomb of the font three times. And as we do we call on the Trinity to enable them die to sin, and rise to the freedom of Christ's life. In this context we can see that the deeper the font and the fuller the immersion, the more easily everyone present understands the power of the symbols.

For all those baptized in Christ, a curious thing happens. As Jesus fully immersed himself in our world, so we are fully immersed in Christ. But we are not spared from the world as if we are initiated into a reclusive religious sect. We are sent out to the world knowing, because of Jesus, that we are loved by God and pleasing to him. We are sent out with faith, hope, and joy to fall into the arms of the world and discover that here, too, is where Christ dwells.

SECOND SUNDAY IN ORDINARY TIME

1 SAMUEL 3:3b–10, 19
1 CORINTHIANS 6:13c–15a, 17–20
JOHN 1:35–42

Most of us have seen those Christian billboards that try to catch the attention of the passer-by.

Among the better ones are:

> Church parking lot full—For Members Only. Trespassers will be baptized!

> Free Trip to Heaven. Details Inside!

> C'mon over and bring the kids.
>   God.

> Searching for a new look? Have your faith lifted here!

> Loved the wedding, invite me to the marriage.
>   God

> The Ten Commandments—for fast relief, take two tablets.

> Will the road you're on get you to my place?
>   God

> If you're headed in the wrong direction, God allows U-turns.

> Come work for the Lord. The work is hard, the hours are long and the pay is low. But the retirement benefits are out of this world.

> What are you doing on earth—for Christ's sake?

Billboards are a new and novel way of calling people to make some form of response to the life of faith, even if that is to reject it. Often through humor they try and resent a welcoming and engaging face for the church to the wider public.

The readings from the First Book of Samuel and the Gospel of John all involve call and response. The first reading plays out what many people think the call of God is like—a booming voice telling us what to do. John's Gospel is more subtle. The earliest apostles are called in two ways and neither of them involves loud voices with grand requests. Andrew follows Jesus because of what John the Baptist says. Simon Peter comes to Jesus through word-of-mouth, his brother Andrew's recommendation.

What these readings collectively indicate is the various ways in which people are drawn into the life and service of God. Sometimes, because we want certainty, we hope and long for a more dramatic indication of God's will. Some people get it. Mostly, however, the experience of Andrew and Simon Peter is the more common one. We follow our desires, play our hunches and pursue that which intrigues us. As time goes on, our experience indicates the path that will lead to the most hopeful, faithful, and loving choice. What is especially encouraging about the Gospel is that Andrew goes after whatever it is that Jesus has. He lives with, or experiences, Jesus' company for a day and then becomes his recruiting officer.

In so many ways, of course, things are different for us now. Rather than us seeking out where Jesus lives, we are given opportunities to experience his life and invite him to come and make a home with us. But whatever the differences in the process, the end result is the same. Just as Samuel, Andrew and Peter could have no idea where their response to God's call would lead them, so we cannot either. All we know is that it will cost us something, maybe everything.

Responding to God's call in Christ is not for the faint-hearted and we shouldn't pretend it is. It involves loving our enemies, working for peace, forgiving those who have wronged us, and making the world a just place for all God's children. If these charges make no claim on us in our daily lives, then, chances are we are listening to voices that endlessly give us the runaround, rather than being hooked up to the source of life that makes sense and gives meaning to all our connections in this world and the next.

THIRD SUNDAY IN ORDINARY TIME

JONAH 3:1–5, 10
1 CORINTHIANS 7:29–31
MARK 1:14–20

Seeing that today's Gospel is set by the water's edge, this story seems appropriate.

One day, three men were hiking and unexpectedly came upon a large raging river. They needed to get to the other side, but had no idea of how to do so. The first man prayed to God, "Please, God, give me the strength to cross this river." In an instant God gave him big arms and strong legs, and he was able to swim across the river in about two hours, after almost drowning a couple of times.

Seeing this, the second man prayed to God, "Please, God, give me the strength and the resources to cross this river." In an instant God gave him a rowboat and he was able to row across the river in about an hour, after almost capsizing the boat a couple of times.

The third man had seen how this worked out for the other two, so he also prayed to God saying, "Please, God, give me the strength and the resources—and the intelligence—to cross this river." In an instant God turned him into a woman. She looked at the map, hiked upstream a couple of hundred yards, then walked across the bridge!

The three men's prayers were all about gaining something: strength, resources, and intelligence. Today's readings are about gaining things too. Unlike the instant answer to the hikers' prayers, Jonah, Paul, and Mark know real gain usually comes less dramatically and quickly, and involves letting go of something as much as it involves taking it on. In the Christian life this is called conversion, and it's at the center of our life of faith.

Christian conversion is not a once-in-a-lifetime moment. It can happen everyday in a rich variety of ways. It involves a change in attitude as much as a change in lifestyle.

All three readings show a different facet of conversion. Jonah calls the Ninevites to social conversion. St. Paul, who reveals a very strong expectation that the end of time is near, calls the people of Corinth to a conversion of mind. And through relating the call of Simon, Andrew, James, and John, St. Mark tells us about personal conversion.

These days we regularly hear God's call in personal terms. It's sometimes called "me and God" theology. Modern hymns reflect it best. We regularly sing about how Jesus died "for me," or that "Here I am, Lord" or that "I will follow you." Individually these lines are all true; the problem is that they tend to play down the more ancient and biblical social dimensions of our call to conversion. In the Bible even though God and Jesus call people to conversion through personal relationships, there is no hint that this is where it stops. Every call leads to the wider community, to the people of Israel in the Old Testament, and out to the entire world in the New Testament.

Today's readings provide a litmus test for our conversion. If our faith has become a self-help club, where we talk about "my" God, "my" prayers, "my" church, "my" Mass, we are in need of conversion. We don't need to leave God's personal love for us behind, we just need to see it as a necessary preparation for belonging to the people of God as we engage with the world at every level. We are challenged to reject the idea that it's me-and-God-against-the-world, and welcome the idea that it's us-and-God-in-the-world.

May we gain the strength, resources, and intelligence we need to be converted personally and socially again this Ordinary Time.

FOURTH SUNDAY IN ORDINARY TIME

DEUTERONOMY 18:15–20
1 CORINTHIANS 7:32–35
MARK 1:21–28

Sometimes when we think we are making a little progress in the spiritual life we can become aware of all the destructive things within us. In this regard we are in very good company. Nearly every mystic in the church's history reports the same pattern: The closer they felt to God, the more aware of sin they became. It stands to figure, doesn't it? The more light there is in a room, the more sharply defined dark corners become. Rather than be discouraged by our growing spiritual awareness, we can see it as a step in the right direction.

In Mark's Gospel the evil spirits regularly recognize who Jesus is before anyone else does. The light highlights the dark.

In today's Gospel the unclean spirit asks Jesus an interesting question, "Have you come to destroy us?" We know that this is precisely what Jesus comes to do for us—to destroy the power of evil, destruction, and death in our lives. Some Christians are prone these days to doubt the existence of evil. I think this is a mistake. It follows surely from the Christian belief in free choice, that evil *is* a reality and some people can, and do, give themselves to its work.

We don't need to give it undue attention, for we believe that the power of good will win out in the end, but the reality of evil is the only way I can begin to explain Hitler, Pol Pot, Stalin, and even some very destructive behavior much closer to home.

When we were baptized in Christ, on our behalf our parents and sponsors were asked, "Do you reject Satan, all his works…and all his empty promises?" I like this last phrase. Most of us are not given over to grand acts of evil, but we can be allured by the promises evil makes. For example, evil often promises us greed in place of generosity, envy in place of admiration, sex in place of love, revenge in place of forgiveness. Each time we go down these destructive paths we see what dead ends they are, appearing to have no way out. This is because the promises are empty and evil, and they always fail to deliver on the glamorous sales pitch they make.

Sadly, however, the fleeting sense of power or pleasure that destructive behavior gives us means that we are prone to being allured again and again. How do we work to claim Christ's destruction of evil in our lives? St. Ignatius Loyola offers us nine tips for working out the signs of the good spirit and the falsehood of the bad spirit. It's called Christian discernment.

1. Trust the commonplace, the ordinary, the everyday.
2. Live in the here and now.
3. Don't make a decision when we are down; allow the crisis to pass.
4. Be suspicious of "the urgent."
5. Be humble enough to take wise advice wisely.
6. Learn the patterns of the good and bad spirit—follow one, train the other.
7. The good spirit connects us. The bad spirit divides, isolates, locks us in our fears.
8. Get your head and heart in dialogue—we need both.
9. No work for the coming of the kingdom is too small, irrelevant, or inconsequential.

Believing in evil does not mean we have a convenient excuse for all the world's ills. As Jean Paul Sartre said, "Evil triumphs when good people do nothing." But we have not been thrown in the deep end of this struggle without help. To keep choosing life and a love that drives out fear, we have to see evil, name it, and do something about it.

So let's pray that we can work out the patterns of the bad spirit in our lives and change them; respond firmly and quickly when we see destructive behavior, and see the task as a lifelong project.

FIFTH SUNDAY IN ORDINARY TIME

JOB 7:1–4, 6–7
1 CORINTHIANS 9:16–19, 22–23
MARK 1:29–39

In the time of Jesus, almost everything people couldn't understand was put down to a demon or an evil spirit. In the Talmud, which is a large work that began to be written shortly after the time of Jesus and that contains the collected teachings of the rabbis, several pages are devoted to the healing of "fevers." Even though we have become more advanced in our medical knowledge, it's surprising how this thinking still persists. While most people don't blame evil for their ailments, they can think God has a direct hand in sending an illness or an injury. Such faulty theology cannot be reconciled with the New Testament.

There is not a single instance where Jesus inflicts pain and suffering on others. He regularly tells us we have to carry our cross and bear our burdens, but this is vastly different from personally laying a cross on our shoulders or giving us the burdens in the first place. By contrast, every time Jesus encounters suffering and pain he works to heal it and restore the person to new life.

The differences between the healing of Peter's mother-in-law and the other healing stories in the first chapter of Mark's Gospel are striking. Rather than in a public space and in front of crowds, this personal healing occurs in the privacy of Peter's house. By contrast to the command for the demons to be gone, in his bedside ministry Jesus never mentions a demon and uses no words, instead he gently takes her by the hand and helps her to her feet. Unlike the others whom Jesus heals, whose response we never hear about, the healing of Peter's mother-in-law leads her to an act of service. Given all the details Mark gives us of this encounter, it's a pity he never tells us her name.

Sometimes we can think of Jesus' miracles, then and now, as acts of dazzling power. The problem with this idea is that if we see Jesus as going around "zapping" people it's hard to figure out why there were times when he could not perform any miracles at all, or that they happened in stages. Whatever else miracles are, they are deep, personal encounters of faith.

As Catholics we believe in the power of miracles and that the source of them is always the grace of God. But we do not have to see them as something done to us from without. Rather, we can see them as unlocking something from within. For some people, Jesus' word or touch set free in them the healing power God has placed in them. For others, it came through another person's intercession. The same holds true for us today. Furthermore, being anointed, celebrating penance or Eucharist, going to a place of pilgrimage, fasting, being prayed over, or meditating can have a similar effect. Looked at in this way, we can see why some people are healed and others are not. If a personal encounter with Jesus did not always lead to healing, then why should it surprise us that some other encounters these days do not always unlock God's healing within us.

Small- and large-scale miracles are happening everyday. Today's Gospel reminds us that they do not happen for show or for the sake of the crowd. They are realizations of faith. Taking Peter's mother-in-law as our model, we are healed and strengthened so that we can witness to God's saving power, serve the kingdom of God in any way we can, and continue to wait on the Lord.

SIXTH SUNDAY IN ORDINARY TIME

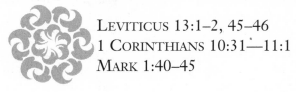

LEVITICUS 13:1–2, 45–46
1 CORINTHIANS 10:31—11:1
MARK 1:40–45

Sometimes translators of the Bible get it wrong for all the best reasons. We are used to hearing in today's Gospel that Jesus was "filled with pity" when he encountered the leper, but the Greek word Mark uses is more accurately translated "anger," not "pity." With the exception of the cleansing of the Temple in John's Gospel, and for a variety of reasons, generations of translators found it hard to imagine Jesus angry. Jesus' anger, however, provides a wonderful insight into him, and a strong challenge to us.

Anger tells us that something is wrong. It is an important and valuable emotion. Anger is value-neutral. It's what we do with it that defines its effect in our lives. Some of us sit on it and stew. Others gain from their anger energy to right the wrong.

People who had any type of skin disease in the ancient world were called lepers. They were treated shamefully. They had to live outside the villages and towns, call out "unclean, unclean" when they came near others, could never attend the Temple, and were considered cursed by God and so excluded from the chosen people. No wonder Jesus was angry when he encountered the man with leprosy. Here he also confronts a social class system that robbed this man of his human dignity and religious laws that robbed him of hope.

There are two details in this story that are especially important. The man with leprosy feels comfortable enough to go straight up to Jesus, put his case, and ask for healing. We are told that Jesus touched him. Social and religious laws were being broken everywhere in this encounter. But Jesus' healing of the man isn't just about challenging social laws and taboos. Jesus tells the man to fulfill his religious obligations so that he can attend the Temple again, and rejoin the community. Jesus was interested in converting all those he met to the higher laws of love and compassion.

We are challenged this Sunday to trust holy anger. This is not only about fighting for our rights when we have been wronged, but more so, it's fighting for the dignity and rights of others. It can take many forms, taking the lot of those yet to be born or who are near natural death, fighting for future generations by calling for a just care of the earth. And it can be about standing up for those people in our home, parish, workplace, neighborhood, country, and world who are treated shamefully, excluded, derided, or declared unclean.

Why should we bother? Because this Sunday Christ comes to us, again, and declares that despite what we might think about ourselves, or what we have been told, there is nothing in us that cannot be healed or is beyond hope.

May the Eucharist give us the love and compassion of Christ to fight for others' dignity because of the dignity we have received from him. May we trust our anger and pray that it be like that of Jesus, and so turn us into agents of change for a more just church and world.

SEVENTH SUNDAY IN ORDINARY TIME

ISAIAH 43:18–19, 21–22, 24b–25
2 CORINTHIANS 1:18–22
MARK 2:1–12

Given that Mark's Gospel was the first one in the New Testament to be written, today's extract could be the earliest evidence we have of intercessory prayer, or better still, intercessory action. The crowd around Jesus is so packed that the friends of the man with paralysis get creative and, literally, go in over the top. There is no sense in today's Gospel of "we shouldn't" or "we can't." There is only boldness in presenting the man before Jesus. Imagine if his friends didn't do this, he might never have known Jesus' healing touch.

Most of us have known moments when we felt desperate. Sometimes when we are ill in mind, body, or spirit, or worse still, when someone we love is in a similar state, we can have bloodied hands from banging on the doors of heaven, asking for God to do a miracle.

In today's Gospel Jesus heals the man dramatically presented before him by his friends. While the physical restitution was the most obvious, it would not have been the only part of the man Jesus healed that day. We can imagine the memories and other afflictions that would have accompanied the man's paralysis. There would have been emotional and spiritual restoration as well.

The same is true of us. If, for all our efforts, our actions and prayers are not answered in the way we would like, we can be left feeling abandoned and forgotten by God. It is not a cop-out, however, to console ourselves with the thought that maybe what we are seeking is the wrong gift from God, either for ourselves or the one for whom we are praying. There are many types of paralysis, equally crippling, and not all of them are physically obvious.

Whatever we ask of Jesus, today's story informs us about his attitude toward our suffering. He initially tells the man, "Your sins are forgiven." Later he says, "Stand up, take up your mat and go to your home." In first-century Palestine, both statements were almost identical. To us, these statements are vastly different. In Jesus' time all illnesses were curses sent by God because of sin. Jesus counters this belief by saying that no illness is from God, no suffering is sent to us because of sin.

How many of us need to hear this? After years of thinking our own paralysis has come about because God is punishing us, this Sunday we hear the Lord say, "Stand up, take up your mat and go to your home." This does not necessarily mean our problems will not need attention in the future. This side of death, we are always unfinished creations, God's "work in progress." But we are reminded that it is always Christ's desire to make us well and whole on every level where we need his healing and peace. We also see the power of friends who support and pray for us and lay our needs before God. What an act of unselfish love intercessory prayers and actions really are.

May we leave behind the Christian heresy that holds that God uses spiritual, mental, or physical pain to get even with us. In its place may we hold onto the image that whatever our paralysis might be, whatever our mat might look like, and hopefully with the support of selfless friends, we can rise up this Sunday and walk into freedom and new life.

EIGHTH SUNDAY IN ORDINARY TIME

Hosea 2:16b, 17b, 21–22
2 Corinthians 3:1b–6
Mark 2:18–22

Have you noticed that weddings have been doing big business in the theaters in recent years? On the stage there is *Mama Mia* and the *Abba Musical*, and on DVD there is *A Guy Thing*, *Just Married*, *Sweet Home Alabama*, *The Wedding Singer*, *My Best Friend's Wedding*, *Muriel's Wedding*, and *Monsoon*. These are just a few of the films that revolve around the theme of marriage. While they are all comedies, underneath the surface they have very serious things to say about fidelity, love, and commitment. The biggest wedding film of all time is *My Big Fat Greek Wedding*, where we meet Toula, a frumpy Greek-American girl who, as a result of falling in love with the Waspish Ian, is transformed into a confident woman able to go outside her fiercely nationalistic family.

The scenes surrounding Toula's marriage are instructive about today's Gospel. For all the months of meticulous planning, contemporary wedding celebrations last seven or eight hours at most. Once the bride and groom leave for their honeymoon, the wedding banquet is over. Weddings were very different in Jesus' day. Everyone in the family and the village was involved, celebrations lasted a week, and the couple did not leave the village for a holiday. Like today, it was unimaginable that wedding guests would not eat or drink anything at the celebrations. Unlike today, wedding guests needed a lot of stamina to get through the occasion!

The stories in the second half of the second chapter of Mark's Gospel are marked by Jesus fighting with the scribes and Pharisees regarding the law and meals. These fights hinge on who can be invited to the table, how much food can be eaten, and when it can be consumed. For Jesus the sign of his coming kingdom was the variety of people who responded to the invitation to the feast and the generous provisions that were made so that everyone could enjoy the banquet.

This sort of thinking and practice did not fit with the rigorous, legalistic mentality of the Pharisees, who were good people trying to do the right thing. The problem is that they lost sight of the fact that religious faith is about a living and dynamic relationship with God, his children, and the world, not just the adherence to rules and laws, as important as some of them might be. As soon as we forget that all laws need flexibility, interpretation, and compassionate administration, then we are in danger of becoming the very thing Jesus condemns. "The sabbath was made for humankind, and not humankind for the sabbath" (Mk 2:27).

For instance, fasting is a good thing, especially in a society that is becoming increasingly obese while other people in the world continue to die each day of starvation. To go without food for a period can be a good wake-up call to seeing God's justice at work in our lives. Yet even when good practices lose sight of their purpose, they can take on a dangerous life of their own. That's why Jesus tells us to cast aside laws that serve no purpose and to put a new spin on the best of our traditions that will connect them to the experience of our society here and now.

And how do we know which laws should go and which can stay? Maybe those featherlight wedding films contain some important wisdom after all. The laws that should be written on our hearts are those that help us to be most faithful, loving, and committed to Christ, all our brothers and sisters everywhere, and the world in which we live. May the Eucharist, this taste of the banquet of eternal life, give us strength for this mission and stamina for the celebrations to come.

ASH WEDNESDAY

JOEL 2:12–18
2 CORINTHIANS 5:20—6:2
MATTHEW 6:1–6, 16–18

An anonymous author has written a "Lenten Song" that can be sung to the tune of "My Favorite Things" from *The Sound of Music*. Even if we don't sing it, we get the idea.

Sackcloth and ashes, and days without eating,
Mortification and wailing and weeping,
A hair shirt that scratches, a nettle that stings,
These are a few of my favorite things.

Penitence, flagellants, memento mori,
Spending nights sleeping on rocks in a quarry,
The sound of a cloak'd solemn cantor who sings,
These are still more of my favorite things.

Tossing and turning and yearning I'm spurning,
Passions aflame like an ember-day burning,
Corpus and *carnis* and wild drunken flings,
Forsaken are they for my favorite things!

(Chorus)
When it's Christmas,
When the tree's lit,
When the cards are sent,
I simply remember my favorite things,
And then I can't wa-a-a-a-it till Lent.

There are some Catholics who think that a satirical, humorous verse should never begin an Ash Wednesday homily. After all, over the centuries this season has been marked by the call to very tough acts of self-denial and penance. And rightly so! But today's Gospel tells us it's not just the acts of mortification that are important, but that even more central is the attitude that accompanies them. Jesus tells us that when we deny ourselves anything, we should not put on a show but be discreet and go about our lives as normal. The Preface to today's Mass goes as far as describing Lent as "this joyful season."

The self-denial of Lent is not meant to be part of a keep-fit program, as good as that might be. We don't give up food, forgo alcohol or chocolate to get slim, prove to ourselves we're not alcoholic, or that we have great will power. We give up, or take on things, this Lent because it helps to change our mind-set for the better. Our sacrifices remind us that as our bodies crave certain food or drink, so our souls crave God. And unlike the obsessive way we can act when we are looking to satisfy our cravings for things around us, our spiritual cravings, as single-minded as they can sometimes be, are marked by a lighter and joyful quest.

Lent is the time when we choose again to live life to the full because one day we will die. And if we want to prepare for the best possible, most loving and peaceful death, then being selfless, sacrificial, and generous is the way to live, not only because others benefit from our denial of self, but also because Jesus showed us that this is the way to eternal life.

So let's wash our face, anoint our heads, not babble like the pagans, and joyfully face up to our dyings because of the selfless way we live our lives.

FIRST SUNDAY OF LENT

GENESIS 9:8–15
1 PETER 3:18–22
MARK 1:12–15

Have you ever noticed that Jesus begins and ends his public ministry in the wilderness? These deserts are the geographical bookends of the greatest story ever told. In today's Gospel we have Jesus in the desert for forty days. Much later, when condemned to death, Jesus is led out of the city and crucified at Golgotha, another dry and desolate location. In both places Jesus is tempted. In Mark we are never told what Satan's temptations in the desert were about.

Luke and Matthew fill in those details. On the cross, however, Mark tells us that the crowd tempts Jesus to work a miracle, come down from the cross, and save himself. In the first desert, Jesus is ministered to by the angels and emerges to proclaim that the kingdom of God is close at hand. In the later desert, Jesus is ministered to by his women disciples and is put to death as a consequence of the way he lived out the kingdom he proclaimed.

It's clear from all the Gospels that the desert and the temptations stayed with Jesus throughout his life. What a comfort this is to us. Many of us do not need to go out and find a physical desert to know its claim on our lives. Temptations do not know geographical limitations. Indeed, the greater the number of options, the more temptations we have to take a destructive path.

When we look at how the desert is used in the Bible, mythology, art, literature, and the cinema two competing images emerge. The first is that the desert can be a place of loss and ruin where some great heroes have gone and not returned. In another equally venerable tradition, journeys to the desert, while filled with a mixture of pleasure and pain, are abundant with revelation, transformation, and re-creation.

These two descriptions do not have to be contradictory. As we find in Jesus' example, we do not have to give into the temptation that the desert is only about loss, but find a path there to negotiate a way out of it so that we can emerge re-created, the richer for the experience.

It's important to remember in our own particular deserts that temptation is not sin. To be tempted by something is not the same as doing it. Temptations are the allures that make destructive choices look good. In one sense, the bad news is that we know from the lives of the saints that the closer we get to God, the more temptations increase. The good news is that we can learn how to deal with them.

Usually, temptations have a context and a history. They can come when we are feeling most deserted and vulnerable, and they normally strike us at the most susceptible points in our character. To deal with them we need to be aware of their pattern, the way they con us into believing that the destructive behavior is "not that bad," will be "just this once," or "for the last time." As well, it helps if we are aware of the danger signs in our lives that can weaken our defenses. Tiredness, boredom, anger, alcohol and drug use, lack of good communication, and a poor self-esteem are common realities that can leave us more exposed than usual.

This Lent, as we venture with Christ into our figurative deserts, let's do anything that helps our self-esteem, deals with our anger, attends to why we might work or drink too much, and ensures that we are less stressed. Against what we might think, these activities could be the most helpful ways we can make sure we emerge from our desert the better for having been there.

SECOND SUNDAY OF LENT

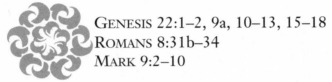 GENESIS 22:1–2, 9a, 10–13, 15–18
ROMANS 8:31b–34
MARK 9:2–10

This week's first reading, the call for Abraham to sacrifice Isaac, is one of the most frightening passages in the Bible. While I take it seriously, I am relieved I do not have to take it literally. The idea that as a test of faith God could require infanticide from a parent is more than my faith could bear. We could not hold as strongly as we do to the seamless garment of life, and also believe that our God is capable of calling for murder—the cold-blooded, unjust murder of an innocent child.

The back story to the Genesis text could be that Abraham thought the way to serve God was to show the Lord how serious he was about his devotion. In a world where other religions practiced human sacrifice, maybe Abraham thought that this might please the Lord as well. Maybe, in the fervor of devotion, he prepared to sacrifice his only son. But something happened that day. As he placed his bound son on the altar, something snapped in Abraham. Imagine the moment—a boy looks up into the face of his father and wonders why, in the name of God, is he about to kill him? And then as Abraham raises his knife, he freezes. Maybe Isaac was saying, "Why are you doing this, Dad? Don't go through with it Pop! Let me live!" Whatever happened at that moment, one of the most important religious events in our world took place. A transfiguration of a great man occurred. Abraham couldn't do it. Not because he wasn't capable of it, but because he saw very clearly that God didn't want it. Later he said it was as if an angel spoke to him. One did—an angel of life. "Do not lay your hand on the boy or do anything to him." Abraham saw that God wants nothing to do with violence and death, that he wants us to cradle our children, not kill them. This luminous religious insight starts to mark out how different the one, true God of the Hebrews was from all other gods. And this is our God.

By the time of Jesus, Christians came to see that God does not want ritual sacrifices either—no sheep, no goats, no bulls. Sometimes we can think that the death of Jesus is like that of Isaac, but, goes this line, that this time around the Father of Jesus saw it through and sacrificed Jesus on the altar of our sins. The atoning death of Jesus, however, was not sought by the Father or the Son, it was a consequence of the faithful love Jesus had for the reign of God in this world and the next, and his love for us.

Jesus refused to be unfaithful to the kingdom of nonviolence, forgiveness, and peace he lived. Then, as now, this way of life, literally, threatens the hell out of those people who trade in violence, power, and death. One way to deal with the threat is to eliminate it. But in Jesus, God had the last word and enabled us to find a way out of offering up all our children for sacrifice—the way of faith, hope, and love. As a result of such love, nothing can separate us from Christ, not "hardship, or distress, or persecution, or famine, or nakedness, or peril, or the sword. No, in all these things we are more than conquerors through him who loved us."

As we pray for our own religious transfiguration in the Father's love this Lent, may the Eucharist give us hope that no matter what altar of sacrifice we sometimes feel laid upon, God never wants us to kill ourselves, or anyone else. Lent is about mercy and survival, because true obedience to God, even in its demand for what can sometimes be a hard love, is never destructive. It always leads to life.

THIRD SUNDAY OF LENT

EXODUS 20:1–17
1 CORINTHIANS 1:22–25
JOHN 2:13–25

In recent years the Ten Commandments have become an unusual staging ground for various groups within the church. Some people complain that young Catholics don't know them by heart. This position is countered by those who say that rather than being able to recite them we should live them, though it's hard to see how we can do one without the other. Still, others rightly claim that Jesus summarized them in his new commandments, "To love God with all our heart, mind, and soul and to love our neighbor as we love ourselves."

The problem with teaching the Ten Commandments is not what they say, but how they say it. The idea of "coveting" anything, but especially "wives, slaves, ox, and ass," are all a bit dated these days.

In an article entitled "Preaching to the Modern Pagans," journalist Bryan Appleyard tells how he interviewed a person who kept quoting the Ten Commandments at length. Later, he decided to read them for the first time since childhood and he was struck by their insightfulness into the human character. Appleyard thought all the Ten Commandments needed was a makeover so that we can reclaim the power of them.

We are used to hearing the first commandment say, "I am the LORD your God, who brought you out of the land of Egypt, out of the house of slavery; you shall have no other gods before me." Appleyard says this basically means be serious.

"You shall not make for yourself an idol, whether in the form of anything that is in heaven above, or that is on the earth beneath, or that is in the water under the earth." Get real.

"You shall not make wrongful use of the name of the LORD your God, for the LORD will not acquit anyone who misuses his name." Be humble, we are creatures not the creator.

"Remember the Sabbath day by keeping it holy." Be quiet.

"Honor your father and your mother, so that your days may be long in the land that the LORD your God is giving you." Respect age.

"You shall not murder." Do not kill, for all murder is suicide.

"You shall not commit adultery." Mean what you say.

"You shall not steal." Do not steal, or all the world will die.

"You shall not bear false witness against your neighbor." Honor others; their frailties are usually your own.

"You shall not covet your neighbor's house. You shall not covet your neighbor's wife, or his manservant or maidservant, his ox or donkey, or anything that belongs to your neighbor." Appleyard concludes that in today's language this means, be kind, be generous and don't screw around. (Adapted from Bryan Appelyard, "Sinai of the Times," *The Australian Magazine*, March 7–8, 1998, pp. 21–25.)

So by putting some ancient words into the modern vernacular we are exhorted this Sunday to seriousness, facing reality, humility, creating space, respecting age, honesty and fidelity, and we are bluntly told to stop killing and stealing. There is nothing old-fashioned about these challenges. As in other instances, we can see that it's not what our tradition has to say, but sometimes it is the way we say it that can be the problem.

And today's Gospel tells us of the consequences of moving away from these guiding principles. I think we need to take Jesus' anger very seriously. Rightly we have emphasized the love and compassion of Jesus over recent decades because for far too long the steadfast love of Christ was underemphasized. We should never think, however, that it cancels out the anger God feels when he sees an unjust world filled with people who know better and do nothing.

God has given us the Ten Commandments, the Law, the Prophets, and Jesus his Son, so that we might know the Way, the Truth, and the Life. When we are called to account for how we spent our lives, whom we loved, and how we made the world a better place for all, most of us will not be able to plead ignorance. May our Eucharist this Sunday enable us to be mindful of what the Ten Commandments say, but even more so may it give us the courage and strength to live them out in a world that needs witnesses to them more than ever before.

FOURTH SUNDAY OF LENT

2 CHRONICLES 36:14–16, 19–23
EPHESIANS 2:4–10
JOHN 3:14–21

As Christians in the world we cannot help but be influenced by the developments that happen around us. Indeed, we believe that many of these advances are gifts from God given to us to enjoy. But not all developments in thinking and practices are for the better.

One alarming development is the false thinking that we cannot judge other people, or that we should not be judged. The wider community regularly maintains that no one is in a position to judge another's behavior or statements. This approach holds that everyone's words and actions are of equal value. This position may not be Christian, but it hasn't stopped it from finding a home among us. We regularly hear statements from Christian men and women like "We're not in a position to judge" or "You can't judge them" and "If it's fine for them, then it's fine." This thinking has a name. It's called moral relativism and it tries to claim that the morality of behavior is only determined by the person who does the act, or the context within which the action is taken.

Our Catholic tradition teaches us that a context is very important in trying to work out if someone is to blame for what they say and do, but that a person's particular circumstances never change the fact that the words or actions are in themselves wrong. We hold that, while all human beings have equal value and dignity, we do not believe that everyone's opinion and actions are of equal worth. We believe that "right judgment" is a gift of the Holy Spirit and that it's best exercised with humility and compassion.

When I hear people say I should not "judge" others, I assume they are telling me that I should not "condemn" other people. There is a world of difference between judging and condemning. To judge is to make an assessment. To condemn is to damn. As Christians we judge because we have to keep discerning how the things of the world can be reconciled with the things we hold to be true. Condemnation is the prerogative of God alone, who sees all, knows all, and loves all. In today's Gospel, however, John tells us that even God has forfeited his right to condemn the world, but has sent Jesus to be the world's light, life, truth, and savior.

The Gospel reminds us that if we feel condemned for what we have done and said, then it's because we have condemned ourselves, not because God condemns us. John tells us that even when we find ourselves lost in the darkness of our most destructive behavior, the saving love of Christ is always available to us, inviting us to come out of the darkness into his light.

What a great metaphor the light and dark is for making the best judgments in our own lives. Alarm bells should always ring when we find ourselves not wanting anyone else to know what we have said or done. Secrecy is often the ally of sin, and the more open and transparent we are, the more confident we can be that we are walking as children of the light.

May this Lenten Eucharist enable us to let go of the desire to condemn others and ourselves, and to receive again the compassionate, just, and humble gift of right judgment that helps us to see the darkness for what it is, and keeps us walking in the light of Christ.

FIFTH SUNDAY OF LENT

 JEREMIAH 31:31–34
HEBREWS 5:7–9
JOHN 12:20–33

If ever you get the chance to travel to Turkey, make sure you go to the Roman ruins at Ephesus. The trip is instructive for all sorts of reasons, not least because two thousand years ago Ephesus was a seaport and now you have to drive inland for over an hour to get there. I wonder what our cities will look like in two thousand years. But Ephesus, the place to which the great letter in the New Testament was addressed, is worth the trip. The Roman ruins there, especially the library, are extraordinary. For Christians, however, three other places there capture the imagination. There are the ruins of the hall in which the important Council of Ephesus met, and there are ruins of a monastery built over what is claimed to be the final home of St. John, the Beloved Disciple. There is also the much more dubious claim that Mary's final house, and the site of her assumption, is on top of the mountain overlooking the ancient city.

There are good reasons to believe that the Gospel of John was written in Ephesus, seventy years after Jesus' death. I like to think about the context in which the scriptures were written, not just because it helps me understand some things in the text, but also to appreciate that our scriptures were inspired by the experience of a flesh-and-blood community.

Ephesus was a center of learning, trade, government, and religion in the ancient world. We also know that the early Christians were greatly persecuted and martyred there. The early church was filled with stories of betrayal, torture, death, and heroic witness to the faith. The stakes for believing in Jesus were very high. And it was the heroic witness of these martyrs that eventually led to the conversion of the Roman Empire to Christianity. It should come as no surprise to us then that John's Gospel should have a special focus on sharing in the sufferings of Jesus and the glory to come.

The words of Jesus in today's Gospel must have been very important to a community that was awash with the blood of their fellow believers. Our foremothers and forefathers in the faith counted themselves blessed to die as Jesus died, alive in the faith of God's love for the world. Just imagine how that community of martyrs first heard these words, "Unless a grain of wheat falls into the earth and dies, it remains just a single grain; but if it dies, it bears much fruit."

By comparison we have it easy today, but martyrdom comes to all believers in different ways. In the broadest sense, a martyr is one who is prepared to pay the price for holding true to Christ. For us now this might mean making serious choices about the company we keep, the business ventures we enter into, the nonviolent protests we mount, forgoing luxuries so that others in our world might have necessities, and even remaining faithful to the vows and promises we have made. Christian faith sometimes bites hard, and when it does we know we are sharing in the martyr's lot.

And what should be our response when our faith in Christ costs us something big? Jesus models it for us in today's Gospel, "…what should I say—'Father, save me from this hour'? No, it is for this reason that I have come to this hour. Father, glorify your name."

May this final week of Lent, then, see this flesh-and-blood community be like our forebears in Ephesus and actively seek out ways of sharing in the martyr's lot by letting go of what is not essential and focusing on the One who loved us to the end.

PASSION SUNDAY (PALM SUNDAY)

Procession: MARK 11:1–10 *or*
JOHN 12:12–16
ISAIAH 50:4–7
PHILIPPIANS 2:6–11
MARK 14:1—15, 47

In the third verse of the rousing hymn *"How Great Thou Art,"* we sing:

> And when I think that God his Son not sparing
> sent him to die I scarce can take it in.
> That on the cross my burden gladly bearing,
> he bled and died to take away my sin.

This verse enshrines a long-held tradition that Jesus died as a necessary atonement to God for our sins. From this perspective, Jesus' suffering and death was the price of the ransom paid to evil so that we might share in God's life. Alternatively, the death of Jesus is seen as the only thing that satisfied God's anger at our sins, and got God to love us again.

We should be very careful about what we sing! On the one hand, this theology rightly shows us the extraordinary love Jesus has for us. On the other hand, it says some very difficult things about God. What loving creator, for example, would say that the torture and death of his beloved Son is the only way he can be happy about his creatures? What just judge, no matter how angry he or she might be at the crimes laid out in the courtroom, would allow an innocent man to die for the guilty? And how powerful is God over evil if the only way to keep it in check is through human sacrifice? These are serious questions and they have an impact on our everyday life of faith, and can sometimes alienate us from believing that God is our all-loving Father in heaven.

Today, we rightly hear a lot about victims—people, who through no choice or fault of their own, have been dealt with wrongly by others who are free to act otherwise, and who know better. In some of the ways we think about the passion, Jesus becomes God's victim. Through no fault of his own, and seemingly powerless in the face of his Father's will, Jesus becomes a victim of God's need for a sacrifice, a ransom, or atonement. As a result, many of us can feel that sometimes we are God's victims too, because if God wanted Jesus to suffer and die, why should we be surprised or complain when we receive large crosses to carry as well.

Mark's account of the passion tends to reinforce Jesus as victim. Mark has Jesus eating with the outcasts, his friends betraying, denying, or deserting him. He tells us that Jesus is terrified at the prospect of death and calls on his "Abba" or "daddy" to help him out. In the end he accepts "the will of God" but even then feels abandoned by God on the cross.

I often think we misread what Jesus is referring to when he accepts God's will in the garden. Rather than refer to the particular will of the Father to see Jesus suffer and die on Good Friday, I think it's more helpful and consoling to understand it as referring to God's will that Jesus remains faithful to the way he lived. If by doing that Jesus threatened the religious and political authorities of his day so much that they have to murder him, then his death is the ultimate sacrifice which reveals how far God was prepared to go out of love for us. This reveals to us that Jesus came "to live," and that by faithfully living this life he was put to death by the powers of sin. Through the cross we see the price to be paid in confronting sin in our day and obediently living out the demands of God's kingdom of justice and peace.

This Holy Week let's celebrate that God spared nothing in showing us how to live. As we pray on Jesus' life, death, and resurrection, may we move from being victims of a bloodthirsty God to choosing again to follow Jesus' example and live lives that are faithful, loving, and obedient. May we also appreciate that this life continues to, literally, threaten "the hell out of" those opposed to the reign of God in our world, but that as Jesus was faithful to God and God to Jesus, so they will remain faithful to us as well, no matter what.

HOLY THURSDAY

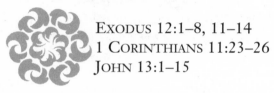

EXODUS 12:1–8, 11–14
1 CORINTHIANS 11:23–26
JOHN 13:1–15

Two of the most powerful Catholic women in the twentieth century saw the connection between service and hospitality, between the washing of feet and the feeding of the poor.

As a young Loreto nun teaching at a private girl's school in Calcutta, Mother Teresa came to see that her real vocation lay with caring for those who were dying from malnutrition in the streets. She never wanted to found large-scale hospitals. To this day, her congregation's homes are clinically basic and more interested in befriending the poor than in restoring everyone to full heath. Mother Teresa often argued that loneliness was the world's greatest and worst disease.

Dorothy Day once helped a nun take a homeless man to a soup kitchen in lower Manhattan. She felt drawn to return there and work. In time the experiences at the soup kitchen led to her become a Catholic and found the Catholic Worker movement with Peter Maurin. Throughout the world Catholic Workers continue to feed the poor and advocate for a more just society.

These two saintly women met in Calcutta on Holy Thursday. Dorothy Day recalls, "It was 1955 when I visited Calcutta and saw an unknown woman, vigorous and purposeful, feeding and caring for skeletonized human beings carried in from the streets by city ambulances. She fed them slowly and carefully and would talk consolingly to them in Bengali, Hindi, or English. As I stood behind her some of them held out imploring hands to me, seeking, I supposed, some consolation. I turned away in revulsion. I could see helping such a person in an emergency situation, but to do it every day? I asked Mother Teresa how she managed to do it. "Our work calls for us to see Jesus in everyone...each one is Jesus in a distressing disguise."" (Quoted in Eileen Egan, "Polar opposites? Remembering the kindred spirits of Dorothy Day and Mother Teresa," *Catholic Peace Voice*, Fall, 1997.)

Holy Thursday calls each of us to see the connection between service and hospitality. If the Eucharist has any impact on our lives, then at least it should leave us conscious of the injustices in the world and should give us a desire to want to get down and dirty in fixing up the problems.

There are often two blocks that stop us from doing this. The first block is that when we get down to work on the world's problems we believe that our efforts won't make much of a difference. It shouldn't come as a surprise to discover that Mother Teresa and Dorothy Day both had great devotion to St. Thérèse of Lisieux's "little way," where every thing is valued and no contribution, prayer, or thought is considered unimportant. Something is always better than nothing. The second block in our path is the belief that we are too powerful to get dirty. Mother Teresa and Dorothy Day had plenty to say about how personal power corrupts the human heart. Both thought that it was impossible to be a true follower of Jesus and have no practical contact with "Jesus in a distressing disguise."

And the reason we bother with this Christian social work is not that it makes us feel good. It's because it's what Jesus did for us. He saw us in our poverty and welcomed us to his banquet. He got down and got dirty washing our feet and told us that if we want to follow him then this is how we should spend our lives.

And to help us do it he left us the Eucharist, the meal for saints and sinners, where we gain the strength to get down and dirty with Christ as we help him make the world ridiculously hospitable and radically just. On this Holy Thursday may Dorothy Day and Mother Teresa, who understood what today's feast is all about, pray for us that we may be found worthy of the example of Jesus the Lord. Amen.

GOOD FRIDAY

ISAIAH 52:13—53:12
HEBREWS 4:14–16; 5:7–9
JOHN 18:1—19:42

We have just listened to so many powerful words we don't need too many more. Except that some of us come here hoping that the Lord's Good Friday casts light on *our* good Fridays too. And it does.

If we've been betrayed by friends and abandoned by companions, denied by those closest to us, falsely accused, and had our integrity questioned, then Jesus is here for us.

If we've been judged and condemned, pushed from pillar to post, and had our emotions laid bear, then Jesus is here for us.

If we've felt the full weight of our burdens and the loneliness of dealing with them on our own, then Jesus is here for us.

If there have been squabbles over possessions as we have been held out to dry, then Jesus is here for us.

And if we've been through the heartbreak of having someone we love die, or the thousand other deaths that constitute our lives, then Jesus is here for us.

He comes to us as our faithful companion, who will never deny or falsely accuse us.

He comes to us not to expose us to condemnation but to save us, and to raise us up with him in the power of the resurrection.

He comes to us to tell us that it doesn't matter what we possess, where we come from, and what we do, it only matters where we're going from here on in.

And he comes to help us see that where there was death and grief and heartbreak there can now be life and comfort and peace.

This is Good Friday. It's made good because our God in Jesus Christ remained faithful to his Father, to us, and to his kingdom of justice and love. No matter what crosses we have carried here this afternoon, lay them down and wait upon God's love, because Jesus is here for us.

EASTER VIGIL

GENESIS 1:1—2:2; 22:1–18
EXODUS 14:15—15:1
ISAIAH 54:5–14; 55:1–11
BARUCH 3:9–15, 32—4:4
EZEKIEL 36:16–28
ROMANS 6:3–11
MARK 16:1–7

A magician was working on a cruise ship in the Caribbean. The audience would be different each week, so the magician did the same disappearing tricks over and over again.

There was only one problem. The captain's talking parrot saw the shows each week and began to understand how the magician did every trick. Once he understood this, he started shouting in the middle of the show: "Look, it's not the same hat." "He's hiding the flowers under the table." "See, all the cards are the ace of spades?"

The magician grew to hate the captain's parrot.

One day the ship had an accident and sank. There were only two survivors—the magician and the parrot. Together they drifted on large piece of wood.

They stared at each other with hate, but did not utter a word. This went on for a day and another and another.

On the third day, the parrot in desperation said: "All right, I can't work it out. I give up. Where did you hide the ship?"

For many people Easter can be seen as a great magical trick. Without us seeing how, Jesus escapes from the tomb and the show goes on. But what we are celebrating is not magic, but the glory and love of God.

This comes to us in all sorts of extraordinary ways, but most especially it takes human form in our brothers and sisters who are about to join our Catholic family of faith. It's hard to get fully accurate numbers, but we know that around the world the population of a medium-size city will enter the Catholic community this Easter, somewhere between 80,000 to over 100,000 people.

What is most consoling to us is that not all these converts are in the developing world, as good as that would be. Despite the terrible scandals we have all had to confront in recent years, there are, thank God, adults in developed countries, too, who still want to find a home among us.

The ceremonies around adult baptism or reception into the church are among the most moving ones we have. They can pull us up short. Just when we begin to take our faith in the Risen Christ for granted or become discouraged at our inability to live out Christ's love, justice, and peace in the church and the world, along comes an intelligent, reflective, and searching person who stands up in front of us and says that they want what we have.

Our catechumens and converts are not coming into the church all starry-eyed about who we are. They know we are a community of loved sinners who are struggling to live out the good news of Jesus. They know that sometimes we get it right, that, outside government, our church remains the largest provider of welfare, education, health care, and trained personnel for the developing world. That, collectively, we give more money to alleviate disease, poverty, and injustice than any other nongovernment organization in the world. They see that the real strength of the Catholic community is found in you, our laypeople, who, in nearly every corner of the globe, bring the love of Jesus Christ to bear in your homes, workplaces, and local communities.

They also know that sometimes we get it dreadfully wrong, that we don't practice what we preach, and that we have to hold each other to account for our sinfulness and failings so that we can all be converted again and again by the Risen Christ's love.

And so just when we might take the gift of faith in Christ or our membership in the church for granted, Jesus sends us the witness of our catechumens and converts to challenge and console us. Like Mary Magdalene and the other Mary in the Gospel, they have gone on a search for the Lord. And sometimes through events that seemed like earthquakes, or in much more gentle ways, they have found a pointer to the meaning, direction, and new life they were seeking. And in this search they met Jesus. He calmed their fears, called them by name, and showed them the Way, the Truth, and the Life. With great joy Jesus sent them to join us where we gather and to announce to us, again, the good news we need to constantly hear: "Christ is risen, just as he promised." "The reign of sin is over." "Death is no more."

We are not celebrating magic here. This is the holiest of all nights because of God's faithful love that has given all of us the gift of resurrection faith in Jesus Christ the Lord.

Happy Easter.

EASTER SUNDAY

ACTS 10:34a, 37–43
COLOSSIANS 3:1–4 *or* 1 CORINTHIANS 5:6b–8
JOHN 20:1–9 *or* MARK 16:1–8
Afternoon: LUKE 24:13–35

A man was driving along the road when he saw the Easter bunny hop into his lane. He swerved to avoid hitting the bunny, but couldn't do so. The basket of eggs went everywhere. The driver felt guilty and began to cry. A woman saw the man and pulled over. "What's wrong?" she asked. "I accidentally killed the Easter bunny," he explained. The woman knew exactly what to do. She went to her car, pulled out a spray can, walked over to the bunny, and sprayed the entire contents all over the little furry animal.

Miraculously the Easter bunny came back to life, jumped up, picked up his eggs, waved at them, and hopped on down the road. Not far away, the Easter bunny stopped, turned around, and waved again. He kept doing this for as far as they could see.

The man was astonished. "What in heaven's name is in that can you sprayed on the Easter bunny?" The woman showed the man the label. It said: "Hair spray. Restores life to dead hair. Adds permanent wave."

For many of our children, the bunny and his or her eggs are the most important thing about Easter. Over the millennia, Christianity has had a gift for domesticating local traditions and festivals, bringing them on board and making them our own. The name *Easter* comes from the Anglo-Saxon spring festival in honor of the goddess Eastre. Her symbol was the rabbit, and the giving of eggs were signs of new life bursting forth as winter withdrew. These associations only make sense in the northern hemisphere, but we can see why the early Christians could be so adaptable and inculturated with this local festival.

In both hemispheres, Christians today celebrate Jesus being raised from the dead. In the New Testament there are two traditions about how the disciples come to know about Jesus' resurrection: the empty tomb and the apparitions of Christ.

Today's Gospel belongs to the empty-tomb tradition. On Magdalene's urging, Peter and John run to the tomb, find it empty, and come to at least an initial belief about the resurrection of Jesus.

We do not believe that God simply revived Jesus' corpse in the tomb, as our driver resuscitated the bunny in today's story. Easter Sunday does not celebrate the resuscitation of Jesus, but his resurrection. We know his glorified body was not the same as his human body because Jesus' presence could be encountered in several places simultaneously, and he is reported to walk through walls and to vanish. The link between both resurrection traditions is the importance of Jesus' death. In the empty-tomb accounts, as in today's Gospel, the writers give us extraordinary details about the grave clothes. In the apparition narratives, there are usually references to Jesus' wounds.

Whatever way they came to experience the resurrection of Christ, the disciples knew that this was Jesus who actually died and was buried and that their personal encounter was with the one who was crucified.

What God did through the death and resurrection of Jesus is what Christians have done with local customs and festivals ever since: He entered into it, understood it, took it on board, domesticated it, and vanquished its power. As a result we believe that God empathizes with the full limitations of our human mortality and promises that he remain faithful to us in death as he remained utterly faithful to his Son Jesus.

That is why on this day 1,600 years ago St. John Chrysostom could say on behalf of us all:

> Hell took a body, and discovered God.
> It took earth, and encountered Heaven.
> It took what it saw, and was overcome by what it could not see.
> O death, where is your sting?
> O Hell, where is your victory?
> Christ is Risen, and you, o death, are destroyed!
> Christ is Risen, and evil is cast down!
> Christ is Risen, and angels rejoice!
> Christ is Risen, and new life is set free!
> Christ is Risen, and the tomb is emptied of its dead;
> for Christ, having risen from the dead,
> becomes the first-fruit of those who have fallen asleep.
> To Him be Glory and Power forever and ever. Amen!

SECOND SUNDAY OF EASTER

ACTS 4:32–35
1 JOHN 5:1–6
JOHN 20:19–31

The earliest Christian community focused strongly on the wounds of the Risen Lord for two reasons: to affirm the fact that Christ, now raised from the dead, was the same person who had lived with them; and also to make sense of the physical wounds being inflicted on them for Christ's sake.

The story of Thomas, even with its mystical details, counters a magical notion of what the resurrection is about. Jesus bears the marks of his torture and death. His glorified body, though different, is connected to how the disciples knew and loved him. They can recognize him through his words and his wounds.

We know the community of Ephesus, for which this Gospel is written, was experiencing great persecution. Is it any wonder, one generation after from the earliest disciples, that the sign of Christ's risen presence are his marks of suffering?

Our own world continues to be intrigued by manifestations of Jesus' wounds. Over recent years films like *Stigmata*, *Dogma*, *Agnes of God*, and *Daredevil* give a hysterical and cynical prominence to the stigmata. There are regular believe-it-or-not documentaries that usually follow suit. Even some pilgrims flocked to Padre Pio's monastery in the south of Italy to see if his hands really bled, or if his wounds really wept. This desire to see outward signs of inner faith is a long way short of Jesus telling us today, "Blessed are those who have not seen and yet come to believe." Our day-to-day lives should be the clearest manifestation of the cross and resurrection of Christ.

It seems, however, that words and wounds still make a claim on us today. You and I know that we don't have to go to a stigmatic to see Christian battle wounds. We carry within us the death of the Lord. We all have our wounds. And we also know that, for many of us, it is precisely when we are wounded most deeply by life that our doubts in the presence of God can be greatest.

The Easter story is not that we should be ashamed of this, or pretend it doesn't happen. Today's Gospel reminds us that it is into this chaos that Christ comes with words of peace, with empathy from the one who was wounded for our sake, and with the mission to forgive as we are forgiven. And that's what happened to Thomas. Christ took his fears, doubts, and disbelief and transformed them into a powerful Christian witness that has sustained generations of us who struggle with life and faith.

Jesuit poet Gerard Manley Hopkins puts it this way in this epic poem of faith, *The Wreck of the Deutschland:*

> Thou mastering me
> God! giver of breath and bread;
> World's strand, sway of the sea;
> Lord of living and dead;
> Thou has bound bones and veins in me, fastened me flesh,
> And after it almost unmade, what with dread,
> Thy doing, and dost thou touch me afresh?
> Over again I feel thy finger and find thee.

So at this Easter Eucharist we are offered the same opportunity to discover that the stone rejected within us, or among us, is the one that God wants to touch afresh. And you know what? When we see this happening, when we see God taking into the hands of God the part of us we consider most unlovable and using it for good, then we want to cry out with the psalmist, "This is the work of the Lord, a marvel in our eyes."

THIRD SUNDAY OF EASTER

 ACTS 3:13–15, 17–19
1 JOHN 2:1–5a
LUKE 24:35–48

Sometimes the lectionary cuts a gospel story off too soon. Today we hear from the last chapter of Luke's Gospel, where there are

four accounts of how the disciples came to believe in the resurrection of Jesus. In the first two stories, Mary Magdalene and then
Peter come to see that Jesus has been raised from the dead
because they found his tomb empty. The third story is set on the
road to Emmaus. Today's Gospel is where Jesus appears to the
apostles and disciples en masse, but it finishes at verse 48. In next
few verses Jesus tells the disciples that he is sending them out to
be his witnesses in the world, and then he ascends to the Father.

The church finishes the passage early because it does not
want to preempt the feast of the Ascension, but by doing so it does
the story an injustice. We are used to hearing how the road to
Emmaus mirrors what we do at Sunday Mass. But if we include
Luke, chapter 24, verses 49 to 50, then we can see that today's
Gospel does the same thing. The verbs tell the story. In today's
Gospel Jesus is present to the disciples—he gives himself to them
to be seen and held, eats with them, teaches them about the scriptures, and commissions them to go out.

As a result of that first Easter, we gather here each Sunday to
remember and make Easter present again. This is the reason, for
example, we talk about the forty days of Lent when in fact there are
forty-five days from Ash Wednesday to the Easter Vigil. In or outside the Easter season, Sundays are always days of the Resurrection.
And just as on the first Easter Sunday, we believe that Christ continues to invite us here, teaches us about how to understand the
scriptures and live them out in our daily lives, is present to us, to
have and to hold, in his word, this community, the presider and in
a special way in the Eucharistic meal, and that he sends us out to
proclaim his saving love with heroic joy.

To enable us to do all this, we receive the same gift Jesus gave
the first disciples as well, the gift of peace. But sometimes we have
to get creative about how we achieve it, like the old man who purchased a retirement home near a high school. He spent the first
few weeks in peace and contentment. Then a new school year
began. The very next afternoon three young men came down his
street beating merrily on every trash can they encountered. The
crashing percussion continued day after day, until finally the old
man decided to take some action. The next afternoon, he walked
out to meet the young percussionists. He called out, "You kids are

a lot of fun. Will you do me a favor? I'll give you each a dollar if you'll promise to come around every day and do your thing." The kids were elated and continued to do a bang-up job on the trash cans. A few days later, the retiree approached them again, "Look," he said, "I haven't received my income check this month, so I'm not going to be able to give you more than twenty-five cents. Will that be OK?" "A lousy quarter?" the drum leader exclaimed. "If you think we're going to waste our time beating these cans around for a quarter, you're nuts! No way, mister. We quit!" And the old man enjoyed peace and quiet for the rest of his days.

So as Christ sends us forth today, may we be wise about how we can create some happiness and peace around us as well.

FOURTH SUNDAY OF EASTER

ACTS 4:8–12
1 JOHN 3:1–2
JOHN 10:11–18

Sometimes a piece of theater can be so powerful it stays with you for your whole life. Many years ago I saw Jesuit dramatist, Michael Moynahan, perform his mime entitled *Come-Passion*. It starts with a clown happily doing tricks and juggling for the audience. Soon, Jesus is led in by the soldiers and is crucified. The clown watches in horror. When Jesus dies and the soldiers go home, the clown remains at the foot of the cross. He removes the nails from the hands and feet of Jesus and cradles the corpse in his lap, as in Michelangelo's *Pietà*. He weeps for the evil that saw a just man crucified. Just then, the soldiers return and find the clown grieving over the body of Jesus. They crucify the clown. The clown suffers and dies on the cross. As they leave, Jesus is raised to life, he sees the suffering clown, removes the nails, cradles him in his arms, and holds him for what feels like an eternity.

When I saw this mime you could have heard a pin drop in the theater, and there wasn't a dry eye in the place. Compassion is not pity, sympathy, or commiseration. Those words imply that we stand outside an experience and feelingly look in on it. Compassion is about "fellow feeling." It's what the Good Shepherd embodies, and what Easter is all about—God meeting us where we are as we are so that we might be carried onto new life. If we are worthy followers of Jesus we will all have our fair share of Good Fridays, but Easter Sunday tells us that just as the Father remained faithful to Jesus, so Jesus will remain faithful to us, as one with us.

In recent years, the bishops, who are often called shepherds of the local church, have come under extraordinary scrutiny. And rightly so. All of us who are living the Christian life are accountable for what we have done and have failed to do, and the bishops are no exception. It's a tough time to be the local shepherd. The flock is highly educated, and we no longer follow anyone's lead with a herd mentality. We want to know our shepherd, hear his compassionate voice call for justice for victims everywhere, but especially ones who have been injured in any way by the church. We want to be confident that what our local shepherd says and does is what Christ the Good Shepherd would say and do.

Over these past years our sense of dismay has come from a very few bishops who have chosen the so-called good name of the church, it's social status and power, their public profile, and even the threat of moral and financial liability over the voices of the most vulnerable members of our flock.

Today's Gospel reminds us what Christian leadership should look like. Jesus didn't liken it to princes in palaces or governors of provinces. His metaphor was of a compassionate shepherd who sleeps in the field with his flock, one who knows them so well and loves them so dearly that he lays down his own life for them.

Let's pray that we always have the leaders we deserve, ones whose compassion is so transparent that it inspires us to be the same—even toward them.

FIFTH SUNDAY OF EASTER

ACTS 9:26–31
1 JOHN 3:18–24
JOHN 15:1–8

Until I spent time on a vineyard ten years ago, I always heard the parable of the vinedresser as a tough, "shape up or ship out" message. I always imagined God as the vinedresser having a field day loping and cutting my dead branches, trimming my unproductive stems, and up-rooting all the rot that undermines my fruitfulness.

It always felt like a violent activity. But what we see is not what we get.

It was a pleasant surprise, then, to actually see a vinedresser in action. Far from an act of violence, the care paid by the dresser to each stem is extraordinary. He or she carefully inspects the branch, delicately cutting only the smallest amount so that the vine will be healthier and more productive. A good vinedresser pours over the vines and from experience knows that to cut too much or too little will deprive the vine of its distinctive character. Every cut is measured and aimed to prune back only the diseased branch so as to bring about greater growth for the whole vine and a bigger yield for the vineyard. The vinedresser is not violent with the vine, but extremely tender. The first hearers of today's Gospel would have known that this metaphor is anything but a "shape up or ship out" message.

This parable is a profound insight into the Christian life. We can claim to belong to the Christian family all we like. We can come to Mass every Sunday, but if the fruit we produce is bitter and poisonous, if we are unforgiving, unjust, and uncaring, we cannot claim to be on the vine of Christ's love. And if that's the case we are in desperate need of the gentle hand of the vinedresser, who only wants to see us bring forth the yield he knows we are capable of achieving.

The Reverend Billy Graham once said, "Being a member of the church no more makes you a Christian than living in a garage makes you a car." That's the point of today's Gospel—God will not judge us by what we say or the public face of goodness we can turn on; we will be judged by the our acts of love in and through our kindness and compassion.

This metaphor of the vineyard also reminds us that we are connected to each other. There are moments in our life of faith when we hear or see other Christians saying or doing things we cannot countenance. We can try and disown them by retreating into our denomination, but we are all connected in Christ's vineyard. We need the courage to tell them the truth as we see it, and charitably point out the problems we have with what they think is right. And we need the humility to listen when they challenge us.

It's even harder when the diseased part of the vine is in our own Catholic section of the vineyard. Our first instinct can be to lop off the branch, just to get rid of it. But as any vinedresser knows, this is the last resort. Whether we find it easy or not, Christ calls us to limited surgical interventions over amputations every time. This is tough love. Even though there are people within our community who have committed terrible crimes and betrayed our trust, the Gospel calls us to hold on to them until it's clear that, no matter what intervention we make, they are dying on Christ's vine already. And even then, we hope and pray that our action toward them might see a new growth within them that could be the beginning of a possible grafting back onto us in the future.

In the face of the world's "shape up or ship out" principle, today's Gospel challenges us to hang in there with each other, in season and out of season, because as the old folk hymn sings, "They'll know we are Christians by our love, by our love. Yes, they'll know we are Christians by our love."

SIXTH SUNDAY OF EASTER

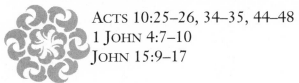 ACTS 10:25–26, 34–35, 44–48
1 JOHN 4:7–10
JOHN 15:9–17

The Italian film, *Life Is Beautiful*, vividly portrays the truth of today's Gospel. It shows a father convincing his five-year-old son that the concentration camp is an elaborate game that the Nazis had invented to test the Italians. Some members of the Jewish community criticized this film because they claimed it made light of the Holocaust. Writer and director Roberto Benigni, however, argued that the heart of the film lies in the fact that most parents will do anything to spare their children the reality of evil. Most parents who have seen and wept through the film know exactly what he's talking about.

And if parents could take such risks and go to such lengths for their children, how much more has God done for us in Christ Jesus. We are the only world religion to believe that our God took our form and died out of love for us so that we might understand the love God has for us, and the love we are called to have for each other.

It isn't, however, just any old love Christ calls us to practice. It's not about a fleeting feeling or having a warm fuzzy inside. Jesus tells us today that the character of Christian love is the degree to which it's sacrificial. This is a challenging way of working out whom we really love, isn't it? The people we love are those for whom we are prepared to sacrifice something of ourselves, maybe everything.

If that's the case, we could decide to stop telling people we don't love that we love them. The goal of the Christian life is to love everyone, but until we achieve that, the more we lie about love the more we lower its currency. It's perfectly acceptable to like, enjoy, be fond of, respect, admire, and be grateful to others, and not love them. There are a very few people for whom most of us would be prepared to lay down our lives. This criteria sorts out our intimates fairly quickly.

We could also decide to stop saying we love things, animals, ideas, or organizations that cannot love us back. Human beings can only truly love other human beings. Jesus did not die for an ideology or an institution. He was put to death because of his uncompromising love for all humanity everywhere. If we find ourselves saying we love our pets, house, car, job, our ideology, even our church more than we love other human beings, then we're in trouble.

That's what I like best about the model of loving that Jesus gives us in today's Gospel. Just when we might expect to find him using the analogy of a family, he talks about us being his friends.

Sometimes we can hear people lament that they are "stuck" with their families, and that they prefer their friends. It's an instructive moment, usually born out of a bitter and unloving history.

We choose our friends, and the strength of any particular friendship is usually found in how we know their history and story, and they know ours, in the way we give them time, attention, and affection. A true friendship is mutual. Jesus loves us, his friends, enough to know us, be available to us, challenge and forgive us. And his love is mutual. The only thing stopping us from having a deeper relationship with Christ is our desire for it.

But Jesus also shows how friends are prepared to give their lives for one another. That's what we celebrate each Sunday, that Jesus the Lord showed the quality and care of his love for us so that we might be empowered to go out and enable others to know and experience his love in the joyful way we sacrifice ourselves for them.

No one promised us that the Christian life would be easy. All we have is our brother Jesus and all our friends, our family in faith, to support us in every loving sacrifice we make.

SEVENTH SUNDAY OF EASTER

Acts 1:15–17, 20a, 20c–26
1 John 4:11–16
John 17:11b–19

In today's Gospel Jesus speaks about entrusting his glory to us. What an extraordinary gift to have received, similar to what St. Paul refers to when he talks about us holding our treasure, Christ, in our earthenware jars, our bodies. In the second century St. Irenaeus said, "The glory of God is humanity fully alive."

Recently I met Brian, a fifty-two-year-old business executive. He told me that twelve months ago he had a massive heart attack. "I was at a fund-raising tennis day for my kid's parish school. I hadn't played for years. After a few tough games, I felt some pain in my chest and arms. Can you believe it? I ignored it and played on." Brian lived in the fast lane. "I was ignoring my family, working very long hours, had too much stress, did very little exercise, and ate badly. I was a disaster waiting to happen—and it did! My hour came, well almost. I collapsed at the net and needed to be resuscitated at the hospital. I'm the luckiest guy I know. And it's the best thing that ever happened to me."

As Brian recovered he had an important conversation with the hospital chaplain. "He said he had never met a person who, on their deathbed, said that they wished they'd spent more time at work. A light went on in my head. When I got better I got a different job, started to look after myself and enjoy my family. I go to the gym with my children three times a week. Somehow I thought I was invincible and didn't have to care for myself. And now, though I might be less well-off financially, I am definitely happier. And so is my family."

How we look after our bodies is a good take on how seriously we believe that Jesus entrusts his glory not only to us, but also in us.

Over the centuries the church has not helped us have a good image about our bodies. By the fifth century, Christians were convinced that the body and the soul were separate entities within us. The soul was pure and good. The body could lead us into sin. Until recently Christians were taught to be suspicious of their bodies and to purge them so as to let the spiritual win out over the physical. It was a long way from St. Paul telling us to glorify God with our bodies because they're temples of the Holy Spirit!

And while we need to be careful that we don't become narcissists and end up worshipping our bodies, if we see them as the earthenware jars holding the Lord, then being committed to getting fit, and staying fit, is a way to show God's glory working in us. It also brings a balance into our lives, a pride in ourselves, and demonstrates that we understand that the spiritual life also involves how we spend our time and energy away from the church as well.

May these final weeks of the Easter season enable us to make the best possible choices about where we put our bodies, and what we put into them, so that we might take up the challenge of St. Irenaeus's words, "The glory of God is humanity fully alive."

ASCENSION OF THE LORD

ACTS 1:1–11
EPHESIANS 1:17–23 *or* 4:1–13
MARK 16:15–20

Aren't we lucky we don't take the scriptures literally? If we did it would appear from this week's Gospel that only multilingual, snake-wrangling, poison-drinking exorcists, with a gift for healing, would be seen as the genuine Christian article. That would leave most of us out in the cold.

This passage, however, is a dramatic addition to Mark's Gospel to show that even though Jesus is now at the right hand of God, he sends his disciples out to the whole world to carry on his ministry, and that he will protect us when trials come. And even though there have been tragic and shocking chapters in our two-thousand-year history, it's good for us to remember what God has done in and through us as we have gone out and proclaimed the saving love of Christ. Today 33 percent of the world's population are, at least nominally, Christian, numbering 2.1 billion people, making us the largest religion in the world. Our Catholic family accounts for just over half this group. We have around 1.1 billion Catholic brothers and sisters worldwide. Many Christians continue to be persecuted or discriminated against for their faith, and some continue to die for their love of Christ, which impels them to seek justice for all.

But the feast of the Ascension is not just an opportunity for us to look back on how we have tried to fulfill the command of the Lord to go out to the world. Indeed, this feast is primarily focused on where we are going from here on in. The ascension promises us that just as the Father raised Jesus from the dead, so too the Father, Son, and Spirit will welcome us into heaven as well, to be at Christ's right hand for eternity. This parable demonstrates the point.

In 1939 a father and son were famous art collectors. When World War II broke out, the son volunteered. In 1944 the son died in battle while rescuing another soldier. A year later, a young man came to see the father. "Sir, you don't know me but I was with your son when he died. I want you to know he didn't suffer.

I know you both loved art," he went on, "and though this isn't much, I want you to have it." He gave the father a package. Inside was a portrait of the son. It was rough work, but the father welled up with tears. "It was the least I could do for your son because he saved my life."

A few months later, the father died. At the art auction that followed, investors gathered from around the world. The first item up for bid was the portrait of the son.

The auctioneer tried to start the bidding, "$200... $100...Any bids? Any at all?" The investors called out, "Skip this one. Where are the Rembrandts?" Just then a man spoke up from the back. "I'll give you ten dollars for the painting. It's all the money I have." It was the gardener at the father's estate. So the auctioneer brought down his gavel. "Sold for ten dollars!" An investor called back, "Can we now get on with it?"

But the auctioneer continued, "The auction is over. According to the will, whoever bought this painting would inherit the estate, including all the art."

No matter what they said, the wealthy investors couldn't buy their way into the inheritance. Only the one who had the eyes of love, and knew what he was looking at, inherited everything the Father and Son had to offer.

May we go out from this feast of the Ascension so confident of our spiritual inheritance to come that we lavish its riches on all we meet right now. Because when it comes to Christ's kingdom, there's plenty for everyone.

PENTECOST

GENESIS 11:1–9 *or* EXODUS 19:3–8a, 16–20b
or EZEKIEL 37:1–14 *or* JOEL 3:1–5
ROMANS 8:22–27
JOHN 7:37–39

Recently I heard a friend's Bose "sound wave" speaker system. For a small box it gives the best sound reproduction I have ever heard. In comparison to the hi-fi I own, its bass notes are strong and true, which gives the music a sense of presence, a foundation upon which the treble rises and falls as the music dictates. This machine allows an exceptional clarity to the sound so that the composer's work can be properly heard.

In the Acts of the Apostles today we are told that the crowd who heard the earliest disciples of Jesus understood them in his or her own language. Now that's clarity! It wasn't so much the gift of tongues the earliest disciples received as much as their hearers received the gift of ears, of listening.

When it comes to listening in the church today, some people mistake mono for stereo, uniformity for unity. At the first Pentecost, the earliest Christians had no such difficulty; they knew that speaking the same language was not as important as was careful listening to one another.

The early church was a very complex and diverse community. Like today, they had their struggles with one another. Within a few years of the first Pentecost, there were fights between Peter and Paul over Jewish and Gentile converts. There were people who died for the faith and others who betrayed them to the authorities. Some Christians thought they were for Paul or Apollos rather than for Jesus, and still others thought the end of the world was nigh. Through it all, however, the bass notes played: the life, death, and resurrection of Jesus Christ.

The Second Vatican Council helped us recover the most ancient tradition in our faith, that in various, unexpected, and inculturated ways the Word of God has been present in all peoples, in every culture. We now hold that whenever the gospel has been proclaimed in a new land, it compliments the best in that culture as well as correcting aspects of any culture that oppress, demean, and diminish the women and men within it.

In this process, what is born between Christ and an individual culture is an inculturated faith, which takes as seriously as the early church did the context in which our faith is proclaimed and lived.

Pentecost faith holds that while we build our faith on the faith of all the believers who have gone before us, we have the responsibility to listen to our contemporary culture and put it into conversation with the gospel. That's why courage is one of the Holy Spirit's preeminent gifts. We are not allowed to retreat from the world but are sent out to enter into conversation with it, and hear in this dialogue the symphony God is composing here and now between the treble of our daily life over the continuing bass line of Christ's life, death, and resurrection.

Let's pray that this Pentecost Eucharist hones our ears as well as prepares our tongues to clearly receive and proclaim the gospel of Christ in the marketplaces of our own day and age.

MOST HOLY TRINITY

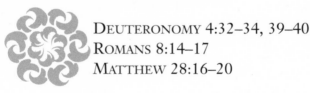

DEUTERONOMY 4:32–34, 39–40
ROMANS 8:14–17
MATTHEW 28:16–20

One of the things we often hear in times of domestic, local, or international crisis is that "everyone pulled together." We are rightly proud, and a few times amazed, at how people can set aside their differences and strive for the common good. Sometimes this experience of working together has the long-lasting benefit of breaking down boundaries. Other times, sadly, old enmities, prejudices, and suspicions return when the crisis is over.

Trinity Sunday celebrates that whether we are in crisis or not, in season and out of season, the Father, Son, and Holy Spirit do nothing but "pull together" to love and save us. What we glimpse as the best attribute of our family, town, or nation defines who our Christian God is, and what they see, how they judge, and the way they act toward the world.

A famous icon of the Trinity depicts the Three Persons at a table where there are four place settings. The final place, in the lower half of the painting, invites the viewer to take the seat and join them. It's profound theology and masterful art, but we can quickly misunderstand it.

We are not just personally invited to join in the very life of God, and pull together with them in their loving and saving of the world. The seat at the table is reserved for all of humanity.

In practical terms it is impossible to profess belief in the Trinity, on the one hand, and then work at things that pull the human family apart, on the other. It is scandalous to hold to the Father, Son, and Holy Spirit and be known as a racist, bigot, and sexist, to not care about refugees or those who die each day of starvation. We cannot keep signing ourselves in the name of a Triune God and then work hard at getting richer and more secure while the rest of humanity grows poorer, and lacks the necessities for human dignity. Gandhi once said, "I love the New Testament and the Christian ideas about God and I would take the waters of Christian baptism tomorrow if I saw Christians practice what they preach."

Trinity Sunday is not about theological mathematics—working out how three goes into one. It's about gaining the strength at the Eucharist so that we pull together to see that all of God's children have the opportunity to hear the good news of how much God loves us as Father, Son, and Holy Spirit. By what we say and do, may they have a share in our privilege at having a place at God's table. Most people will learn about the saving love of God primarily through the way they observe us seeing, judging, and acting.

It's not by accident that in our Catholic tradition the usual moment we invoke the Trinity is when we make the sign of the cross. It reminds us that "we cannot have our cake and eat it too." Every time we profess the Trinity we recommit ourselves to die to self so that God's saving love may be realized for everyone, everywhere.

So let's not only profess our belief in the Three Persons that make up our one God, but live the life that goes with it, "In the name of the Father, the Son, and the Holy Spirit. Amen."

BODY AND BLOOD OF CHRIST (CORPUS CHRISTI)

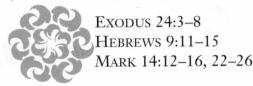 EXODUS 24:3–8
HEBREWS 9:11–15
MARK 14:12–16, 22–26

In years gone by the major focus of this feast of Corpus Christi was a procession that usually concluded with benediction of the Blessed Sacrament. Many of us have warm memories of benediction: a bejewelled cope and monstrance, the flickering candles, the Divine Praises and Latin hymns. It all worked to create a magical atmosphere. As richly theatrical as it was, the magical side of the ceremony was part of the problem.

In medieval times Catholics rarely received Holy Communion. So much so it was in this context that the church ruled that we had to communicate at least once a year. In the absence of communion, veneration of the Blessed Sacrament took on a great significance. Seeing the host was thought to impart an intense power.

Although in the last hundred years we have been encouraged to receive communion more frequently, the magical properties ascribed to the host persist in some people's devotional thinking.

As Catholics we believe that Jesus is really and personally present to us in the broken bread and shared cup of the Eucharist. And although we believe that Christ is present in the scriptures, the assembly, and the ministers of the church, we hold that Christ's presence under the form of bread and wine is one filled with the greatest intimacy and uniqueness.

The Eucharist is not intimate and unique because it is magic. It's not intimate and unique because we gaze upon the elements. The body and blood of Christ are intimate and unique symbols because earthly signs are transformed by God's love, and are consumed in faith. And as we eat and drink these elements Christ becomes part of us, and we come alive in Christ.

By receiving into our hands the bread, blessed and broken, and the cup, poured and shared, we say "Amen" to becoming the same in Christ: blessed, broken, poured out, and shared in love. We commune with God and he with us in the Eucharist so that just as earthly gifts are transformed into Christ so through us will be the entire world, and all things in it.

There is a huge and important difference between grace and magic. One is a trick for show. The other is the power of love, which expresses itself in faith, hope, and service.

In a profound poem French Jesuit Didier Rimaud challenges those of us who love the Eucharist to see it linked to the liberation begun in the Exodus, consummated in the resurrection, and working in our world today.

> In remembrance of you,
> We take the bread of Easter in our hands,
> This Bread do we consume:
> It does no longer taste of bitter herbs, nor of unleavened bread.
> It is the bread of a land promised us where we shall be set free.
>
> In remembrance of you,
> We take the wine of Easter at our feast,
> This wine do hold dear.
> It does no longer taste of bitter springs, nor of dark salty pools.
> It is the wine of land promised us where we shall be made whole.
>
> In remembrance of you,
> From exile we return.
> In remembrance of you,
> We walk across the sea!
> (Translated and set to music by Christopher Willcock, SJ)

No wonder the early Christians called the body and blood of Christ "food for the journey." May the Eucharist strengthen and embolden us to help God liberate and transform the world through how we spend out lives.

NINTH SUNDAY IN ORDINARY TIME

DEUTERONOMY 5:12–15
2 CORINTHIANS 4:6–11
MARK 2:23—3:6

A family of great cooks handed down from mother to daughter their many good recipes and cooking tips. One of the more curious instructions contained in one recipe came from the family's great-grandmother who had written that the joint of the leg of lamb had to be broken before baking it. The woman's several daughters, and in turn their daughters, obeyed this instruction believing that the wisdom was not to be questioned.

On doing some research on the family's papers, however, one of the great-granddaughters found a thank-you card from the original family cook to her husband. It read, "Dear Arthur, thank you so much for the gift of the new, large baking dish. I can now desist in breaking the leg of lamb, for the joint will now fit nicely."

This story goes to the heart of what Jesus is teaching us today. Mark's Gospel is an action story. Within the first three chapters Jesus has confronted evil spirits, gathered his disciples together, and taken on the religious authorities three times. Here he is in trouble with the Pharisees again, first for eating corn, and then for healing the paralyzed man. The problem is not that he does these things, but that he does them on the Sabbath. The Jewish law of the time was very clear—you could only work to heal someone on the Sabbath if they were in danger of death. Clearly the paralyzed man was not about to die. Jesus just thought the Sabbath law was wrong, and that the man's affliction demanded an immediate response. It wasn't good enough to say, "Come back tomorrow and I will look after you then."

Laws are not good in themselves. In fact laws exist because others have not lived up to their responsibilities and do not respect the rights and dignities of others. Some people, however, insist that almost all laws must be obeyed to the letter. As Catholics we do not hold this to be true. There aspects of certain laws in civil societies that the church considers to be morally questionable, or wrong, such as rest and remuneration for labor, taxation, land rights, gun control, abortion, and capital punishment. Sometimes where a law is so wrong, the church instructs us that we are not morally obliged to obey it.

All laws, then, religious, civil, personal, and even family rules must serve a clear and coherent good for them to be moral and binding upon us. And their purpose must be able to be explained; else we will descend into the farce of saying that "we obey the law because the law says so."

And as Jesus shows in today's Gospel, all law cannot be applied the same way in every case. Law is meant to serve humanity and attend to our needs and it needs intelligent and skillful interpretation. All too often, when we don't want to look at deeper issues in our church or society, we want a quick fix to make us feel better, so we demand tougher laws or greater obedience. Think of the number of times when elections focus on law-and-order issues. Often an analysis of the crime rate in our area or state shows that it is almost the same as, or less then, it was at the time of the last election. Unfounded fear regularly drives the law-and-order brigade. It can be true in the church as well.

The problem is that if we get fixated on obeying the letter of the religious law we can become as blind as the Pharisees. In today's story, even though they witness the healing of a man with a withered arm, their response is a hardening of heart and conspiring to kill Jesus.

There are only two occasions in the New Testament that we are told Jesus got angry: in this text, and in the clearing of the Temple in John's Gospel. It indicates how affronted Jesus was to blind obedience to religious laws. But we are also told that Jesus grieved for the Pharisees because they just didn't get what he was offering. They didn't get him.

Wouldn't it be a tragedy if when we meet Christ his response to us were anger and grief because of our righteous and unbending attitude to the religious law? Let's pray and work hard to make whatever changes we need to in our lives, and in the life of the church, to make sure that never happens.

TENTH SUNDAY IN ORDINARY TIME

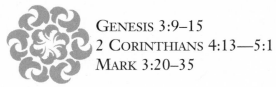

GENESIS 3:9–15
2 CORINTHIANS 4:13—5:1
MARK 3:20–35

Some parts of the New Testament are described as recording the "dangerous memory" about Jesus. This usually refers to a text or story that casts Jesus in a very different light from the one we are used to hearing. It's dangerous because it can be interpreted in a variety of ways.

Today's Gospel is one of those dangerous-memory texts. There are a few of them in Mark's Gospel, which was the first one to be written. It comes as a shock for us to realize that people in Jesus' hometown thought he had "gone out of his mind." Worse was to come, for it seems that Mary, who is named in Mark's Gospel, and his family seem to agree with the townsfolk and go to try and "restrain him."

Father Richard York vividly fills in some of the gaps in the story for us when he writes, "[S]ome of the neighbors came to Mary and said, 'You need to do something and quick! Your son is out of his mind! He's gone mad!' Some even suggested that if she didn't do something, they would. Mary was overwhelmed with a flood of emotions: embarrassment, shock, hurt, maybe even some guilt. She and Jesus' other relatives discussed it, but were convinced that the ugly reports were true: Jesus was mentally ill! Even some of the scribes and religious authorities were saying the same thing. So they hurried out to find Jesus and to seize him and involuntarily confine him, for *his* sake and for *theirs*. They came to the house where he was teaching. 'Your mother and brothers are asking for you,' he was told. Jesus replied, 'Who are my mother and my brothers? Anyone who does the will of God, that person is my brother and sister and mother.'" (See *www.healthieryou.com/j34.html*)

There is no getting around this story: At least in the early part of Jesus' ministry, some people and even his family had some doubts about his psychological health. The critical Greek word used by the writer of Mark's Gospel is *existemi*, which literally means that a person has lost his or her mind. Unfortunately the word we would use today is *nuts*.

We can see why people may have thought that Jesus was mentally ill. He was casting out demons, taking on the usually unassailable Pharisees, upending centuries of religious traditions, and saying the kingdom of God was at hand. Imagine if you met someone who had this record?

I think this is a wonderful story on many levels, enabling the dangerous memory of Jesus to bring us comfort today. First-century Palestine had little doubt about the origin of physical and mental illness: They were all curses by God, the consequences of sin or of being possessed by demons. Either way it was a dreadful stigma to carry. In our day we have become more sophisticated about the origin of disease and destigmatized most physical illnesses, but the stigma around mental illness remains.

Because we don't understand mental illnesses as well as we should, we fear it. And because we think it is uncontrollable, we are often anxious around those who outwardly suffer with it, or those whom we know who are undergoing treatment. This is understandable, but unfair. All of us carry a certain level of mental or emotional illness; in some of us these psychological or chemical symptoms are more organized and acute. So one of the best consequences of today's Gospel could be for us to educate ourselves about the causes and treatments for mental illness today.

Moreover, I think today's Gospel gives support to parents who cannot work out what's going on with a child of theirs, and to those families who have to deal with a relative whom they think might be mentally ill. These families have the mother of Jesus as a patron saint in the first instance, and the relatives of Jesus in the second.

Their patronage is stronger when we see what Jesus has to say about his family's presence outside where he was preaching. He seems to reject them, which can so often be the reality when we reach out to those closest to us who are battling an emotional disorder.

Jesus is, of course, saying something much more inclusive about the nature of the Christian family. He was outlining for us that we are not just his friends nor his servants, but that we belong to his intimates, we can be his mother, brother, or sister. And if we radiated that intimacy to the world, we would be a very dangerous force for good indeed. So let's go and do it.

ELEVENTH SUNDAY IN ORDINARY TIME

EZEKIEL 17:22–24
2 CORINTHIANS 5:6–10
MARK 4:26–34

"He did not speak to them except in parables." This text, of course, is not meant to be taken literally. In Mark's Gospel Jesus uses thirteen parables, and we regularly hear Jesus tell the people many things without telling them a parable. What this famous phrase does do, however, is underline how important stories were in the teaching ministry of Jesus. Parables were the media of first-century Palestine, and Jesus was one of the most skilled users of them.

Jesus did not invent the parable. The rabbis had long used them to explain the Hebrew scriptures, or to drive home a point of Jewish law. Jesus inherited a tradition of parables that were memorable, visual, and contained a moral lesson. And because most of the people in Israel were involved in farming, many of the rabbi's and Jesus' parables drew on analogies from that world. Jesus' parables have a majesty about them. They are immediate, simple, and profound. Where he broke away from the rabbis in regard to the parables he used was in their content. Jesus almost exclusively uses them to describe what the kingdom of God is like.

Today we hear about two elements of the kingdom—how it spreads, and who finds a home with it. There are two ways to look at the parable of the sower. The farmer is God scattering the seed. It might start out as an insignificant presence, but will later blossom into a glorious tree. A more accurate reading is that we are the farmer and Jesus sends us out to scatter the seeds of the kingdom.

If people are disposed to receive it, then the kingdom grows up into a generous stalk, ready for the harvest at the end of time.

In the second parable, the kingdom is compared to a tree that grows up to give shelter to all the birds of the air. We know from the fourth chapter of the Book of Daniel that it was common to describe foreign nations as "birds of the air." This parable not only draws on a rich metaphor from nature, but also tells us that the Gentiles, or foreigners, are finding a home in the kingdom, which is referred to as a tree.

In the first parable, faith can't be forced; it can only be attended to while God gives it growth. Our Christian history is littered with the tragic consequences of those who did not understand this, of those who bought faith with the sword. In some parts of the world we have much for which we need to repent. But for the most part now we know that the best seed we can plant anywhere, from our own backyard to foreign soil, is the witness of our faith, hope, and love of neighbor.

In the second parable, God surprises us with who finds a home among us. We should never underestimate how radical the idea was in Jesus' days that Gentiles could be among the chosen people. I think we still struggle with this, being altogether too confident when it comes to sharing our perch, of who is an unacceptable foreigner. God continues to confound us by his generosity, and to challenge our hospitality.

In a sense, and through no fault of our own, I think we have become too sophisticated for our own good. The immediate, simple, and profound message of Jesus' kingdom can be somewhat lost in the grandeur of our liturgy, the arguments of canon law, or the disputations of theology. This is the risk the church runs when it moves too far away from the ordinary things of life, and ordinary people's lives.

It might be that it is time not only to tell the stories of Jesus, and the truths of our faith in him, more simply and directly, but also to let others tell their stories of how they have been nurtured in the most surprising of ways, and how God has given them room to grow and flourish. After all, the seeds of the earth have to respond to the sun and soil, and the birds have lots of choices about in which tree they make a nest.

We just want to be sufficiently faithful to Christ that we will be seen as offering rich soil and strong, welcoming branches.

TWELFTH SUNDAY IN ORDINARY TIME

Job 38:1, 8–11
2 Corinthians 5:14–17
Mark 4:35–41

If we follow the time line closely in Mark's Gospel, the event in Jesus' life we hear about this Sunday rounds off an action-packed day. Jesus has a serious run-in with his townsfolk, his mother, and family; he has taught five outstanding parables, explained the detail of one of them, and then in the evening ventures out on the lake, encounters a storm, and calms it. Talk about a busy day! The context matters.

Throughout the first four chapters of Mark's Gospel it is increasingly clear that Jesus has divine powers. He drives out demons, he heals the sick, he teaches with authority, and he repeatedly speaks about God's kingdom as if from firsthand experience. Now in the space of six verses, all our suspicions are confirmed, not in words, for that will come later, but in deeds.

There are lots of giveaways in the text. The calming of the storm is the first "nature miracle" in Mark's Gospel. Like many expectant brides anticipating their wedding days, the Jews believed that God, and God alone, destined the weather. He was the master meteorologist. It's clear that some of the other miracles that Jesus did were not a surprise to those around him. The Pharisees don't seem to take exception that Jesus heals people, just that he does it on the Sabbath. This leads us to conclude that others did these things as well. But no one else gets nature to obey a command. That is God's prerogative.

Three Old Testament stories have a strong influence on this one. First there is Genesis, where God's Spirit "hovers over the waters" from which creation springs forth. Second there is

Exodus, where the Red Sea parts and the Israelites make their bid for freedom in the promised land. Finally there is Psalm 107, where God "made the storm be still, and the waves of the sea were hushed! Then they were glad because they had quiet, and he brought them to their desired haven."

The first hearers of the Gospel would have easily drawn the dots between those stories and this one. By invoking these images, Mark is not just saying that Jesus is a man God likes and is using to do some spectacular things, but now he is revealed as a man who can command nature. He is the Son of God. In fact to underline the continuity among all of Jesus miracles, Mark says the command Jesus used at his first healing miracle in chapter one is the same as gives here at his first nature miracle: Be Still!

So that's how the story works on a theological level, but it also had another importance for Mark's community. Most scholars think that this Gospel was written for the earliest church in Rome. We know that these believers were persecuted from the beginning. Images of storms, waves, and being swamped were then, as now, metaphors for the rough patches in life, and so we can imagine what this story meant to the Christians who were paying with their life for believing in Jesus. Mark reassures them that Christ hears their pleas and will not be outdone in fidelity.

And what was true for them is true for us. Roy Campanella picks up the complexity of our prayers in adversity in "A Creed for Those Who Have Suffered":

> I asked God for strength, that I might achieve.
> I was made weak, that I might learn humbly to obey...
> I asked for health, that I might do great things.
> I was given infirmity, that I might do better things...
> I asked for riches, that I might be happy.
> I was given poverty, that I might be wise...
> I asked for power, that I might have the praise of men.
> I was given weakness, that I might feel the need of God...
> I asked for all things, that I might enjoy life.
> I was given life, that I might enjoy all things...
> I got nothing I asked for—but everything I had hoped for.
> Almost despite myself, my unspoken prayers were answered...

Not that we believe that God directly sends us infirmity, poverty, and weakness, but if these are the storms of life that are presently swamping us or whipping up around us, then we can indeed experience the miracle of Christ's power in obedience, wisdom, dependence, and joy.

And maybe the sort of position we are meant to take when the storms in our life hit is the same one as Jesus—the prone position. For as Psalm 4 says, "I will lie down and sleep in peace; for you alone, O LORD, make me lie down in safety."

I don't know about you, but I am going to have to work on that one!

THIRTEENTH SUNDAY
IN ORDINARY TIME

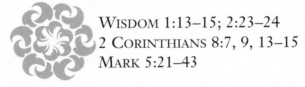

WISDOM 1:13–15; 2:23–24
2 CORINTHIANS 8:7, 9, 13–15
MARK 5:21–43

For most of us, the devotion to St. Jude as the "hope of the hopeless" is not taken all that seriously. We do not attend to the instructions of those dreadful chain letters that parade as prayer guides, because they reduce God to being an unpredictable tyrant: "I will do what you want only if you jump through these hoops." For the record, we do not have to write out a prayer nine times and leave it in nine churches for God to listen to us, or for him to take our prayers seriously. Still, St. Jude's patronage does exercise a power in the modern imagination because there are many more people living desperate lives in our community than we could credit.

This Sunday's passage of Mark's Gospel is among the most moving in the New Testament. There are four key actors in the narrative: Jesus, Jairus, his dying daughter, and the woman with the hemorrhage. Three of the four of them are desperate. Jairus is in danger of losing his beloved child. The daughter is about to die.

And the woman in the crowd, chances are, was a gynecological mess. Some of us can relate to these desperate situations, others of us have ones of our own.

It is also good for us to remember that the recipients of Jesus' healing and saving love on these occasions were two women. It's hard for us to imagine how sexist Jesus' society actually was in comparison to our own. And on this score we still have a long way to go. Women were not just second-class citizens, they were possessions of their husbands, fathers, sons, or brothers. Girl children were not anywhere near as important as boys, and a hemorrhaging woman would defile any Jew who came near her. These women were dispensable in first-century Palestine. But this girl was not dispensable to Jairus, and neither of these women were dispensable to Jesus. In the first part of the fifth chapter of this Gospel, Jesus heals a man possessed with demons who lives among the graves. That was as outcast as a man got in Jesus' time. Now, in the very next story, Mark tells us about how Jesus does the same for women. There was no room for patriarchy in the ministry of Jesus.

This is not the first time in the Bible when someone was raised from the dead. God brings the dead back to life in Ezekiel's Valley of the Bones. But even more of a parallel to Mark's story is found in the First Book of Kings. Elijah prays at the bedside of a widow's son that God will raise him from the dead. God answers the prophet's prayer. And, of course, we know that the raising of Jairus's daughter prefigures what God will do for his Son Jesus at the end of this Gospel.

At every stage Mark lays out the unbounded compassion and power of Jesus. He drives out unclean spirits, heals the sick, commands nature, and now restores life to one woman who had been socially dead for twelve years and a girl who was physically dead at twelve years of age. Jesus' power, however, is not meant to be a spiritual "shock and awe" campaign. He simply tells the woman who was healed to go in peace, and he strictly orders Jairus's household not to tell a soul. If we have faith in Jesus, it is because of his saving love, not because he is wonder-worker.

So to us. There are times we can feel absolutely desperate over something that is happening in our own lives. Sometimes our desperation is over something happening in the lives of others we love. Powerlessness is a gut-wrenching experience. Whether it's a social death, in the profoundest sense, a physical death, or anything in between the two, this Gospel is our life buoy. Jesus' compassion and saving love is unbounded. His companionship of us in our quiet desperation is strong and constant. All we need is faith.

We may not have the spectacular results we are after, but we will receive healing and peace, restoration and new life in ways often unimaginable to our prayer.

Trust me! St. Jude won't mind. It is Jesus, not Jude, who is the hope of the hopeless. For those of us who need him, let's claim his power right now. For those of us who are not feeling so hopeless at present, pray for those of us who are.

FOURTEENTH SUNDAY IN ORDINARY TIME

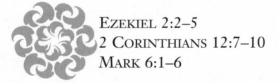

EZEKIEL 2:2–5
2 CORINTHIANS 12:7–10
MARK 6:1–6

We know the Gospel of Mark was written for a mainly Gentile audience, probably in Rome, because Mark often has to explain Jewish customs and beliefs and he has to translate into Greek a variety of Aramaic phrases. We also know from the Gospel that the community was undergoing crisis and persecution, and that people were dying for their belief in Christ. One of the other issues they had to face squarely with Gentile converts was: Why should I believe that Jesus is the Messiah, when most of the Jews don't? Today's reading about Jesus' rejection at Nazareth begins the explanation.

In the Gospel we would expect to find Jesus' hometown accepting and welcoming him with open arms. Jesus' ability to teach so well, his wisdom, and deeds of power, however, cause so much offense that the hometown crowd turns on him because he claims too much for himself. Jesus, literally, gets the hell out of there. A couple of chapters earlier we have already had a hint of the trouble Jesus would face at Nazareth when his mother, family, and the hometown crowd think he has gone out of his mind. But now Jesus has to flee Nazareth, and in Mark's Gospel he never returns.

There is an important detail about the consequences of Nazareth's disbelief: Jesus could work no deed of power there. Sometimes we can think of miracles as Jesus going around "zapping" people, a power he can turn on or off at will. But the reality in the Gospel is that the real miracle was not so much the act of power, but the depth of faith that preceded it. This remains true today.

For Mark's community, however, the stories of Jesus' suffering and rejection must have been very consoling. Jewish converts were expelled from the synagogue, and no doubt Gentile converts were excluded from the pagan sects as well. Maybe their own families rejected some of them, and more than a few would have had to leave town too. In this context their fate was an identification with that of Jesus. It gave meaning and direction to their plight. It gave them hope.

The experience of rejection, misunderstanding, and frustration is also a reality in many of our lives. Even having Christian faith these days can see us derided as fools, or pushed out of certain circles. In this context, we can draw on the same hope and courage that has always sustained the Christian community.

On a more worrying level, however, as a community we can run the risk of acting like the residents of Nazareth. No matter how much wisdom, authority, or goodness some people demonstrate in our Christian community, it seems some are told that they are not acceptable, we take offense at them and drive them away. Some Catholics have simply walked away from us because our community disbelieves that Christ's gifts can be manifest through them as well. This is true of people I know who are divorced and remarried, Catholic women who have had an abortion, gay Catholics and women who feel called to the ordained ministry. Whatever the complexities of their situations, I have heard people in these situations speak of the hostility they have felt from, and painful treatment they have received at the hands of the universal and local church. Nazareth did not value who was in its midst because it thought it knew better.

Today's Gospel also has a practical impact in our homes and communities, where we don't get away with very much and where affirmation can be sparingly given. This can be taken to unhealthy extremes when parents and siblings speak highly of their spouse, children, brothers, or sisters to everyone except to the person being praised. We are often so worried about a family member "getting a big head" that they never hear from us the encouragement they deserve.

As Christians we should look for opportunities to build up and praise those we know and love.

It was too late for Nazareth after it rejected Jesus. But it's not too late for us. May it never be said that we despised wise people who have something to teach us, and that we dragged down those whose gifts and talents reflected the power of God.

This Sunday Jesus reminds us that it's never too late to stop our disbelieving.

FIFTEENTH SUNDAY IN ORDINARY TIME

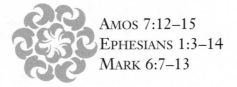

Amos 7:12–15
Ephesians 1:3–14
Mark 6:7–13

Many centuries ago the pope decided that all the Jews had to leave Rome. Naturally there was an uproar from the Jewish community. So the pope made a deal. He would have a religious debate with a member of the Jewish community. If the Jews won, they could stay. If the pope won, the Jews had to leave. The Jews realized that they had no choice. Problem was that no one wanted to debate the pope. The only volunteer was a poor, simple, old man named Moishe, who opened the door to the synagogue each Friday night. Not being used to words, Moishe asked for only one addition to the debate—that neither side be allowed to talk. The pope agreed.

The day of the great debate came. Moishe and the pope sat opposite each other. The pope raised his hand and showed three fingers. Moishe looked back at him and raised one finger. The pope waved his hand in a circle around his head. Moishe pointed to the ground where he sat. The pope pulled out a wafer and a glass of wine. Moishe pulled out an apple.

The pope stood up and said, "I give up. This man is too good. The Jews can stay."

Later, the pope explained what happened: "I held up three fingers to represent the Trinity. He responded by holding up one finger to remind me that we believe in the same one God. Then I waved my hand around my head to show that God was all around us. He responded by pointing to the ground, showing that God was present right here. I pulled out the bread and wine to show that God has given us the Eucharist. He pulled out an apple to remind me of original sin. He had an answer for everything. What could I do?"

Meanwhile, Moishe explained to the Jewish scholars how he won the unwinnable debate. "Well," said Moishe, "first he said that the Jews had three days to get out of Rome. I told him that not one of us was leaving. Then he told me that this whole city would be cleared of Jews. I let him know that we were staying right here." "And then what clenched the debate?" asked the rabbi. "I don't know," said Moishe. "It was strange. He took out his lunch, and I took out mine!"

Life always depends on how we read the signs!

In today's Gospel Jesus tells the twelve apostles that they should embody three signs: simplicity of lifestyle, dependence on others, and hospitality. These instructions are such a contrast to what most of us value today, where it is often the rich and powerful, the independent and the inhospitable who are thought to be the best leaders.

For Jesus, however, the one truly sent in his name is the one who knows that another's worth comes from who they are, not what they have. It doesn't matter whether we're rich or poor. It's the way we use our money for others that reveals whether our wealth possesses us or not.

For Jesus, being "a rock and an island" was not a sign of strength but one of fear and despair. A strong Christian is the one who rejoices in our dependence on each other, and is always grateful for the interconnectedness of life.

For Jesus, making room for others, especially those in legitimate need and even when it makes a large claim on us, is a preeminent sign of his kingdom.

The Christian life is about reading the signs of the times. May our eucharistic signs of his presence amongst us, the bread and wine, change us today, to match it with the best in being simple in lifestyle, happily dependent, and extravagantly hospitable with our time, talent, and energy for the sake of the kingdom of God.

SIXTEENTH SUNDAY IN ORDINARY TIME

JEREMIAH 23:1–6
EPHESIANS 2:13–18
MARK 6:30–34

I know very few people these days who work from 9:00 a.m. to 5:00 p.m. The eight-hour day seems to be a thing of the past. Where priests regularly encounter these new work patterns is when we see young people who are preparing for marriage in the church. Sometimes to arrange a meeting we have to resort to a 6:30 a.m. or 10:00 p.m. meeting. Some young people are working sixty hours a week; they take work home and work on the weekends. We know from surveys that they eat out most of the time, that they party hard when they get the chance, and that Sunday is spent on the home front, going to the gym, or sleeping. Then on Monday they start the process again.

Two things drive this obsessive work practice: competition in the job market, and the financial bonuses offered to the employees.

The problem is that this practice cannot be a long-term strategy. At the other end of the scale we all know people, only in their thirties and forties, who are burnt-out and feel used by a ruthless commercial marketplace.

This culture of exhaustion is not confined to the young corporate raiders. Most people in our country have never worked as hard, with so many claims on our time and energies.

Excessive demands on one's time, no matter how great the needs and rewards, were issues for Jesus and the apostles as well. The best translation of the Greek text for today's Gospel says that, after the apostles returned from their missionary journeys, "there were many coming and going and they had no leisure, even to eat."

Jesus' call to "come away to a deserted place all by yourselves and rest a while" is not just about good work practices and ethical employment policy. It is about humanizing our work, making sense of what we do, and seeing our work as means to an end, not an end in itself.

The social teaching of the church, especially in Pope John Paul's statements about labor and the rights of workers, repeatedly stresses three aspects of work: It gives us dignity—so governments and employers must not allow a work culture to develop where we lose our sense of personal importance, where we are treated like just another cog in the wheel; work enables us to improve the standard of living for us and our families; and through working we develop our talents and gifts that build up society as a whole.

Rest from work is a key factor in the success of all three aspects being achieved in any community. A culture of exhaustion militates against them. The bottom line in all this is appropriate boundaries.

Even Mark tells us today that, though Jesus was moved to compassion by the needs of the crowd, he also knew that their needs were not the only ones that had to be met. Jesus teaches his disciples, and us, that the balance between work and rest is an obligation of faith. This applies equally to work inside and outside the family home.

So this Sunday's Gospel carries a critical message for the modern world. Rest, recreation, and leisure are not indulgences about which we should feel guilty. They are rights defended by Christ that protect our human dignity.

I hope today you have a well-earned break.

SEVENTEENTH SUNDAY IN ORDINARY TIME

2 KINGS 4:42–44
EPHESIANS 4:1–6
JOHN 6:1–15

Recently I was invited to a relative's home for dinner. This family has been having more than a little trouble with their thirteen-year-old daughter, who is going through a particularly defiant and rebellious stage. The young girl was not happy with the vegetables her mother served at dinner and so she refused to eat them. The uneaten vegetables became the staging ground for an adolescent conflict. Trying to coax the girl into eating, her mother calmly used some lines I'd heard before. "Wasting food is a sin" and "There are starving people in the world who would be grateful for what you don't want." With that the girl jumped up and left the dining room. A few minutes later she returned with an oversized envelope and a marker pen. She began to stuff the food into the envelope and, as she did, she angrily asked, "What starving people do you want me to send these vegetables to?"

Who said being a parent was easy? Celibacy had never looked better!

In today's Gospel, after the five thousand have been fed, Jesus says, "Gather up the fragments left over, so that nothing may be lost." Some of us have never truly been hungry, so it can be hard to fully appreciate how wasteful our developed world must appear to those who watch their families die of starvation. People who lived through the Depression or have lived through wars often carry the scars of being hungry. To this day some of them are on guard against waste. Others try to numb the memory of want by overindulging.

For most of us in the developed world, especially thirteen-year-old middle-class kids, hunger has only ever been fleeting, and we are presently eating ourselves into obesity.

Some people would prefer to think of the story of the feeding of the five thousand exclusively in spiritual terms. There is no question that today's Gospel refers to the Eucharist where all are spiritually nourished by Christ our host. It also refers to the eternal banquet where hunger will be no more.

But this Gospel asks us to look at our world through the eyes of Christ's kingdom where the mighty will be cast down from their thrones, the poor will be raised up, and the rich who will not share will be sent away.

There is such a thing as healthy guilt. It's where we become aware of what we have done or failed to do in bringing about Christ's kingdom in our world. Given that it is entirely unnecessary for over thirty thousand people to die each day because of lack of food and water and the diseases this brings, guilt on our part seems a reasonable response. It becomes a healthy moment in our lives when we decide to change our priorities, and call for similar changes in the priorities of our nation, which spends more on bombs than starving babies.

I often wonder what God thinks when he hears wealthy nations say that the reason they refuse to share more with the poor is because these poorer nations often have unelected despots who divert their country's wealth into Swiss bank accounts or nuclear and conventional weaponry programs. Even in the face of these complex issues, we could find a way to feed the hungry who might, one day, be empowered to take charge of their nations.

"What starving people do you want me to send these vegetables to?" the thirteen-year-old asked. To which I wanted to reply, "Put your own name on the envelope because your own level of comfort makes you the neediest person in the world."

May the Eucharist enable us to do on earth what is done in heaven, where the hungry are welcomed and fed, the leftovers are gathered together, and nothing is wasted.

EIGHTEENTH SUNDAY
IN ORDINARY TIME

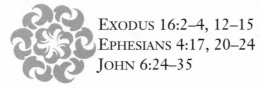

EXODUS 16:2–4, 12–15
EPHESIANS 4:17, 20–24
JOHN 6:24–35

We know from several sources that the ancient Greeks had a tradition of giving a meal to those who were about to set out on a journey. Before long, the gift of the meal extended to other gifts necessary for travel: clothes, food, and blankets. In Greece this custom came to be called the *ephodion*. In Latin this was translated as *viaticus* meaning "of or pertaining to a road or journey." In Roman temple worship there was a traditional belief that the final meal of a dying person gave them strength to cross over the River Styx from this side to the other.

Because Jesus had left us the Eucharistic meal in his memory, one can see why the early Christians took up a similar idea in regard to communion and even used the same name: viaticum. By 325 it is recommended that communion be given to the dying as "food for the journey." We still do. In recent years this ancient phrase in relation to the Eucharist has reappeared and become popular. Rather than exclusively refer to the last communion we might take in this life, however, "food for the journey" as used in the twenty-first century, has come to mean the life the Eucharist gives us to live out our faith each week. This entire tradition finds it roots in today's Gospel.

Following the feeding of the five thousand, the crowd thinks that when Jesus says he is the Bread of Life he is simply referring to the source of their next meal. If this were true it could put a new spin on what some might mean when they use the term, "cafeteria Catholicism." The poor old crowds and the disciples in John's Gospel are always getting their wires crossed when they listen to Jesus. They rarely understand his deeper message.

Jesus, however, is referring to himself as the fulfillment of all appetites, where we will never be hungry or thirsty again. Appetites are important things. They demand regular attention. Physical appetites tell us that we need nourishment, hydration, exercise, or sleep. We have learned to read our body's signs and if we ignore them we die. We also have emotional appetites, where we need affection, acceptance, and a listening ear. If we ignore these signs our mental health deteriorates and our quality of life is compromised. Jesus, however, also alerts us to our spiritual appetites. These are the needs we have for him, for meaning and purpose, for faith, hope, and love. If we ignore these appetites, we can be lost in regard to where we came from, why we are here, and where we are going.

As the sixth chapter of John's Gospel goes on, Jesus becomes clearer about the hunger and thirst he has come to fill. And as he does, the crowd's wires get uncrossed and they're shocked. Jesus, the Bread of Life, is interested in us fulfilling our physical, emotional, and spiritual appetites in this world as a way of glimpsing the life to come in him, where all our hungers and thirsts will be fulfilled.

Now all of this can seem rather theologically heady, a bit "out there." Michael McGirr in *Finding God's Traces* enables us to see how the "food for the journey" has its origins in our dining rooms.

> It is unfortunate that the family dinner table is not as common as once it was. Some people grow up learning to eat on the run. In some households the same meal can be eaten at the same time in five different parts of the same building: in front of the TV, beside the computer, on the back deck and so on. Creating a family table is easier said than done, especially in a fast food age. But it's worth the effort. The table is the gathering place, the place to listen and talk. Food and stories sit down together.
>
> The family home is sometimes called "the domestic Church". The meal table is a mirror image of the Eucharist, in which we hear stories from our faith tradition and are fed the Bread of Life. Grace before eating can help us to draw together some of the threads of the day, to give thanks for what each person has been doing, to remember those who are suffering or hungry and to remind ourselves that the family table is also the table of the Lord, the place where God sits among us, is patient when we argue, laughs at our funny stories and knows whose turn it is to stack the dishwasher.

NINETEENTH SUNDAY IN ORDINARY TIME

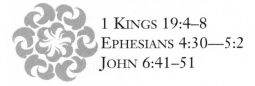

1 KINGS 19:4–8
EPHESIANS 4:30—5:2
JOHN 6:41–51

Around the world there are women's shelters run by the St. Vincent De Paul Society called "Manna House." It's an inspired name for such an important work. Women and their children, in the midst of fear, and having suffered terrible abuse, are welcomed into a safe haven where they can be loved and looked after. It's a temporary respite where broken families can piece their lives back together and be revived for the journey ahead.

What happens at Manna Houses for women at risk happens for each of us when we come to the Eucharist. We receive manna from heaven. It's our stop on the journey of faith so that we can go out spiritually revived to be the face of Christ in the world. Sometimes we need this "manna come down from heaven" when we are spiritually most at risk.

I love the fact that as Catholics we believe that Christ is present in ordinary gifts of bread and wine blest and offered at the Eucharist. We don't just believe that Christ is present in sunrises, sunsets, and in natural beauty, we also believe that God comes to us in a special and unique way in the simple, ordinary things of life. And it is in what we do with these gifts of bread and wine that Christ is really present. The earliest Christians called the Eucharist "the breaking of the bread." It is to the broken bread and the poured cup given into our hands to which we say "Amen" and so affirm our belief that Christ is present here.

We often need to be reassured of Christ's presence when we are in the desert periods of our own life. We can feel we are wandering around in the wilderness looking for some sign of God's life. For all of us who are broken in mind, body, or spirit, or who are pouring ourselves out in love for other people, communion is precisely the time Jesus meets us where we are. Is it any wonder that the Eucharist means so much to us? May we never feel as though we are not good enough to be here, for Jesus has invited us to be at his table where we are loved and cared for.

As important as the Eucharist is, however, it is not "ours," in the sense that we can selfishly hold on to the gifts we receive here. We are given Christ in word and sacrament, so we can become Christ.

In a sense Jesus says the same thing in today's Gospel when he talks about how the Father draws people to faith.

Sometimes we can fall into the trap of thinking that faith is only an intellectual exercise. As important as good thinking and the power of strong arguments might be, the truth of faith is best demonstrated on an emotional and intuitive level when others see the power of God's saving love active in the way we live our lives. This is what really captures people's attention, and draws them to ask what gives our lives this quality, direction, purpose, and meaning.

So may this respite from the journey of faith dispel our fears, revive us for the task ahead, and enable us to live as though the only Bible others will read will be our lives, and the only sacraments that will captivate them and draw them to Christ will be our justice and joy.

TWENTIETH SUNDAY IN ORDINARY TIME

PROVERBS 9:1–6
EPHESIANS 5:15–20
JOHN 6:51–58

In the early 1970s there was an edition of *Reader's Digest* that told how a jet crashed in the Andes Mountains. It was a good case study in moral reasoning. The issue was that some of the survivors of that crash resorted to cannibalism to survive. The question the author posed was "Is it ever ethical to eat another human being?"

Whatever the extreme and specific ethical arguments for cannibalism might be, the thought of eating another person is repulsive to most of us. Yet many people outside Catholicism often think that we are Christian cannibals, feasting on Jesus' flesh and blood.

The best traditions in the church have always been very careful in the language they use about how Jesus is present in the Eucharist. We are not cannibals. We are not eating Jesus' liver, brain, and bones.

In the catechism when it speaks of the Eucharistic real presence, it never refers to "Jesus" but always to "Christ." The distinction matters. The Eucharist is a sacrament of Easter. It is the glorified, Risen Christ who is wholly and truly present under the form of bread and wine at the Eucharist.

Popular piety and legends that speak too explicitly about the physicality of the Eucharist have not helped us have sensible thinking. As a Catholic I believe that Christ, raised by God from the dead, is truly and personally present to me in the Eucharist. "How" is a question that misses the point of the gift.

Chapter six of John's Gospel is a discourse on the Eucharist. It is also, and at the same time, a discourse about Jesus' passion and death and our mission to follow in his way. For Jesus, the new Moses, not only gives bread to the people, but also in his passion, death, and resurrection he gives us himself. This is why the church has always linked the events at Easter with the celebration of Eucharist.

Why have we been given this unique gift? The Eucharist is not meant to be a feast for a privileged few. It's not a private devotion. It's not meant to be something that only assures us of our own particular salvation. It is meant to be something that empowers all Christians to go out and transform the world with love and goodness for Christ's sake.

The church has always linked what we do away from the Eucharist with what we celebrate at it. This doesn't mean that all of us can rush out and feed the world's poor. It does mean that most of us can assist other groups or people who do precisely that. And it does mean that when we think about who we will vote for as political leaders, we ask about their platform in relation to those in our country and world who are suffering the most.

Sometimes we can think of the Eucharist as a magical act. Jesus counters such a notion in today's Gospel when he tells us that he gives us himself "for the life of the world." The Eucharist does not turn us into cannibals; it's meant to make us radicals, radically committed to all God's people everywhere.

TWENTY-FIRST SUNDAY IN ORDINARY TIME

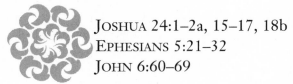 JOSHUA 24:1–2a, 15–17, 18b
EPHESIANS 5:21–32
JOHN 6:60–69

I have some sympathy for the response of the Jews to Jesus' hard teaching in today's Gospel! For a Jew to be asked to drink blood is as abhorrent as it gets. It is the same as demanding that an ultra-Orthodox Jew eat pork!

In almost all the stories in the Gospel of John there are insiders and outsiders, those who understand the message and those who take Jesus too literally and are offended or confused.

The flesh and blood given for the life of the world is at one and the same time the passion, death, and resurrection of Jesus celebrated in the Eucharist. Jesus was not, literally, offering his arm for his followers to chew! He was referring to the gift he was soon going to give his followers: the example of utter fidelity to God's kingdom even unto death, and the meal of that kingdom, the Eucharist.

We are the recipients of both gifts and the commission to live them out. The Bread of Life and the Cup of Salvation are given to us for our mission in the world today and for our journey toward the world to come.

The other response in today's Gospel gives us great hope. In spite of being confused and deserted by his friends, Peter hangs in there with Jesus. He holds on to faith when all the signs show that a hasty retreat may be a better course of action.

We all know people who remain faithful in the most extraordinary of circumstances. Some of these we can understand—parents with sick children or spouses with ill partners. It's heroic, but understandable.

But sometimes fidelity is heroic and inexplicable: when a spouse welcomes back his or her partner after an adulterous affair; when a foreign-born priest or religious will not abandon an oppressed community; when a person will fight a just cause and be persecuted all the way to the end. These are powerful signs of faithful love at work too.

It's a fine line to know when fidelity is dying to self, not killing self. We are called to the former and often seduced by the latter.

James Keenan in his book, *Virtues for Ordinary Christians*, says that fidelity is the bottom line of the Christian life. He argues that the church has spent too much time preaching about infidelities and too little time teaching about those things that strengthen fidelity. "Each person," he says, "has two major moral goals in life: to be just and to be faithful."

Being faithful to his Father, and to us, sums up what Jesus does for our salvation and is exactly what he calls forth from the disciples in today's Gospel. Perhaps because we too easily think it is something difficult, we presume that being faithful to our friends is hardly a moral issue. Yet once we see that friendship is the key to the moral life then we can come to see that living the moral life is about the ordinary interactions of our day.

James Keenan writes, "To this end we may need to make more calls, write more letters, cook more dinners, take more strolls, linger a little longer with a friend. We may also need to disengage ourselves from the habit of counting or measuring what the other does or does not do or say." Until recently, however, rather than talk positively about fidelity we have spoken for too long and hard about infidelities.

But when have we been taught to practice acts that strengthen fidelity? The Gospel today reminds us that the focus should be on the positive, that fidelity is at the heart of the moral life. Being faithful to his Father, and to us, sums up what Jesus does for our salvation, and it is exactly what he calls forth from the disciples in the Gospel today.

Perhaps because we too easily think something is difficult, we presume that being faithful to our friends is hardly a moral issue. Yet once we see friendship as the key to the moral life then we can come to see that living the moral life is about the ordinary interactions of our day.

TWENTY-SECOND SUNDAY IN ORDINARY TIME

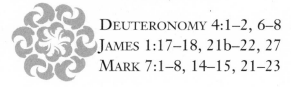

DEUTERONOMY 4:1–2, 6–8
JAMES 1:17–18, 21b–22, 27
MARK 7:1–8, 14–15, 21–23

I like watching, and am sometimes amused at, the theatricality of the State of the Union address. The president shakes hands with everyone on the way in and out, and the audience likes everything he says so much they get up on their feet after each statement. The speech is about talking up what he has achieved and telling the Congress where he wants to go.

Today's Gospel is Jesus' State of the Union address. Like the U.S. president, Jesus may have done the local cultural equivalent of shaking hands when he came in, but he received no standing ovations for what he said, and he had to fight to get out alive when he was done.

Imagine any contemporary political leader saying that his policies are going to be good news for the poor, that he wants to let prisoners go free, make sure the oppressed are given justice and heal the sick. Like the hometown crowd in Nazareth, we would think his goals were laudable.

Imagine the same leader, however, telling us these great acts were not going to be for the local community or our nation at all. Rather, he was going do all this for the nations around us whom we despise. My hunch is that we would be moved to rage as well.

After Jesus announces his program of what God wants in the world, he goes on to invoke the biblical stories of the times when, though there were great needs in Israel, two of their greatest prophets went to the Gentiles and defended their rights to a just and dignified life. Israel despised the Gentiles.

Jesus says that what God wants is for Israel to be like Elijah and Elisha. This is what fills the crowd with rage. The faith of the Gentiles was a very difficult issue for the early church. They were written off by everyone as irredeemable. Even Jesus seems to have been surprised at their faith and acts of love. The church has to be constantly on guard that we do not fall into the same trap of being too sure of who it is that can be bearers of God's kingdom.

The work of salvation is God's and not ours. Every time we seem to have worked out precisely who can and cannot board the salvation train, God usually undermines our expectations, judgments, and prejudices.

Christ is always there for us, but his kingdom only comes alive in our communities when we admit we are poor, we want to be set free, we want to see how the world actually is, we seek an end to our own oppression, and we face up to the ways in which we oppress others.

This is the saving message Jesus makes his own from Isaiah. What is just as powerful to me, however, is where he stops reading from that same book. He reads up to Isaiah 61:2a. He does not complete the verse because it goes on to announce God's vengeance on the world.

Jesus knew that vengeance was not part of God's desire for our salvation. In this matter, too, we have to keep reminding ourselves that God is not primarily interested in judging us, but that God wants to seek out and save those who are most lost and broken.

I would like to think that if I was in Nazareth when Jesus put down his scroll, I would have stood and cheered and yelled for joy. I think, however, I may have been challenged to silence. Every time we think we have God nicely packaged, we are spectacularly undone.

May the Eucharist, this meal of those of us who know we need Christ, help us to work for the kingdom he actually proclaimed and not the one we constantly try to build in its place.

TWENTY-THIRD SUNDAY IN ORDINARY TIME

ISAIAH 35:4–7a
JAMES 2:1–5
MARK 7:31–37

I read on the Internet the true story about a baby girl who was seriously ill in a neonatal ICU. The pediatric specialist said there was very little hope. The baby's five-year-old brother, Michael, kept begging his parents to let him see his sister. "I want to sing to her," he kept saying. Children were not allowed in the ICU, but Michael's mother eventually insisted that he be able to see his sister. When he got to the crib he sang: "You are my sunshine, my only sunshine, you make me happy when skies are grey." The nurse reported that as Michael sang, the baby's pulse rate began to calm down and become steady. "Keep on singing, Michael," encouraged his mother with tears in her eyes. "You never know, dear, how much I love you. Please don't take my sunshine away." The baby recovered and left the hospital three weeks later.

I am not pretending for a moment that Michael's song healed his sister, but we should never underestimate the power of human support and love. It helps us to be healed.

The Gospel story of the healing of the deaf-mute is striking because it is one of the few stories where the crowd makes the request of healing from Jesus. This is understandable given that the man cannot speak for himself, but the scene, as Mark writes it, is very touching. Mark tells us that the crowd brought the man to Jesus. "They" beg Jesus to heal him, "they" are ordered not to tell anyone about the miracle, but "they" go straight out and tell everyone about it.

In our own way we bring the deaf and the mute to Jesus each time we gather. This is what the Prayers of the Faithful are all about. This is why they are so important.

When we visit another parish we can tell a lot about it by the care with which the intercessions are composed and compiled. If they only attend to the needs of the parish and never with the wider church or the world, if they focus on the needs of the Catholic world and never on the plight of those in crisis, who may not share our faith or may hold to another or no faith, it says so much.

The church has always believed in the power of intercessory prayer. Not that God needs to be reminded what our world needs. God knows that better than we know it. But intercessory prayer sorts our priorities and establishes who has a claim on our affections and concerns. It also enables others to know that we stand in solidarity with them.

And miracles still happen when we are one with those for whom we hope and pray. Sometimes the first miracle that occurs is that we notice the needs of some group beyond our immediate circle. Their suffering moves us and we choose to help them.

Let's pray that Christ removes our blindness, opens our ears, and loosens our tongues so that we speak up for those who are most in need of a healing word that brings them justice and peace.

TWENTY-FOURTH SUNDAY IN ORDINARY TIME

Isaiah 50:5–9a
James 2:14–18
Mark 8:27–35

At the very end of Peter Weir's film about World War I, *Gallipoli*, Frank Dunne (played by Mel Gibson) is racing back to a frontline trench with the news that the attack has been called off. Meanwhile, Major Barton is commanded to "order the men over." In doing so he is sending them to certain death. In the scenes that follow each man prepares for his final moment on earth. Some write notes to their families, some weep at the futility of the entire exercise, some have a cigarette, and one recites the twenty-third Psalm.

Just as they prepare to attack, Barton offers these words of encouragement: "All right, men, we are going. I want you all to remember who you are, you are from the Tenth Lighthorse Brigade. Don't forget it! Good luck."

Knowing who we are gives us dignity. Being called by name presumes intimacy. In the Hebrew scriptures, knowing and using another's name was to have power over them. This is one of the reasons why God's name is never spoken by Israel. No one has power over God.

In the Christian scriptures, however, names are readily and generously used. We are invited to call God by name and Jesus assures and shows us that God knows each of us by name and we are all invited to use the family name. The days of distance are over.

In Mark's Gospel, especially, the moment when Peter names who Jesus is, the entire story changes. Everything in the Gospel so far has been preparing for this moment. Until now only the evil spirits know who Jesus really is and they have been ordered to remain silent. Now Peter names that Jesus is the anointed one, for whom Israel has longed and hoped. Everything that follows in the Gospel is a consequence of this revelation.

Peter's confession of faith in and about Jesus is instructive about the God in whom we believe. Jesus does not seem worried about naming rights and religious conventions. His power does not come from his secrecy, but from his generosity of heart, his authoritative teaching, and his intimacy with those around him. People felt known and loved by him.

This is the face and name of our God. Not some remote being aloof from our day-to-day struggles, but one who is with us at every step of our life.

Old habits die hard, however, and Peter wants his Messiah to be powerful and strong in standing up to the authorities in

Jerusalem. Jesus knows that the real love and intimacy of God is not found in acts of might and domination, but in the extraordinary love of the cross.

And all of us who are called by his name are challenged to do likewise and lose ourselves in being generous of heart, authoritative in the stand we take on matters of conscience and truth, and intimate with those around us.

The soldiers at Gallipoli in World War I were slaughtered, but they died knowing who they were. May we never have to suffer the same agony or folly as they did. But may the way we live out the suffering and pain of our own life demonstrate the dignity of knowing that there is meaning and hope even in our darkest hours and that our known God is one with us even through the valley of death.

TWENTY-FIFTH SUNDAY IN ORDINARY TIME

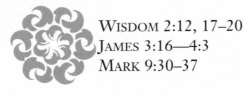

WISDOM 2:12, 17–20
JAMES 3:16—4:3
MARK 9:30–37

It's hard to see what the disciples don't get when Jesus tells them in fairly plain language that because of the way he lives and what he says he will be put to death by the power barons of his day. The disciples seem to think the passion is going to be an event out of *Boy's Own Annual*, where the ensuing campaign will see greatness thrust upon them.

In this context, Jesus takes the smallest and most vulnerable in their society and teaches the disciples that greatness comes through care of the least.

This is a powerful lesson. Greatness in the world—power, connections, wealth, influence, reputation, and learning—only counts for something in the kingdom of God when put at the service of the most vulnerable of our society. Greed, riches, and pride are so alluring, so seductive for us in the church, as much as for those outside it, that we need to regularly examine our consciences to assess the motivations and results of what we are doing, and why we are doing it.

When I read today's Gospel, however, I also feel sad. I cannot help but reflect on how unintentionally prophetic Mark was in linking the prediction of Jesus' passion with the status of a child.

The safeguards now needed in response to the criminal and scandalous behavior of a very few leaders in the church mean that many bishops, priests, religious, and teachers can no longer follow Jesus' example and take children in our arms. I fully understand why this is the case, but the fact that we have to be so careful about the care of our children and have strict protocols and legalization that covers such behavior toward children is a necessary and, nonetheless, tragic moment.

It's also a moment for us to remember the passion of those who have had to endure the trauma of destructive behavior. As the Jews say of the Holocaust, "To forget is to commit the same mistake again."

At its most basic level the latter part of today's Gospel reveals what we would expect of Jesus—he likes children and they like him.

It's amazing how a couple of pieces of information can sometimes change the way a scriptural story is read, and its importance for our lives today.

We know from other documents of the same period as the New Testament that children in the ancient world had no rights. They were possessions of their fathers, and they could be bought and sold, exploited, and even killed without any recourse to the religious or civil law.

One way in which a child was publicly claimed in this society was that only their immediate family could touch them. The story, then, of Jesus embracing the child in public was in itself a social challenge to accepted customs. But it's much more than that. In taking the children in his arms, Jesus declares that they are possessions of no one, but they belong to us all as gifts. In the family of God, children are accorded the dignity and respect we would give to God.

Today's Gospel tells us that those who deserve our attention and esteem are the ones who are the least, the most at risk, or those who put their talents and gifts at their service by making the world a better place for them.

Just as he did in the marketplace of Galilee when he took the children in his arms, Jesus has a habit of turning our world's values upside down.

TWENTY-SIXTH SUNDAY IN ORDINARY TIME

NUMBERS 11:25–29
JAMES 5:1–6
MARK 9:38–43, 45, 47–48

Given today's Gospel, I wonder how our Christian brothers and sisters, who insist on the literal truth of the scriptures, avoid cutting off their hands and feet, plucking out their eyes, and worrying abut how hot hell is! I'm not sure about them, but I know my feet have taken me to places I wish I'd not gone, and when I got there my eyes saw things I wish I'd not seen. Still, in spite of the times I've let myself down, I am glad I'm still in one piece, and not all that worried about the worms and weather in hell!

Jesus was a skilled and powerful communicator. And like all great teachers he used metaphor and exaggeration to make his point. In Mark's Gospel, Jesus takes evil very seriously. He is always conscious of it around him and is aware that it comes from within us, and without us. Jesus teaches us today to stop doing the destructive things that prevent us from loving God, each other, and ourselves.

Sinful behavior often falls into two categories of human activity: habitual and compulsive. Habits are unusual things.

There are good habits, like saying "please" and "thank you." There are habits that can start out well intentioned enough, but end being obsessions, like caring for one's physical fitness. And there are habits that bring moments of relief or let us off the hook—like lying, dishonesty, and stealing—but always end up being destructive.

Compulsive behavior, however, is of a very different order. Gambling, drinking, shopping, smoking, violence, work, sex, eating, drugs, pornography, money, and the Internet are fairly common modern manifestations of compulsive behavior. As heartbreaking as these addictions are, they are the presenting problems of deeper issues related to self-esteem, personal history, desire, fantasy, and even genetic disposition.

One of the comments I've heard people make about their compulsive behavior is "I found myself doing it again and I am not sure how or why." No doubt there are some people who feel so lonely and get so depressed about their habitual or compulsive behavior that they contemplate severing an arm or a leg, or gouging out an eye.

Jesus underlines that we have to stop our destructive behavior and offers three pieces of practical advice so we can. First, do whatever helps. For some people the most unusual solutions attend to the deeper issues and help us piece our lives back together. It doesn't matter whether others approve of it, or it's related to religious faith, for as long as it doesn't lead to other destructive behavior, then "whoever [or whatever] is not against us, is for us."

Second, accept help. None of us can battle through life carrying all our burdens on our own. Steps four to six of AA are concerned with sharing the exact nature of our burdens as a means of coming to terms with them. Our family and friends are not mind readers and we need to seek out wise counsel and follow it wisely. The help and support we receive could be like the cup of refreshing water Jesus tells us about today.

Finally, habitual and compulsive behavior always has a pattern. Only when we regularly examine ourselves to see where, when, how, and with whom we are most likely to walk away from God's love can we work out why we do it and change the pattern.

And when we really know ourselves as we are, and not as we would like to be, we have the chance to choose life over death more often than not.

TWENTY-SEVENTH SUNDAY IN ORDINARY TIME

GENESIS 2:18–24
HEBREWS 2:9–11
MARK 10:2–16

During World War II, Mary was one of hundreds of Australian women who fell in love with an American soldier. She married her Episcopalian army major at the side altar in a Catholic church in 1945. He was dashing and handsome and by the time it came for him to return to Baltimore in 1946, they were expecting their first child.

Upon arrival at her new home, Mary found that her brave soldier was not as fearless as she thought. He was completely dominated by his aristocratic, wealthy mother who made it clear from the beginning that she opposed the marriage. Mary's life in the family home was a nightmare. The tensions boiled over when Brendan was born. Regardless of the promises his father had made in Australia to have their children baptized Catholics, the soldier waged no war against his mother, who declared that if any grandchild of hers was baptized a "papist" she would disinherit the three of them. The major buckled under the maternal pressure and demanded that Brendan be baptized an Episcopalian.

Mary was devastated. She gathered her few possessions together, had her son baptized a Catholic, and fled home.

In 1950, by now a divorcee, she met Maurice, a wonderful man who wanted to marry her and be a father to Brendan. When they went to see the local parish priest, he told them they could not be married in the church and if they contracted a civil marriage they ran the risk of going to hell for eternity. They were tough days. Catholicism was one of the reasons Mary left the United States. In turn, the very church she defended shut her out.

In today's Gospel, Jesus speaks directly about marriage and divorce. In Jesus' day only a few women had rights before the law. These were wealthy women from the priestly families. They could divorce their husbands. The vast majority of women, however, were seen as possessions of their fathers, husbands, or sons. A husband could draw up a divorce writ for any reason he wished and so force his wife out of their home into destitution or humiliate her by sending her back to her own family. No wonder Jesus lays down the law so strongly about fidelity and commitment. His new interpretation of the Law of Moses defended women's rights to dignity and security.

Every Catholic parish today has parishioners who are divorced and remarried. In the face of the negative messages you hear, I want them to know how much we admire their often heroic faith, how much God loves them, and how grateful I am that they hang in here with us. The problem for the church is that, on the one hand, we want to keep affirming the permanence of married love, and yet, on the other hand, we have an increasing number of Catholics who are divorcing. We are caught between the fine ideal Jesus teaches and the frail human condition we all carry in different ways. We have not got the balance right yet.

The church's remedy to marriage breakdown is an annulment. An annulment is not a Catholic divorce. A civil divorce says the parties that were married are not now. An annulment says that there were factors, often unknown to the couple on the day of the wedding, which meant that there was never a full and true Christian marriage in the first place. The sacrament is therefore null and void.

Some Catholics, and certainly people who are not Catholic, cannot face up to the long, complex, and legal process involved in an annulment. It can be a traumatic experience. Others argue that the church might step away from the more recent legal approach to dealing with marriage and, like the Orthodox churches, use the sacrament of penance to nullify the sacrament of marriage.

Whatever the process, Christian teaching on this issue must always be metered with compassion.

From 1951 until 1993, Mary and her second husband did not receive the sacraments. She instigated annulment proceedings in 1990. In 1993 as they received communion for the first time in forty-two years, the small congregation knew that they had been away from the church for too long. We also knew that God had never moved away from them, embracing them in his arms, laying his hands on them every day and blessing them.

At that Nuptial Mass in 1994, Maurice's best man was Brendan, born in Baltimore in 1946. Maurice had legally adopted Brendan the day after he married Mary. And as we all received communion, with tears streaming down our faces, we understood that it is to human, frail, and open hearts that the kingdom of God belongs.

TWENTY-EIGHTH SUNDAY IN ORDINARY TIME

WISDOM 7:7–11
HEBREWS 4:12–13
MARK 10:17–30

John Calvin, one the founding fathers of the Protestant Reformation, reacted against what he saw as medieval Catholicism's adherence to the sacramental law as a means to salvation. "If you keep the law, the law will keep you." He was right to condemn the preaching of some Catholic priests of his day. Calvin maintained that since time began God predestined those who, by faith, would be saved. Calvin argued that the rest of humanity would be lost. It was impossible to know for certain, Calvin argued, who was who.

Within a few years, however, his own congregation in Geneva wanted to know how anyone could be sure they were on the right path to salvation. Calvin's disciples taught that strict and right behavior was an indication of who belonged to those elected by God to be saved. Not dancing, drinking, swearing, or gambling, plus working hard, saving one's money, and the careful observance of the Ten Commandments became the benchmarks of the elect. Within a few generations of Calvin's death, it is easy to see that the observance of the strict, Protestant, moral code had replaced the seven sacraments as a way of being assured of heaven.

The rich young man in today's Gospel wanted to be assured of salvation too. He was a good man, an observant Jew and someone Jesus looked on with love. But he was hoping the law would save him. He wanted to be sure of gaining heaven by jumping through the right hoops, at the right time, for the right reasons.

Jesus doesn't reject the importance of faithful and good living, but he offers the young man a relationship that would make sense of the choices involved in following him. Without a loving relationship with God, who calls us to live the best life we can, the fulfillment of any law, civil or moral, is a tyranny. We do not believe in a tyrannical God.

We do believe, however, in a God who makes demands of us, who often challenges us in the places where we are most vulnerable. For the young man, his money was an obstacle. He could not embrace a relationship with Jesus because this would have placed in peril his wealth and the comfort that his many possessions afforded him.

For the earliest Christian community, today's Gospel highlights serious issues on which people left their company: the role of the law in following Christ, the divide between rich and poor; the commitment demanded of followers in the earliest community.

In comparison to our forebears in faith, we have domesticated this radical edge of the Gospel.

We often comfort ourselves with the assurance that the law will save us, whereas Jesus tells us that salvation comes from a loving relationship with him, shown in the sacrifice of our lives. To the degree that any law enables us to deepen this relationship with Jesus and to serve his people, then it is helpful and good. If a civil or religious law gets in the way, then it's moral authority over us is questionable.

In a world where the vast majority of the world's wealth and resources are held and used by a predominantly white, educated, and, at least nominally, Christian first world, then the demands of today's Gospel should be as challenging to us as they were to the rich young man. "You lack one thing; sell what you own...then come follow me." It has suited us to move away from this financially hard teaching of Jesus.

The law and money are in themselves neutral things. They can be used for good or evil. At their worst, the law and money seduce us into pride, greed, and power. At their best, they can serve the liberation of all people and enable our world to better reflect the kingdom of dignity, justice, and equality Jesus taught and lived.

Given that all things are possible for God, let's pray that we stop domesticating the gospel but allow it to lead us more deeply into a relationship with Jesus, who looks on us, loves us, and calls us to write the law of love on our hearts in such a way that our lives will be good news to all people.

TWENTY-NINTH SUNDAY IN ORDINARY TIME

ISAIAH 53:10–11
HEBREWS 4:14–16
MARK 10:35–45

One Sunday morning during Mass, the congregation was surprised to see two men enter, both covered from head to toe in black and carrying submachine guns. One of the men proclaimed, "Anyone willing to take a bullet for Christ remain where you are!" Immediately, the choir fled, altar servers fled, and most of the congregation fled. Within a few minutes, out of the two hundred strong congregation, only ten people remained where they were. The man who had spoken took off his hood, looked at the priest, and said, "OK, Father, I got rid of all the fence-sitters, how about we make a start."

In many respects this shocking story makes an important point. I would like to think that faced with such an extreme moment like this I would have the courage of my convictions, but I must admit I have my doubts.

Each Sunday by coming and celebrating the Eucharist we implicitly, and explicitly, state that we want to become like Christ. As the gospels repeatedly tell us, if we follow him in his saving love for the world, then, like him, we must confront injustice, defend the rights of the poor and the oppressed to dignity, give and forgive, heal and reconcile. By saying this, we are clearly not looking for a smooth ride through life.

In concert with the whole church, what most of us have done is domesticate the hard edges of Jesus' teachings to suit our comfortable existences. And then we get a Gospel like today's. The sons of Zebedee want the best seats in the house without knowing what the admission price is going to be. They want the glory without the gore.

Jesus teaches them, and later all the other apostles, that for his kingdom to come on earth as it is in heaven requires of us to drink a cup of suffering and be baptized in a river of sacrificial love. We can't dress this teaching up, or put a good spin on it. There is no resurrection without the cross. No gain without the pain.

For most of us this challenge means doing whatever we can politically and socially to bring the values of the gospel to bear on our different spheres of influence. But Jesus also links this challenge to the act of service. And in this regard some leaders in the church give us mixed messages and let us off the hook.

Whatever the patrimony of the past, today's Gospel reminds us that bishops, priests, and deacons should be excellent models of the humility of service. The leadership Jesus advocates is not monarchical or tyrannical, it is being the least, and being a servant. The Second Vatican Council taught that leaders in the church should be outstanding in humility, charity, and simplicity of lifestyle. Some leaders are just this. Others have domesticated the hard edge of the gospel.

Let's pray that we recover a love for the hard teachings of Jesus, even though they demand so much of us, and that we have the courage to call our leaders to do likewise. These teachings are, after all, what makes us different from the Gentiles, and sorts out who is actually sitting on the fence.

THIRTIETH SUNDAY IN ORDINARY TIME

JEREMIAH 31:7–9
HEBREWS 5:1–6
MARK 10:46–52

One Monday, three priests, a Franciscan, a Dominican, and a Jesuit, were having a hard time on the golf course. The golfers in front of the priests were the slowest and worst they had ever seen. Golf balls were going everywhere. Against golfing etiquette, the group never asked the priests to play through. By the eighteenth hole the priests were furious. At the clubhouse, just as they were going over to blast the group, they were told that the men were blind.

The Franciscan, moved with remorse at how they had spoken about the group, said to the Dominican and the Jesuit, "I am going to say Mass every day that God may grant them a miracle and restore their sight." The Dominican, equally filled with regret, told the Jesuit and the Franciscan that he was going to get the blind men an appointment with the best eye surgeon in town. The Jesuit, however, looked at the Franciscan and the Dominican and declared, "I can't see why they don't play at night!"

To have any type of disability in first-century Palestine not only meant financial hardship, but social segregation. Because Jesus' contemporaries did not understand the causes of disability and illness, they assumed it was, to some degree, a curse sent by God in punishment for sins. They also thought the curse could be caught. So the blind, the lame, the crippled, the leper, and the bleeder were desperately poor and socially outcast. Incredibly in our day, with all our supposed sophistication, some Christians have made similar statements about God cursing gay people with AIDS. Given the way Jesus acts toward those he encounters with illness, we know that God never sends disease as a curse for sin.

Bartimaeus is, however, a desperate man and in the story he acts desperately, calling out until he is heard. And in one of the strangest questions in the Gospel, Jesus asks a blind man what it is he wants. Maybe Jesus wants Bartimaeus to name his deepest desire. Maybe Jesus knows that it is, often, the unseen hurt that is the most diseased and needs healing first. Whatever his motives, Jesus' question gives the man dignity.

American Jesuit dramatist, Michael Moynahan, has written a moving play entitled *Bartimaeus*, which centers around that pivotal question, "What do you want me to do for you?" The action of the parable, as we have it in the Gospel, freezes when Jesus puts the question.

As Bartimaeus considers his options, he hears the voices of those he might have to look at if he regains his sight. The poor remind him that "once before you could see and what you saw disgusted you." The hungry ask, "Do you have the courage to experience and share my hunger?" The elderly inquire whether he wants to see those "put away because we remind you of the frailty of life." The captives challenge him to see those "unjustly bound and oppressed." And finally the self wants to know, "Are you willing to look inside yourself to see your beauty and ugliness, darkness and light?"

It's a gripping scene.

It reminds us all that sight, and the insight that can come from what we see, bestows on us the dignity of having options and the responsibility to do something about what we behold. We are in the position of making choices about what we look at. Not everything in the world needs to be seen. There is enough violence and abuse of human dignity in real life to discourage us from seeking out most fictionalized portrayals of it. We cannot, however, let ourselves off the hook in regard to seeing the world as it is and doing something about creating a better vision of humanity for everyone, everywhere.

Michael Moynahan's play finishes, like the Gospel story, with Bartimaeus requesting from Jesus the gift of sight. But in the play, in a powerful twist, as Bartimaeus follows Jesus on the path, he stops, turns, and sees the human faces behind the challenging voices. He goes back, embraces them, and together they walk the Christian path.

The same question is put by Jesus to us, "What do you want me to do for you?" And if our answer is to have sight or insight, then let us also pray for the courage to shoulder the responsibility that comes with such a gift.

THIRTY-FIRST SUNDAY IN ORDINARY TIME

 DEUTERONOMY 6:2–6
HEBREWS 7:23–28
MARK 12:28b–34

It is amazing to note how leaving out just one half of one verse of the Gospel can affect the Christian life for centuries.

All of us know by rote the command of Jesus that we must love God with all our heart, mind, soul, and strength and we must love our neighbor.

But the second half of verse 31 is not usually quoted because, sadly, it is not as embedded in our memory. It reads: "You shall love your neighbor *as yourself.*"

There are very clear historical reasons why the second part of Jesus' summary of the commandments was quietly forgotten. Given the checkered personal experiences of their own bodies, the earliest monks of the fourth and fifth centuries had very ambivalent feelings about the human body. They thought that, generally, it was to be feared as the instrument through which we would sin. They encouraged us to tame it through prayer, mortification, and penance. Their ideas about the body held sway until Thomas

Aquinas in the thirteenth century, and the Jesuit theologians of the sixteenth century argued that, while the body can lead us to sin, it is also a temple of the Holy Spirit and a vehicle of God's love and grace.

In the sixteenth century Cornelius Jansen denounced Aquinas and the Jesuits and argued that the earlier views were the correct Christian ones. No matter what the church did to denounce Jansen at the time, his thinking took deep root in Europe, the United States, and missionary countries throughout the world. Jansenism, the belief that our body and its desires are evil and that we need to harshly mortify ourselves, is, tragically, still active in Christian thought today.

Jansenism is irreconcilable with today's Gospel where Jesus tells us that the love of God, the love of neighbor, and the love of self are the cornerstones of the Christian law. And the opposite must be true too. We cannot call ourselves Christian if we hate God, hate our neighbor, or hate ourselves.

Some people argue that Western society has already gone too far in the direction of self-love. They maintain that the lengths some people go to achieve a sculptured body, the use of steroids, the growing frequency of eating disorders, the adoration of sportsmen and women, the cult of the gym and of the sex industry all point to a culture too much in love with itself. Some argue what we need is a good dose of self-control. They are half-right.

The problem with the term *love of self* is that we often hear in it an encouragement to "adore self." Nothing could be further from what Jesus is saying. We are called to love our bodies, not worship them. Jesus is not calling us to a narcissistic love, like we see in the sex industry and the gym cults. If we have no sense of our own self-worth, our own dignity, and the personal love of God for each of us, it is impossible for us to give the same to others and to claim from others the dignity we deserve. We will either treat others as our inferiors, on the one hand, or allow others to walk all over us, on the other.

Love of self is not about canonizing a loss of self-control. Jesus shows us by the way he loved his Father, us, and himself that true love always involves sacrifice. If we love ourselves in the right way, we have the self-control to forgo those things that are most destructive in our life and we have the generosity to do for others the things that will enrich their lives. Jesus knew that we can never love others if we hate ourselves.

Let's pray, then, that we will develop our mind, heart, soul, and strength to love the One that has created us in love and love those given into our care with the same love we lavish on ourselves. The gospel of Jesus Christ demands nothing less!

THIRTY-SECOND SUNDAY IN ORDINARY TIME

1 KINGS 17:10–16
HEBREWS 9:24–28
MARK 12:38–44

A few years ago there was a very funny British comedy series entitled *Keeping Up Appearances* in which Mrs. Bucket, which she insisted was pronounced "Mrs. Bouquet," pretended she was a member of the English gentry, when she was, in fact, solidly middle class. She was not happy in her own skin. Today's Gospel could be fairly subtitled *Not Keeping Up Appearances*. In it, Jesus lines up the religious leaders of his day and lets them have it with both barrels. It may come a surprise to learn that hypocrisy is the sin Jesus condemns most frequently in the gospels. He could not bear it. Nor should we.

The scribes in the gospels were the lawyers of their day. They were often referred to as rabbis as well, for they were not just jurists, but also religious teachers—a cross between a priest and an attorney. Most of them were Pharisees and, while some of them were good and holy men, it is clear that many of them were frauds. Some scribes liked to parade their piety before the community. When smaller *talliths*, or prayer shawls, would have done at the required prayer times, some scribes wore very large ones, and all the time. They seem to have hunted in packs and demanded respect, rather than earn it. Throughout the whole life of Jesus they were among his most watchful and determined opponents.

We can take it, from what Jesus condemns in their behavior, that it would have pleased him to have observed the opposite. If that's true then we are called to wear simple robes, not look for notoriety in the community, be happy with whatever seat we get at church or in a restaurant, say short prayers, and be very careful how we conduct our business affairs.

Being powerful and rich is not a problem in itself. As with all gifts it is what we do with them that show us up for who we are. The problem with religious, political, social, or even family power, and the wealth that can come from it, is that it is so seductive. The more powerful and rich we become, the more we can think everything is our due. We can take our eye off the Giver of all gifts and avoid our responsibility to share with those who are left with nothing.

In the second part of today's Gospel we meet the famous widow of the widow's mite, a story of such power that it has a currency well beyond religious circles. In the Jewish Temple, women could only come into the very first of three courtyards in the complex. Not surprisingly it was called the Court of Women. In this area there were thirteen trumpet-shaped boxes where people put in their Temple tax and other financial offerings. Mark gives us great detail about the widow's offering. He tells us that the widow gave "two small copper coins," or a quadran, adding up to one penny. A quadran was about 1/64 of a denarius, which was a worker's daily wage. In today's money that means she gave about $3.75, which is all she had to live on.

Jesus does not praise the widow because she is poor. There is no nobility in poverty. Jesus praises her for being generous and he indicates how the poor teach the rich about what really matters in life, about what it means to be humble.

Most of us were given wrong ideas about humility, that it was about feeling bad about oneself. Michael McGirr in *Finding God's Traces* puts it this way, "Humility is not putting yourself down. It is the acceptance of the truth about oneself. For St. Ignatius Loyola, that truth is that Jesus invites us into a close relationship. In this relationship, we discover absolute dependence on God. No material aspiration or achievement can hold a candle to the dignity that comes from being a child of God. The opportunities which come our way in life should be accepted or rejected on the basis of whether or not they will bring us closer to God."

Jesus challenges us today to avoid being seduced by power, riches, and greed, and to use whatever gifts we have received to build up the entire human family. In such a world scribes would learn from widows, and widows would share in the wealth of scribes.

The Christian life is as simple and complex as that. May we never stand condemned by Jesus saying one thing, and then leaving here and doing the very opposite.

THIRTY-THIRD SUNDAY IN ORDINARY TIME

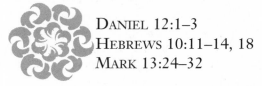 DANIEL 12:1–3
HEBREWS 10:11–14, 18
MARK 13:24–32

The film *The Pianist* won Best Picture at the Oscars of 2003. It is the true story of Wladyslaw Szpilman, who was a celebrated classical pianist in Warsaw during the 1930s. He came from an affluent and intellectual family. Like all Jews of Warsaw, in November of 1940 the Szpilmans are herded into the Jewish ghetto. Unlike most of the others Wladyslaw comes out each day to work as a cocktail pianist in a Warsaw café. Polish Jews and Christians remember and admire his playing. So much so that in the summer of 1942, while the rest of his family are deported to Treblinka, Wladyslaw is rescued from the train by a Jewish collaborator. The Polish resistance hides him in Warsaw. When his whereabouts are discovered, Wladyslaw goes on the run and survives in a city that barely survives the war.

Toward the end of the film there is a magnificent scene where the now-skeletal Wladyslaw is caught by a Nazi army officer hiding in one of the few Warsaw houses left standing. He asks Szpilman what he did for a living, and then invites him to sit and play the piano in the drawing room of the house. In the midst of the almost total destruction of the world around them, Wladyslaw enables beauty to have the last word over the horror of war. It changes both men. It's the first time the pianist has played in years, and his concerto touches something human in the German soldier that leads him to protect Wladyslaw.

In today's Gospel we get a very vivid picture of how the end of the world might break in upon us. It's clear that Mark thought it was going to happen in the lifetime of some of his hearers. It didn't, and many generations later we're still waiting.

This is not to say that the reign of God doesn't regularly break in upon us. Wladyslaw's playing shows how music can do it. We believe that every day more good is done in the world than evil; else this world would destroy itself. And we hold that the source of all love is Christ. So, every time we are kind rather than cruel, patient rather than intolerant, generous rather than selfish, beautiful rather than ugly, the reign of God bursts into our lives.

One translation of verse 27 in today's Gospel reads, "Then he will send out the angels and gather together his elect from the four winds, from the ends of the earth to the ends of heaven." The whole idea of "the elect" has exercised the imagination of generations of Christians ever since this verse was written. The Protestant Reformation was, in part, based on who Christ elects to be his own, how we get elected, and how we stay that way.

John Calvin was especially interested in this question and he rightly linked the goodness of our lives with those elected by Christ. But Calvin and many Catholic scholars have interpreted the meaning of this text too narrowly.

Remembering that Mark thinks the end of the world is soon, that his community is being persecuted for their Christian faith, and that Christianity has not spread all that far by the time he writes this Gospel around AD 65, it's somewhat surprising to read that the elect might be made up of people who come from the ends of the earth. We can safely assume that at this time not many people, beyond the Mediterranean basin, had heard about Christ. Even if this more generous and inclusive reading is not what Mark means when he refers to this world, it would be mean-spirited of us to imagine that all he means in reference to the elect in heaven are only those professing Christians who had died in his lifetime.

The more consoling reading of who is in the elect is to understand it as including anyone, anywhere, whose life enables faith, hope, love, beauty, justice, and peace to break in upon the world.

And so what's makes being a Christian so special? We know who's doing the electing and why, and we have each other as we struggle to live out Christ's reign every day—until he comes again in glory.

FEAST OF CHRIST THE KING

 Daniel 7:13–14
Revelation 1:5–8
John 18:33b–37

Pope Pius XI only established the feast of Christ the King in the Holy Year of 1925. Although rooted in an ancient devotion, this particular feast appears to have its roots in the 1880s when many European bishops were worried about what they saw as the rise of secularization. I'm pleased they're not around today! These bishops were concerned at how governments were increasingly asserting more power over and against the church. Especially in France and Italy, bishops started to venerate Jesus as the Universal King. This devotion took off. By 1922, at the Eucharistic Congress in Rome, sixty-nine cardinals petitioned the pope to establish this feast. Within three years the Vatican had been inundated with requests, and so the solemnity was established.

It's clear from today's Gospel, and the New Testament in general, that while Jesus frequently spoke of his kingdom, is hailed like a king on Palm Sunday, and is facetiously given the title of king by Pilate, his kingship is vastly different from that of Caesar, Herod and even David and the other kings of Israel.

The earliest Christians seem to have understood this very well. We find very little writing or artistic representation of Jesus as a king before AD 324. In that year Emperor Constantine becomes a catechumen and Christianity becomes the religion of the Roman Empire. After this time Jesus starts to appear wearing a crown and holding an orb. Mary is styled as the Queen of Heaven and begins to be pictured as such. This is all understandable as the previously persecuted Christian sect now emerges to become the most powerful unifying force in the Roman Empire. It was a sweet victory, but it meant that whatever was said of the Roman emperor, even more must be true of Christ the Universal King and Lord.

As centuries passed and the Roman Empire passed away, the church maintained many of its now long-standing royal prerogatives and language. Just as an example, to this day the pope and some bishops live in places called palaces. They wear jewels and rings and have feudal coats of arms. Worse still by far, however, is the mentality and behavior of a very few bishops, who seem to think that the church is above the scrutiny of the faithful and the law of the land.

The problem with all these historical accretions is that they directly contradict the way in which Jesus spoke about himself as a king. Almost all references to Jesus' kingship occur within the passion narratives. Today's extract from John's Gospel is among the most famous of them all. "You say that I am a king. For this I was born, and for this I came into the world, to testify to the truth. Everyone who belongs to the truth listens to my voice."

There are not too many kings or queens today who would love their people so much that they would be prepared to die for them. We know from history that when the going gets tough many monarchs get going. But what we get in Jesus as king is one who did not compromise his humanity, who would not yield from his preaching and does not abandon us in our desolation. Jesus' kingship is revealed in his utter fidelity to us—even to the end.

So let's not be seduced by the power, pride, riches, and greed that worldly rulers so crave. Let's keep our own eyes on Christ our King who loved people more than things, who spoke the truth with love, and who died that we might live. And let's not shrink from challenging the entire church to so the same.

Cycle C

FIRST SUNDAY OF ADVENT

Jeremiah 33:14–16
1 Thessalonians 3:12—4:2
Luke 21:25–28, 34–36

Do you remember that during Advent in 1999, when some people thought they were about to usher in a new millennium, a few Christians declared that the end of the world was nigh and that Christ would return on his two-thousandth birthday?

They seem to subscribe to the old adage that "one should never let the facts get in the way of a good story!"

Christianity took over the Roman calendar in what we now call the fourth century of the Christian era. At Rome in 526, a scholarly monk named Dionysius Exiguus compiled a list of the dates of Jesus' birth, death, and resurrection. He assigned dates in the new Christian calendar for each of these events. Given the tools at his disposal, he did an extraordinary job. We know, however, from other historical sources and from the New Testament, where it mentions who the various Jewish and Roman rulers were in Palestine, that Dionysius was four years off with his dating. The church became aware of this mistake in 1582, but to correct it the world would have lost four years! So we have all lived with it ever since.

We can, however, safely assume that Jesus knows the year in which he was born and that, even if we got the year wrong, he would have known he was meant to return in 1996!

The facts are that in every generation we have had people tell us that the sun, moon, stars, wars, famine, tidal waves, and earthquakes, mentioned in today's Gospel, all demonstrate that Jesus is about to return. Clearly, we are still waiting. If only the Christians who give out these dire predictions, every so often, would take as seriously Jesus' words, "You will know not the time, nor the place when the Son of Man will return in glory."

Luke's community thought that Jesus would return quickly and spectacularly. They were surprised that the first generation of Christian believers was dying without seeing it all happen. Given the terrible suffering they were enduring for Jesus, the early Christians no doubt hoped that the end of the world would be soon and would demonstrate to everyone that they were not foolish to cling to Christ in the face of all opposition and persecution. The early Christians knew that there was no point professing faith in Jesus Christ unless our daily behavior reflects his kingdom. It has been a telling point ever since. If every Christian lived out the gospel in his or her daily life, the world would be transformed and Christ would come in spectacular fashion.

I haven't got a clue when the world will cease to exist, but on this, the first day of the church's year, I know that the Lord returns to us every time we love, forgive, share, are compassionate, are generous and sacrificial toward one another. It may not be as grand as dancing suns and tidal waves, but the heroic love of a parent for a child, a spouse for their sick partner, and the first world sharing with the third world are spectacular enough for me to believe that Jesus' kingdom comes on every day, in every hour, at every moment.

May this first Eucharist of the church's year be a taste for us of the kingdom of God that is both present among us and still to come. And may the Advent season sustain us in our waiting and give us courage in our living.

SECOND SUNDAY OF ADVENT

BARUCH 5:1–9
PHILIPPIANS 1:4–6, 8–11
LUKE 3:1–6

The English left their colonies many fine cultural legacies, but one of the best is the ability to wait in line. If ever you have been overseas you know that we do it better than others. In Paris years ago, I remember standing in a very long line for a taxi. I had never seen jostling, shoving, and abuse like it in my life. And when someone pushed in at the top of the line, all hell broke loose—mainly from the elderly women holding their poodles! The locals told me this was normal behavior.

Here, however, until recently, we have been pretty good at standing in line and waiting to be served. I do notice a change in this tradition, however, at the bank, where higher fees mean people rightly expect that customer service will be faster and more efficient.

The success of waiting on line depends on patience, knowing that everything is going as efficiently as possible, and being rewarded at the end for the time and effort we have expended.

In today's Gospel, John the Baptist encourages his followers to be patient, as the wait for the Messiah will soon be over. The Israelites longed to see the day when the Messiah would come. Each generation hoped and prayed that they would be the one to witness the appearance of God's anointed. The Jewish people still hope and pray for this event in every generation.

But Jesus did not come as many expected. Some thought he would arrive in a dramatic event and the end of the world would occur. Others expected a regal entrance or a political overthrow of the Romans. Luke's Gospel repeatedly points out that the very people who longed for the day to see the Messiah missed out because they were looking for the wrong signs.

John the Baptist is the first to see Jesus for who he really is for the world. He recognizes that Jesus' sacrificial love can fill our valleys, lay mountains low, make crooked paths straight and rough ways smooth.

Advent is not a season where we have to pretend that we do not know Jesus is coming and then put on mock surprise at Christmas. Advent is the season when we celebrate a "patient yes." Every year all of us in the church stand in line and remind ourselves of how blessed we are to have seen our salvation in Jesus. We remember the faith of those who longed to see what we see and to know what we know. And we cultivate our patience for life's valleys, mountains, and crooked paths where sometimes we can feel Jesus' absence more than his presence, where only when we look back can we see he was with us all the way.

So, as we all wait together in line this Advent let's say yes to all that salvation holds for us: yes to God's personal love; yes to Jesus' kingdom of justice and peace; yes to every opportunity to serve the gospel; and yes to knowing that our God is a companion to us at every step of our journey, even in the most unexpected ways.

Scottish poet John Bell expresses it this way:

Light looked down and saw the darkness.
"I will go there," said light.
Peace looked down and saw war.
"I will go there," said peace.
Love looked down and saw hatred.
"I will go there," said love.

So he,
the Lord of Light,
the Prince of Peace,
the King of Love,
came down and crept in beside us.

THIRD SUNDAY OF ADVENT

ZEPHANIAH 3:14–18a
PHILIPPIANS 4:4–7
LUKE 3:10–18

The military is a great institution, but it is not famous for encouraging individuality. The entire process of basic training strips away people's individuality so that they can live and work in the group. Military leaders need to be sure that under pressure their men and women will think and act as one. It saves lives. This is one of the reasons they wear uniforms, have very clear lines of authority, and enforce strict protocols in regard to addressing one another, saluting, and the chain of command. Soldiers are meant to think for themselves, and respond to some situations quickly, but they are also trained to take and follow orders.

In our recent history we delighted in talking about the church triumphant being in heaven and the church militant being on earth. As children making our confirmation, we felt very important as we became "soldiers for Christ." We went as far as to talk about some orders in the church as the "militia of the Lord." In this military model, uniformity was the key. Many Catholics loved the idea that everywhere in the world the church was the same, the liturgy was in Latin, and local cultures did not have much of an impact on our life as a church. Obedience was more highly valued than creativity.

This model held some important lessons for human organization and clarity. The only problem is that, taken to an extreme, it seems to contradict what lies at the heart of today's Gospel.

John the Baptist never strikes me as a flexible man. He seems to be an all-or-nothing-kinda-guy. Yet here he is instructing the members of the crowd that a life of virtue and goodness is as specific as the personalities in front of him. Jesus obviously adopted this as his model too, and Luke, the only one to record Jesus saying this, thought it enshrined a vital truth, which we all needed to hear and live.

This approach to the Christian life is one that values creativity as highly as it does obedience. It suggests that there are very specific things that only any individual can do to live out the kingdom of God. It means thinking as creatively and concretely as possible about how the scriptures and the tradition of the church are meant to be applied to our daily living. This is not about all of us keeping the same laws and rules, and all of us looking and acting the same, because it takes seriously the vastly different circumstances and spheres within which all of us operate. What could be demanded of one person could not be expected of the next.

The first and second readings offer us some creative ideas about some virtues that should have deep roots in our daily living: joy, gentleness, freedom from anxiety, and peace. A word about each of them.

Sadly, we Catholics are not well known for our joy. We can be seen to be a rather serious lot who have not yet fully experienced or understood the joy that Christian faith is meant to bring. Today, we are not being called to share in that supercilious happiness that never seems all that in touch with reality, but the type of joy that always looks for the happy things in our life, our church, and our world. If we cannot think of any, then maybe we have become too serious for our own good.

Have you noticed how aggressive people are these days? In both word, action, and speech, we tend to be more forceful than I think we need to be. It's good, then, to have St. Paul encourage us: "Let your gentleness be known to everyone." Now there is a challenge. Even though we should assert our rights to receive that which is duly ours, could it be said of me that I am both an assertive and gentle person?

Anxiety is presently a pandemic in our modern society. If we sincerely want to lessen it, we need to carefully work out the pattern of behaviors and people that leaves us this way. And we need to make some changes, or at least change our thinking in regard to those people and situations. Just talking about freedom from anxiety rarely makes us feel less anxious.

And maybe if we are people who look for things to rejoice over, are more gentle with others and ourselves, and are less anxious, we will share in a greater sense of personal peace that most of us crave.

One of the problems associated with the church militant is the impression we have to uniformly soldier on throughout life. As we prepare for Christmas it would seem that the real campaign we are called to mount is to be joyful, confident, gentle, and peaceful.

For these, this Advent—John the Baptist, pray for us.

FOURTH SUNDAY OF ADVENT

MICAH 5:1–4a
HEBREWS 10:5–10
LUKE 1:39–45

The visitation is one of the most moving scenes in the Gospel. On a human level here are two cousins, unexpectedly pregnant in the most extraordinary circumstances, meeting and offering each other greetings and support. We can see the scene and feel the bond.

In the Gospel of Luke this moment is pivotal. These women meet in the mountains where God has always been manifest to the Israelites. Elizabeth is the Old Covenant made to Israel and she carries John who will be the herald of the Messiah. Mary, literally, embodies the new, and final, covenant in Jesus.

Elizabeth recognizes what is happening here and she embraces all that God is doing for the world. She has tasted the promise of God and now sees its fulfillment.

On a more mundane level, however, a meeting like this would have occasioned much comment and speculation from those outside the inner circle. We only have to imagine it happening today in any small rural town for us to appreciate the human scale of the unfolding drama.

The Iona Community has explored the unwritten history in their story of Mrs. Matthew, Mark, and Luke, *The Village Gossips*.

Narrator: In any small village, news travels quickly. Therefore it is only to be expected that the strange changes in the lives of Mary and Elisabeth might have been food for other people's thought.

Mrs. Matthew: Well, ladies, you know how I'm not one for gossip, but wait until you hear this. You know that old woman Elisabeth, with the man who has not spoken for nine months.

Mrs. Mark: Yes, what about them?

Mrs. Matthew: They say she's had a little boy.

Mrs. Luke: At her age? She's 88 if she's a day!

Mrs. Matthew: Well, that's what I heard and it was on very good authority!

Mrs. Luke: Are you sure you've got the right woman? You're not mixing her up with her cousin?

Mrs. Mark: Who? Mary?

Mrs. Luke: That's her! Now, I'm not one to talk about anybody but wait until I tell you this. She's pregnant!

Mrs. Mark: Never! How do you know?

Mrs. Luke: You can tell. You can just tell.

Mrs. Matthew: Oh yes, you can tell all right. I heard her in the store last week asking for a dress eight sizes too big for her.

Mrs. Luke: There you are. Draw your own conclusions. Now, I know that this will not go any further, but I hear tell that she and a certain young man are planning to leave the district.

Mrs. Matthew: Who is the young man?

Mrs. Luke: The joiner's boy, Joseph.

Mrs. Mark: Never!

Mrs. Luke: Well, that's what they say and I'm not one for gossip.

Mrs. Mark: So, have you heard what they're saying about the so-called Census?

Mrs. Matthew: No. Tell us.

Mrs. Mark: Well, I happened to hear that the reason the Romans want our names, is not to send us birthday cards.

Mrs. Luke: Well, why are they having a Census?

Mrs. Mark: To register us for a "poll tax."

Mrs. Matthew: I heard it was a "community charge."

Mrs. Mark: "A rose by any other name."

Mrs. Luke: They wouldn't do that, would they?

Mrs. Mark: Well I'm just warning you. Mind, I'm not one for gossip.

Mrs. Luke: Nor me.

Mrs. Matthew: Nor me.

The story of the visitation keeps the rumor going that just when we think we can figure God out, predict how God will enter our lives and our world, then God does something none of us can imagine. And the best thing about this rumor is—it's true.

As we wait for Christmas to come again into our lives, let's make room for Jesus Christ, who always gives the gossips plenty to talk about.

CHRISTMAS

Midnight:
ISAIAH 9:1–6
TIMOTHY 2:11–14
LUKE 2:1–14

Last week I was invited to a nativity play at a Catholic primary school. All the parents of third-graders were there. The sister who organized the play told me that she had trouble with the boy who was playing the innkeeper because he had his heart set on playing St. Joseph. Rehearsals had not gone well, but she was sure everything would be fine in the performance.

As Mary and Joseph knocked at the inn, the innkeeper gruffly yelled out, "Who's there?" "Joseph, and my wife Mary," came the reply. The innkeeper did not budge, so Joseph knocked again. The innkeeper barked, "Who's there?" "Joseph, and my wife Mary," came the reply. The little innkeeper put his head around the door and blurted out, "Mary and the baby can come in, but Joseph, you go to hell."

With that, Joseph burst into tears, the shepherds bashed up the innkeeper and the three wise men started attacking the children who were inside the camel costume. Sister turned to me and said, "This wasn't the way it was supposed to go," and it took ten minutes to restore peace.

I thought it was great. And the thing I liked most about it was that it was human and real. For long enough we have cleaned up Christmas too much. The original Christmas must have been a terribly messy affair. After traveling for days in the last month of her pregnancy, the nineteen-year-old Joseph has to help his fifteen-year-old wife have a child in a cave where the smell of animals must have been shocking. This is far from the sanitized image we have on our cards or that we sing in our carols.

The Gospel tells us that God is Emmanuel. God meets us as we are and leads us to find the way to a life that has meaning and purpose, and prepares us for eternal life. No matter if we are sadly alone, or with family, if this is a happy time of year, or a stressful one, if there are fights at Christmas lunch or you have a great reunion of relatives and friends, as a result of the first Christmas, God meets us in our human reality.

Today also challenges the excessive money we spend and the excessive food and drink we consume to celebrate this feast. Nothing could be more inappropriate in marking the moment when Jesus crept in beside us.

The real and long-lasting way we celebrate Christmas every-day is recognizing that, as followers of the babe of Bethlehem, we are sent to bring God's life to bear in our world, be it at home, at work, with friends, in ordinary places, or even in the midst of utter chaos.

Christmas is the feast day when we are given the grace to recognize our own dignity, to search for an even deeper faith and respond to all we meet with compassion because that is precisely what God did for us in Jesus.

Happy Christmas.

HOLY FAMILY

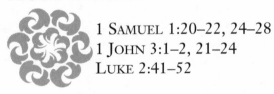

1 SAMUEL 1:20–22, 24–28
1 JOHN 3:1–2, 21–24
LUKE 2:41–52

Christian art has not served us very well in terms of picturing the Holy Family. From medieval times, Joseph is portrayed as being as least eighty, Mary is very young with perfect white skin, and, usually, Jesus has golden curls and a knowing smile.

Now I don't know about your family, but among my clan no one is a canonized saint, immaculately conceived, or the Son of God. Let's face it, the Holy Family is a tough act to follow.

We know only the barest facts about the Holy Family.

Joseph was eighteen or nineteen when his fiancée, Mary, who was fourteen or fifteen, potentially caused great scandal in the neighborhood by conceiving a child, by the power of God, before the wedding. They were a poor, devoutly Jewish family from Galilee. They were as olive-skinned as any Lebanese is today and they lived in a country harshly administered by the occupying Roman army.

The scriptures tell us they knew what it was like to be refugees, to lose their child for three days, and that Mary so misunderstood what Jesus was about that once she went to bring him home; later she watched him tortured and executed by the Romans.

By these traditions the Holy Family has much to say to those in our world who are teenage mothers, are poor, hardworking, religious people, are refugees, or are so-called colored people. They give consolation to parents who can't figure out their children, to children who feel their parents are not on their wavelength, and to anyone of you who has ever lost a child in a marketplace or been through the heartbreak of losing a child in death.

You see, the more we put halos on the Holy Family, sadly, the less we seem to be able to connect their family experience with our own.

Most families are about being generous, loving, stable, and faithful. They stand for security, roots, and identity. Our world needs stable, strong families more than ever before.

Families, however, also fight, can be envious, they break up, are under pressure from all sorts of social lobbies, and, tragically, the family home is the most common place for physical and sexual abuse in our society.

For all our Western wealth and technology, I think it's very hard to have a happy and balanced family life today.

So what's the secret?

Family studies tell us that forgiveness is the key. In our complex world, no one can pretend that forgiveness is easy or that it is a magic wand we wave over deep hurts and harsh words. True forgiveness does not deny reality, it deals with it. But forgiveness is necessary if we are going to follow Jesus. It is also necessary if we want to enjoy a happier family life. Revenge and spite, so endemic in society, are the antithesis of what Jesus taught and lived out.

May this feast of the Holy Family, then, give our families the "serenity to accept the things we cannot change, courage to change the things we can, and wisdom to know the difference."

EPIPHANY OF THE LORD

 Isaiah 60:1–6
Ephesians 3:2–3a, 5–6
Matthew 2:1–12

A woman friend of mine told me that, if there had been three wise women instead of three wise men, they would have known the directions, arrived on time, helped deliver the baby, cleaned the stable, made a casserole, and brought disposable diapers as gifts!

Whatever the gender of the wise, dreaming stargazers in Matthew's Gospel, they point to how radical is the kingdom of Jesus. This story takes on an even greater power when we remember that Matthew is writing for a predominantly Jewish community. Israel considered themselves the chosen people and they hoped and longed to see the Messiah. Yet here are three Gentiles, to whom the promise of the Messiah had not been made, who are among the first to see and believe in Jesus.

One thing Matthew is saying in these shadowy figures is that Jesus has come for all people everywhere. There is no such thing as an outsider in the community of faith in Jesus.

And how we need to hear this Gospel again and again. All too often we set up barriers and boundaries that block the hospitality and diversity that are the distinctive features of Christ's followers.

Matthew's story is also a wonderful interplay between wonder and fear. We are told only five things about the wise men from the East: They follow the rising star, they ask directions in a foreign land, they are overwhelmed with joy at finding the child at Bethlehem, they are warned in their dreams about Herod, and they go home by another road.

Herod, on the other hand, is frightened at the prospect of a pretender to his throne. He whips up similar anxiety all around him in Jerusalem, he uses the wise men to find the child, his deceit is uncovered, and he is left without knowledge and more spiraling fear.

In twelve verses Matthew paints a portrait of wisdom and fear. If we are wise followers of the babe of Bethlehem we need to be shrewd in dealing with power, keep our eyes on the journey that most brings joy and fulfillment to our lives, believe in dreams, and pray that we are never so sure of how God works in our world that we miss seeing the very thing we long to behold.

Matthew also tells us, however, that the enemy of the Christian life is fear. It entraps us and infects those around us. And we are often most fearful when we risk losing power, so we lie, are deceitful, and cheat to maintain our position at all costs. As with Herod, it all ends in death.

So this story is far more than a travelogue of some exotic Persian kings. It is the story of the choices that lie before all Christians everywhere. This Sunday the choice is ours again: Do we want wonder or fear?

Jesuit poet, Michael Moynahan, puts it this way:

O God,
who's hidden deep within
the timeless yearnings
of our hearts,
you trigger something
in us all
that makes us restless,
anxious for discovery
of what will satisfy
new felt wanderlust.

Like the wise before
who searched the sky
and recklessly pursued a dream,
their hope was more than make-believe,
we, too, leave all we know
and travel into unknown lands
driven madly day and night

by what our hapless startling hope
can only guess at.

Our journey's filled
with constant doubt
and ever-present fear.
How will we know
when we have found
travel's impulse,
this craving we call
our heart's desire?

In our search
we leave no stone unturned.
We struggle frantically
to find our happiness
perhaps in this town.

Or when we meet
with failure here
our sight adjusts instinctively
to over the horizon there
where we will next settle
for a resting-place.

Then one day,
as every pilgrimage
must run its course,
when hope is drained
and body broke,
we'll find ourselves in Bethlehem
weary, wounded, travelled out.
And so we'll stumble,
as if by accident,
into epiphany.

How could three travelers
with dust-filled eyes
see such good
in one so young?
Had we come all that way for this?

And once again we bruise our heads
bumping into mystery.
The child found there
will touch and free
the child in us.

And we will feel
somewhat renewed
for having found in him
what lies deepest
in every pilgrim's heart.

O God, who's found in journey's end,
bless all our goings,
fill all our comings,
help us all be freed
and found by you.

BAPTISM OF THE LORD

 Isaiah 40:1–5, 9–11
Timothy 2:11–14; 3:4–7
Luke 3:15–16, 21–22

A funny thing has grown up in the recent life of the church. Older priests tend to give couples who are living together a hard time when they come seeking to be married in the church. It's a mistake, because here is a couple trying to regularize what the church thinks to be an irregular situation. When some of these couples hit a frosty reception in their first meeting with these priests, they choose the park instead. Young priests, on the other hand, in trying to uphold the seriousness of the baptismal commitment, tend to give parents a hard time when they arrive for baptismal preparation. These priests can put the initiation bar so high that the parents feel they can't go through with it.

My attitude, on the other hand, is that I marry anything that moves, I baptize anything that moves, and I bury anything that doesn't! I am not underestimating the seriousness of these moments, but am seeking to make the sacramental occasion as good an experience of the church as I can, in the hope that they will want to return and join us more permanently.

One of the things I like best about baptism is that it is our most ecumenical sacrament. If a Lutheran wants to be a Catholic, or a Catholic moves into the Greek Orthodox community, he or she is not rebaptized. Unfortunately, some Christian denominations, who take selected parts of the scriptures literally, rebaptize other Christians because they worry about the volume of water that was used on the first occasion.

Generally, then, this sacrament unites almost all the world's Christians in Christ Jesus. And this is just as it should be, because the baptism of the Lord tells us that all Christ's followers should be united in celebrating baptism that no one can take away the Christian dignity bestowed upon them by these saving waters.

The thing I like best about the Catholic rite of baptism is how it underlines the dignity of the adult or child being initiated into the life of Christ. Let's think about infant baptism for a moment.

Using actions and words that extend back to the birth of our faith, and in some instances beyond it, we begin by asking the parents what name they have chosen for their child. I always look up the meaning of these names. It is often a revelation as to the child's personality.

Then the parents and sponsors declare they understand what they are doing and are prepared to be Christian role models for this child. In the early church there was not much preparation for the sacrament of baptism. In those days anyone who professed the faith and was prepared to risk his or her life because of it was thought to be ready. A lengthy period of instruction in "the way" of the Christian life came immediately after baptism. Then, as a way to confirm the declarations just made, the child is claimed for Christ by the sign of his cross.

I do all these rituals at the back door of the church, since this is the first formal time we have received the child into the place where the church gathers. It also allows us to process to the font, especially if its at the front of the church, which in turn prefigures all the processions the child may make in his or her life, for confirmation, eucharist, penance, marriage, holy orders, and anointing of the sick. It also reminds us of that day when this new Christian will recess out of the church for the final time at his or her funeral.

After the Liturgy of the Word, we remember that this child has patron saints who are praying with all of us right now in heaven, and we call on them by name. We ask that all that is evil be kept far from this child and, as we anoint the breast, we ask that the child's heart be united in love for God, self, and neighbor. We bless the font, profess our common faith, and then immerse the child into the life-giving and saving bath of baptism.

These days we ask the parents not to bring the child already dressed in their baptismal robe so that after baptism, in line with the more ancient custom, they can be vested in it, as a physical reminder that they have just put on the life of Christ.

Then we anoint them with the church's holiest oil and welcome them into the royal family of Christ, his school of prophets, and the priesthood of all believers. We then present their parents and sponsors with the light of Christ, and pray that the child's ears will soon hear the word of God and that their mouth will proclaim it.

And the reason we have such an elaborate ritual around this child is because we know that because of the baptism of the Lord all people who want to be Christians have to come to see their true identity is in God, that they are beloved by him, and are very pleasing in God's sight.

Let's pray that we keep claiming our Christian dignity by how we choose to spend our lives.

SECOND SUNDAY IN ORDINARY TIME

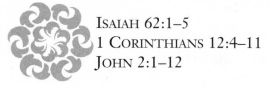 ISAIAH 62:1–5
1 CORINTHIANS 12:4–11
JOHN 2:1–12

Church architecture often tells in stone the story of theology. By the ninth century, as Christian churches in Europe became longer and higher, a shift was occurring in theology as well. Coinciding with the engineering abilities of the builders, theologians reinstated a more severe and distant theology about God. God was "immortal, invisible, God only wise, in light inaccessible, hid from our eyes." Jesus had ascended his regal home in the tabernacle, which over the centuries got farther and farther away from where the people stood or sat.

One of the extraordinary things that occurs in the layout of churches of this time is that as the tabernacle goes back, the Marian altar comes forward, often halfway down the church where people could have easy access to it.

Today's Gospel was used as the justification for this theological and architectural movement. Mary is seen to intercede on behalf of the bride and groom and ask Jesus to do what he can. This is the first sign in the Gospel of John and Jesus is reluctant to perform it, but because his mother asks, he does it.

The changing of the water into wine is not just a sign that Mary and Jesus like a good party! It is a sign of the kingdom of God where joy and life are in abundance, where shame ends and all tears are wiped away. It is no accident that in John's Gospel the mother of Jesus is present at this first sign and remains faithful until the end, right up to the culmination of all the signs—his being lifted up on the cross. Mary not only asks for a sign, she understands that it will cost something for Jesus to give it and for her to witness it.

So for us, the wedding feast at Cana is a taste of the fullness of life we celebrate every Sunday. The Eucharist is always and everywhere a first course in the eternal banquet of heaven. But it is also an invitation to see beyond the signs, to the faithful relationships that require sacrificial love and years of fidelity.

All parents who sacrifice so much for their children, all spouses who remain faithful and good to their wife or husband, all friends who attend to their companions with devotion and care share in the kingdom of God and are the signs of Christ's presence in our world. Every time we are kind, Cana occurs again.

Sometimes these actions can be very lonely and the cost can be high. Today's Gospel, and the traditions of the church that flow from it, tell us we are not alone, especially when the going gets tough.

What I like best about our belief in intercessory prayer, in the healthiest devotions in honor of the mother of Jesus and in our belief in the martyrs and the saints, is that they take seriously the companionship of God's family that transcends time and space.

Through our common Christian faith we are connected to millions of believers who have battled with similar, and sometimes greater, struggles than we endure and yet remained faithful to the end. Led by Mary, who never wants us to feel ashamed or embarrassed, they are our cheering squad in the stands of heaven willing us on in the race of life, giving us a few pointers on the best preparation, the pitfalls on the way, and how to maximize our performance as we strive to do our best and be our best.

Welcome to Cana where one course is richer than the last and the wine only gets better with age.

THIRD SUNDAY IN ORDINARY TIME

NEHEMIAH 8:2–4A, 5–6, 8–10
1 CORINTHIANS 12:12–30
LUKE 1:1–4; 4:14–21

Nine-year-old Joey was asked by his mother what he had learned in his religion class.

"Well, Mom, our teacher told us how God sent Moses behind enemy lines on a rescue mission to lead the Israelites out of Egypt. When he got to the Red Sea, he had his engineers build a pontoon bridge and all the people walked across safely. Then he used his walkie-talkie to radio headquarters for reinforcements. They sent bombers to blow up the bridge and all the Israelites were saved."

"Now, Joey, is that really what your teacher taught you?" his mother asked.

"Well, no, Mom. But if I told it the way the teacher did, you'd never believe it!"

Given the ways the scriptures have divided Christians over the centuries and because previous generations wanted to protect the truth of the Bible, we were often taught that the Holy Spirit dictated the text. In this schema, the real skill of Matthew, Mark, Luke, and John seems to have been their shorthand!

Today we begin reading through Luke's Gospel. And in the opening verses of this extraordinary document, Luke puts paid to the idea that he is simply listening to the whisperings of the Holy Spirit in his ear. What we now call the Gospel of Luke was the first installment of a two-part letter written to his friend and disciple, Theophilus. Epic letters like this one and the Acts of the Apostles, which is its sequel, where the writer praises the deeds of a great man and lists his achievements, were very common in the Hellenized world of ancient Rome. Luke knew how to write it and, more importantly, Theophilus knew how to read it.

It is not a documentary on the life of Jesus, recording a series of facts. If it were, then parts of it and its tone cannot be reconciled with the other gospels. They disagree with each other about many important details. As Catholics we believe the Holy Spirit guided the writing and selection of the scriptural record so that it contains no errors regarding our salvation. A life lived in harmony with the scriptures is its own testament to our belief that the Bible is not a book of facts, it is a book of truth.

Luke knows that Theophilus has already been instructed in the way of salvation in Christ and he makes it clear that the truth of this way is what he is attending to. In this Gospel he paints a vivid and intimate portrait of who Jesus is and why he has the message of salvation for everyone.

These days we often hear people asking others to be "up front" and to "lay your cards on the table." Long before it was trendy, Luke does precisely this in the second part of today's Gospel. At the very beginning of Jesus' public ministry, Luke summarizes the story he is about to tell Theophilus and his community in what is called "the program."

In the tradition of the greatest of the prophets, we are told Jesus has come for those of us who are poor, captive, blind, and oppressed. But, unlike the former prophets, Jesus is not only a companion in our distress or an advocate on our behalf, he has also come to establish the definitive reign of God in our lives. In Jesus, all that Israel longed to see is fulfilled.

And so to us. As the spiritual children of Jesus, Luke, Theophilus, and his community, we are inheritors of a tradition that is up-front in what we are called to do. Our program is explicit. We are called to be companions to the poor, to set prisoners free, to fight oppression, to enable others to confront what they would prefer to ignore, and to boldly proclaim that there is no one beyond God's favor.

As tough as these demands are, they are not optional extras. They define who we are as Christians and how we are sent to change the world.

May the Eucharist give us courage for the task at hand.

FOURTH SUNDAY IN ORDINARY TIME

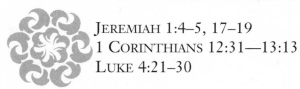

JEREMIAH 1:4–5, 17–19
1 CORINTHIANS 12:31—13:13
LUKE 4:21–30

At the end of today's Gospel we hear how Jesus' hometown crowd was so outraged by his words that they wanted to throw him off a cliff. How things have changed! These days many young adults seek the thrill of bungee jumping where they tie a rope around their ankles and willingly hurl themselves from any available precipice!

It seems that some young people enjoy the challenge of facing down their fears, trusting the generally good track record of those who have done it before them, and publicly showing their courage, even to the brink of death. Those of us not courageous or stupid enough to attempt a bungee jump have to concede that to do it, for whatever reason, is heroic stuff.

Heroic stuff is at the heart of today's readings. Even though the crowd hated what they heard, Jesus preached boldly to his own people. Jeremiah was similarly courageous in his teaching, in the face of enormous persecution from his people. And Paul knows the only reason one can endure hardships and rejection and even be seen as stupid in the eyes of the world is for the sake of love.

The word *love* has to be one of the most misused words in our language. We say we love our house, holiday, car, and even ice cream. But using *love* in this way we scarcely come close to what Christian love is all about.

St. Paul teaches today that love is not primarily about warm, fuzzy feelings and swooning violins. Paul knew that Christian love is an intensely practical business. There is no point in any of us saying we love anyone unless our actions follow the profession we make. Indeed as St. John was to sharply say in his letter in the New Testament, "If you say you love God and hate your neighbor, you are a liar." We can spout the right words about loving God and each other all we like, but if we do not show it in how we live, then we are noisy gongs and clanging cymbals.

There is no way around it, Christian love always and everywhere involves sacrifice.

So, how can we love like this? Why should we love like this?

We can love sacrificially because other people have loved us in the same way. When anyone has been gentle, kind, and patient with us, when they did not insist on their own way, were not irritable, resentful, or enjoy our downfall, we were on the receiving end of love. They showed us how to do it. That's love.

We can take this enormous gamble to love like this only when others have loved us enough to tell us the truth about ourselves and we in turn have spoken the truth to them. That's love.

And we can plunge into the unknown, even to the brink of death, because along with others we have held on to hope in the face of difficult times. That's sacrificial love and that is what Christian love is all about.

The good news today is that we also have legions of companions who have been down this road before us. From Jeremiah to Jesus to Paul to the martyrs and saints and to our own families, we know that it is possible to face down our fears, trust the track record of those who have done it before us, publicly show our courage, even to the brink of death and leap into the future with only three ropes tied to our ankles. On one is written "faith." On the second is written "hope" and on the third and strongest rope is written "love."

Let's pray, then, for the grace to be stupid in the eyes of the world and heroic in the courage it takes to sacrificially love others, and be loved by them, even to the point of death.

FIFTH SUNDAY IN ORDINARY TIME

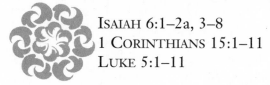 Isaiah 6:1–2a, 3–8
1 Corinthians 15:1–11
Luke 5:1–11

Think about this for a minute!

It is time to elect a world leader, and yours is the deciding vote. Here are the facts about the three leading candidates:

Candidate A associates with crooked politicians, consults with astrologers, has had two mistresses, is severely disabled, chain-smokes, and drinks eight to ten martinis a day.

Candidate B was kicked out of office twice, sleeps until noon, used opium at university, is an undiagnosed manic-depressive, and drinks a bottle of whiskey every day.

Candidate C is a decorated war hero, vegetarian, doesn't smoke or drink, except for an occasional beer, and has never had an extramarital affair.

Who would you choose?
Candidate A is Franklin D. Roosevelt.
Candidate B is Winston Churchill.
Candidate C is Adolph Hitler.

Sometimes the best candidate on paper is the worst leader in reality. Thank goodness Jesus did not hire a management consultancy to help him recruit his earliest disciples. On paper Peter, James, and John would not have got past expressing interest in the job. Jesus recognized, however, that they had the three things necessary for Christian leadership: faith, hope, and love. Not that they had it immediately. We know they constantly misunderstood Jesus and tried to steer him in other ways, they made promises they did not keep, and they abandoned Jesus when the going got tough. But in it all they had the one thing that nearly all great leaders have in their formation: a mentor who knows they are not perfect, forgives their limitations, tells them the truth, brings them back to what they are actually about, and inspires them by what he says and how he lives.

Sometimes we think the gospel always demands a very different lifestyle from the one we have, and sometimes it does, but today's Gospel should be taken seriously, though not literally. Luke tells us that the disciples "left everything and followed him." We know that following Jesus did not demand of Peter, for example, that he abandon his family. And we also know that the disciples returned to their work of fishing a number of times in their life with Jesus. Luke is telling us, then, that to follow Jesus is a radical option and that we have to divest ourselves of anything that stops us serving the kingdom of God. Conversely, it follows that we have to cultivate the very things that draw us on in the Christian life. For most of us the departures necessary in following Jesus are in our hearts.

Furthermore in this story, Luke is also telling us about the great number of converts attracted to the Christian life. We know that some of these were notorious sinners. No doubt the leaders of the early church had anxieties about admitting them. By relating the story of the sinful Peter being called by Jesus, Luke reassures the community that as long as anyone is able to leave behind the destructiveness of their previous life they can, with guidance, become a disciple of Jesus. Luke teaches that it is not for us to condemn anyone caught up in the net of salvation, simply to trust in God's love and compassion that visits the sick and well alike.

May we pray for the humility in the church to accept that God can turn our judgments, laws, customs, protocols, and management strategies upside down and sometimes bring forward from the most unexpected quarters leaders who show us new dimensions to God's power shining through our human weakness.

SIXTH SUNDAY IN ORDINARY TIME

JEREMIAH 17:5–8
1 CORINTHIANS 15:12, 16–20
LUKE 6:17, 20–26

The pope had just finished a tour of the United States and was taking a limousine to San Francisco. Having never driven a limo, he asked the chauffeur if he could drive for a while.

Well, the chauffeur didn't have much of a choice, so he climbs in the back and the pope takes the wheel.

The pope starts accelerating to see what the limo could do. He gets to eighty miles per hour and suddenly sees the lights of the highway patrol in his rearview mirror. He pulls over, but the policeman, seeing who it is, says, "Just a minute, Your Holiness, I'm going to have to call in about this one."

The trooper asks for the chief. He tells the chief he's got someone really important pulled over.

"It's not the Mayor again is it?"

"No, chief, he's more important."

"Is it the governor?"

"No, sir, it's more important."

"Good God man, you have not pulled over the president?"

"No, sir, even more important."

"Who is more important than the president of the United States?"

"I don't know, sir, all I've ascertained at the moment is that this guy is so important he has the pope as his chauffeur."

What we see is often not what we get.

Luke's Gospel falls into this category.

When we hear the phrase, "Blessed are you," it can sound rather patronizing. It can seem that Jesus glosses over all sorts of tough human realities with, "Well done, keep it up, be happy, and we'll fix it all up in heaven."

But reading the Beatitudes in this light is a direct contradiction of what Jesus says in this text and certainly how he lived it out.

The Hebrew concept of a blessing isn't about divine pats on bowed human heads; it's about where the presence of God is to be found. In the Hebrew scriptures, a blessing is the discovery that God is present and active in one's experience, right here and right now.

So the Beatitudes are saying that we do not need to go past our own daily struggles to find the presence of God. Jesus tells us that when we see the poor, the compassionate, the mournful, those who campaign for a just society and suffer because of it, the gentle, the innocent, the peacemakers, and the martyrs, we are encountering, in a special way, the presence of God.

Jesus teaches us that God is not impervious to our pain and happiness, or a great manipulator desiring terrible things to punish us or teach us something. No. The God of the Beatitudes is a companion with us in every experience we go through either personally or as a community.

But Luke goes on to give us the "woes and warnings" and these are as important as the Beatitudes. Luke highlights for us that every blessing carries with it a call, every gift contains a duty to share it, and every right houses within it a responsibility.

This is particularly true of our nation where the vast majority of our citizens are housed, educated, have clean drinking water, a long life span, and enjoy a stable democracy. This places us in the top 15 percent of the world's population. We should discover God's presence in the midst of these blessings, but we must face up to the responsibilities they give us.

It's not good enough to simply be appalled at the widening gap between rich and poor in our own country and around the world. Today's Gospel places at our feet the challenge to do something about it—in our prayer, in our careful use of resources, in what we spend our money on, and how we vote for governments that might affect international change.

The Beatitudes and the warnings call us to become so transparently attentive to justice, development, and peace for all people that what others see in the followers of Christ is precisely what they get.

SEVENTH SUNDAY IN ORDINARY TIME

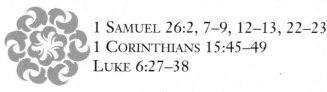

1 SAMUEL 26:2, 7–9, 12–13, 22–23
1 CORINTHIANS 15:45–49
LUKE 6:27–38

Some years ago I came across this story about an annual parents dinner at a Catholic school for profoundly disabled children. A well-known local politician, whose child was in the school, was asked to speak. This is what he said:

> "I would like to pay tribute to the staff at this school. Only parents and teachers know what a joy and a heartbreak it is to have a profoundly disabled child. I always wanted the perfect child, but where is the perfection in my son, David? We are told that God looked at the world and it was prefect, but my son cannot understand things as other children do. David cannot remember facts and figures as other children do. David walks with difficulty and cannot speak. How can God be filled with joy at David?"
>
> The audience was shocked by this pained question from an anguished father.
>
> "I believe," the father continued, "that when God allows a world in which David can now live for fifty years, perfection is found in the way people react to children like him.
>
> "Just recently David and I were walking in our local park. Some boys there had spent most of the day playing baseball. They were serious about this competition. David was very excited and I knew he wanted to join in. David has terrible physical coordination, but I approached one of the boys and asked if David could play. The boy looked around for guidance from his teammates. Getting none, he took matters into his own hands and said, 'Things are tight, we're going to have to get a home run to win, but we'll try and give him a go.' David smiled broadly. David was put in the lineup and called to the plate. I helped him get out there.
>
> "Everyone knew that it was all but impossible for my son to help them win the game. He didn't even know how to

hold the bat properly, let alone hit with it. The pitcher, how-ever, sent down a slow ball so David could at least make con-tact. The second similar ball came and David swung clumsily and missed it. One of David's teammates came up to him and together they held the bat and faced the pitcher waiting for the next ball.

"As the ball came down, David and his teammate swung at the ball and together they hit a strong shot to the crowd. At his captain's urging David ran to first base. Never in his life has David run so fast. He then went on to second base and then on to third, and finally he made a home run. The ball could have been thrown to third base or home, but it wasn't. It was purposefully thrown over each base they aimed for. The young men knew that there was another win-ning moment happening out there.

"That day," said the father softly with tears now rolling down his face, "those boys showed me why God always looks at creation and knows it is very good."

In today's Gospel Jesus says, in effect, "If you love those who love you, what credit is that to you? Be kind, be merciful, forgive, and do not condemn, for the measure you give out is the measure you will receive."

EIGHTH SUNDAY IN ORDINARY TIME

Sirach 27:5–8
1 Corinthians 15:54–58
Luke 6:39–45

At Rome, during the sixteenth century, the most famous confes-sor in town was St. Philip Neri. Popes and paupers sought his counsel and spiritual direction. One day a famous duchess came to him and confessed the sin of gossip. Philip Neri told her to go home and get a feather pillow and return to the steps of the church. Sometime later he met her there and produced a small knife. He told the noblewoman to rip open the pillow. As she did, the swirling wind in the square picked up the loose feathers and they danced around the square and down the lanes.

St. Philip and the duchess watched in silence as the feathers went everywhere. He then turned to her and said, "Now, go and collect all the feathers." To which she protested, "They have gone everywhere, I couldn't possibly find and regather them." "So too with your tongue, madam," St. Philip scolded her. "You have no idea where your words go, and you can never unsay them."

In today's Gospel Jesus teaches us that our words reflect the state of our hearts.

Psychologists tell us that there are three main reasons why people habitually gossip, or "share the news" as men prefer to call it: power, envy, and boredom.

To know something about someone else can put us in a more powerful position with friends or colleagues. By being able to share what we have just heard, we are seen to be current and interesting. But this type of power is destructive because our friends normally assume that when they are absent they are maltreated in the same way. Gossipers have more alliances than friendships.

The most malicious gossip often comes out of envy. Envious gossip often sees people make things up about others and pass it off as though it were true. The worst of tabloid newspapers, television, and radio trades on this destructive vice. There is no place for the "rumor file" in the Christian life. Sometimes, when a company or person has to deny the false accusations made about them, we get what we want—their reputations are tarnished and even their business can be in danger. No wonder medieval theologians called envy a deadly sin.

Boredom, however, is a modern cause for gossip. Our relationships, and the way in which we hold each other's trust and good name to be paramount, are undermined by images from the media about how exciting life should be for everyone. Scene after scene in novels, television programs, and films where confidences are betrayed and lives are raked over for comment and intrigue fill in the boredom in our lives with a distorted portrayal of human behavior. The more we take it in, the more we mirror it in our own conduct.

Jesus does not tell us today that there is no place for criticism, challenge, confrontation, and correction in the Christian life. Just that we have the responsibility to be very careful about what we say about others and how we criticize and condemn them. Jesus reminds us that most of our condemnation of others is what we now call, "projection," where we ignore similar failings in ourselves, but roundly condemn them in others.

May the Eucharist, then, help all of us let go of the need to be powerful, the deadly sin of envy, and be more creative with what we do when we are bored. May it help us make better choices about how we speak, to whom we speak, and what we say.

St. Philip Neri knew it all too well: Most times we cannot know the consequences of what we say and we can never unsay it.

ASH WEDNESDAY

JOEL 2:12–18
2 CORINTHIANS 5:20—6:2
MATTHEW 6:1–6, 16–18

Until quite recently Catholics did not go in for cremation. In some countries bishops would not allow it. These days most Catholics can choose between being buried or being cremated. Given the importance of Ash Wednesday in the Christian calendar, the Catholic ban on cremation is hard to understand.

There is something elemental about ashes. The Church of England's *Book of Common Prayer* says, "In sure and certain hope of the resurrection to eternal life through our Lord Jesus Christ…ashes to ashes, dust to dust. The Lord bless him and keep him, the Lord make his face to shine upon him and be gracious unto him and give him peace. Amen"

As powerful as it is to see a casket committed to the ground, sprinkling someone's ashes over a place that was important to the deceased is even more moving.

Ashes committed to the earth amplify an important facet of today's feast. On the first level it reminds us of our relationship to the earth. Human beings are made up of the same substance as the earth. We might be the crown of creation, but we are in continuity with it. Our being is a more sophisticated arrangement of the building blocks of the natural order. It never hurts us to be reminded of this, because we can quickly think that by being the glory of creation, we are different from it. Our care for the world is intricately linked to the dignity we claim for ourselves.

On another level ashes remind us of our death. We live in a death-denying culture. These days we hide dead bodies, or when we see them we dress them up to make them look as though they are still alive. At their most extreme, the plastic surgery and cosmetic industries are about Western society's resistance to growing old, to facing up to the decline of our bodies, and our death.

But Ash Wednesday brings us face-to-face with our mortality. Today's feast invites us to think about what changes in our life we would bring about if our death were imminent. For all our casual conversation about overseas trips and fancy meals, if most of us had just twenty-four hours to live we would attend to our relationships. Chances are, we would want to tell the people that we love we love them, forgive those we need to, and asked forgiveness of those we have offended. And then many of us would think about God and eternal life.

The Jesuit paleontologist, Pierre Teilhard de Chardin, described death as a "different mode of being," the moment when we move from this world to the next. That's what makes our language of the soul so important. Our soul is the reality that survives our body, and is alive to God and those who love us.

Ash Wednesday ushers in forty days when we can assess if the life we are presently living is the one that, if our death came soon, we would be ready to move from this mode of being to the next. Would we be ready to leave our body behind, so that our soul might enjoy eternity?

In sure and certain hope of the resurrection to eternal life through our Lord Jesus Christ...ashes to ashes, dust to dust. The Lord bless us and keep us, the Lord make his face to shine upon us and be gracious unto us and give us peace. Amen.

FIRST SUNDAY OF LENT

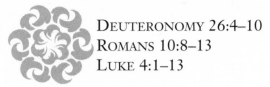

DEUTERONOMY 26:4–10
ROMANS 10:8–13
LUKE 4:1–13

These days, in many parts of the world, Jesuit novices undertake a pilgrimage. For over a week the novice has to walk to a place of Catholic pilgrimage, begging for his food and accommodation. He cannot tell anyone who he is or what he is doing.

One Jesuit writes:

> It's the only time in my life I've been remotely in what we could call a wilderness and I have known hunger. There were many knock backs, but there were a few occasions when people were extraordinarily generous. We are told that we cannot trade off being a Jesuit, but if we are invited into someone's home we can tell them who we are, so that they will not be frightened that they have welcomed Jack the Ripper to stay the night. If the person has offered the garage and a sandwich, however, we cannot use being a Jesuit to get an upgrade from coach to first class!
>
> One woman who welcomed me into her home questioned me at length about where I was from, where I was going and how I got here. Then she declared, "I think I can trust you." So she ushered me into her home, offered a meal that night, breakfast the next day, her guest room. I told this woman who I was and complimented her on her extraordinary generosity. "Well listen, sunshine," she said, "let's face it, I knew you were OK, 'cause you're the best presented, most articulate beggar I've ever met."

In today's Gospel we are told that Jesus was tempted in the wilderness for forty days. Numbers are never randomly used in the Bible. One, three, seven, twelve, and forty all have specific meanings. Forty indicates a time of formation. Luke tells us that Jesus confronts evil head on and is tempted in every way that we are.

We often feel alone when faced with difficult choices and temptations, but especially at these moments, there is one thing we need to remember: Temptation is not sin. Only when we freely and knowingly choose to act on temptation is sin involved. Though one may like to talk about the temptations one has in reconciliation, we never have to "confess" them as though they are sinful actions.

When we look at our temptations they often appear as good things, but often they have a sting in the tail that is always destructive. We need to be very alert to all the consequences of what we do and say, and learn from our experiences. The more we give into temptation, the more immune we become to seeing that there's anything wrong with what we are doing. We can develop whole habits in our living, deceiving ourselves that what we are doing "is not that bad."

Many spiritual writers over the centuries have told us that the worst temptations are greed, pride, and riches. This comes as a surprise to Catholics who have been told for too long that sex is number one. Mystics remind us that we should be wise in how we deal with temptations: Name what's going on, and attend to the pattern of the temptation quickly and consistently.

As John B. Metz, says, "We can say that the three temptations in the desert are three assaults on the poverty of Jesus.... What Satan fears most is the powerlessness of God in the humanity he assumed...so he appeals to Jesus' divinity, he wants God to remain God...but Jesus subjected himself to our plight and opted for us as we are."

We should take great comfort from this: There is no path of temptation along which Jesus has not gone ahead of us to show us we can choose life ahead of death. That's what Lent is always about—a yearly season to keep embracing life and living it to the full.

SECOND SUNDAY OF LENT

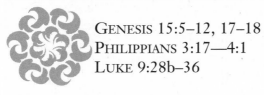

GENESIS 15:5–12, 17–18
PHILIPPIANS 3:17—4:1
LUKE 9:28b–36

An American Jesuit theologian, John Powell, tells the story of a young man named Tommy who was the resident atheist during his Philosophy of God course at Loyola University in Chicago. At the end of the course while he was turning in his final paper, Tommy said to Father Powell, "Do you think I will ever find God?" "No," Powell replied, "but I think God will find you." Tommy walked away.

Years later, Tommy returned to see John Powell to tell him that he had been diagnosed as having terminal cancer. More than ever, Tommy said, he wanted to find God, or at least to be in the right place at the right time to be found by him. John Powell told Tommy to go and tell the people that he most loved in the world that he loved them.

Within a week Tommy reported to Father Powell that in the midst of doing this he had a genuine and significant encounter with God. They had found each other. Tommy died three months later. John Powell reports that the only way to describe the final three months of Tommy's life was to say that, in the process of telling others he loved them, he was transfigured by God.

The transfiguration is no mountaintop light show. In borrowing heavily from similar stories in the Old Testament, it describes, in a dramatic way, how loved Jesus was by God and how this experience was seen and known by his disciples.

So often we hear people say they have not, or cannot, experience the presence of God, and therefore deny that God exists. These readings show us that if we want to encounter God then we have to experience love. This is not an optional extra for the Christian life. As St. John says in his letter, "If you say you love God, yet you hate your brother or sister, you are a liar."

The transfiguration is not a one-time event for Jesus alone. It is meant to set the pattern for all of us to experience the love of

God as sons and daughters through Christ. The problem with the concept of love is that we've devalued the currency. We say it too often about things we don't or can't love. We say, "I love you," to people we don't love, and because we've learned that actions are more telling than words, we don't easily believe others when they tell us they love us. We can feel unlovable and cynical about the whole experience.

But there are three things of which we can be sure:

If we feel distant from God, we only have to guess who has moved away from whom. Nothing we do stops God from loving us.

God loves us as we are, not as we would like to be. As the old saying goes, "You don't have to get good to get God, you have to get God to get good."

Finally, as the song runs, "You ain't nobody until somebody loves ya."

And so for a Christian, being vulnerable enough to tell those we love that we love them is no sentimental exercise but a participation in the heart of God. By taking the risk of doing this, others may clearly hear the voice of God through us and we may discover ourselves transfigured by the personal love of God. In the process, God may move from being an idea, an abstraction, even an object of curiosity, to the focus of a loving experience that can give our lives meaning, purpose, and hope.

Together then let's ascend the mountaintop together, and hear God say to each of us, "You are my son. You are my daughter—and I love you."

THIRD SUNDAY OF LENT

EXODUS 3:1–8a, 13–15
1 CORINTHIANS 10:1–6, 10–12
LUKE 13:1–9

The resource I use to help a couple prepare for marriage has questions for them to think about and discuss between sessions. One of the questions at the end of one of the chapters is "What effect would adultery have on your marriage?"

In one sense this hypothetical question is absurd. Dealing with the consequences of any sin requires time and place, context and contrition. It is even tougher to imagine the effect of any destructive behavior in one's marriage before the marriage has begun. Still, it never ceases to amaze me how this question usually leads the couple to have a very fruitful and frank discussion, not about adultery, but about their values, family history, commitment, fidelity, and growing old together.

Sometimes, however, I cringe when the prospective bride or groom seems to give the green light to their future spouse by saying, "Well, I guess if he or she went looking elsewhere it would be my fault" or "I love him or her so much that I know we could go on regardless." Others say very clearly that it would alter the trust and respect of the relationship, but they hope they could look at the circumstances and rebuild the relationship.

The most mature couples do not gloss over the seriousness of the sinful action, but want to hold on to compassion, forgiveness, and a commitment that it will not happen again.

Couples like these have clearly understood the power of today's readings. The Third Sunday of Lent is all about second chances. In Exodus we have a bush that is alight but does not burn, and in Luke we have a fig tree that does not bear fruit, is earmarked for the axe and saved by the gardener. In both cases, where we would expect to find destruction we find new opportunities for growth, nurturance, and flowering.

Over the centuries the goodness of God that always gives us another chance has not been proclaimed as vigorously as it should have been. We have focused on God's justice as though it was a once-and-for-all, shape-up-or-ship-out sort of message. These ideas can be deduced from today's second reading where Paul seems to argue that God killed the chosen people for their complaining and infidelity.

Paul was a tough man and for him Christian commitment was no picnic. He was aware of how people were suffering and dying for the gospel, so he was at pains to teach the people of Corinth that the commitment demanded from the gospel could entail everything they had. His reading of why the Israelites died in the desert, however, needs to be read against the second chances people get in other stories of the New Testament, especially in the gospels.

We believe during Lent that we enter a holy time in our year and visit a holy place in ourselves where the fire of God's love should burn brightly within us. We are offered these weeks to reexamine our values, family history, commitment, fidelity, and growth so as to chart how best we can grow old with God. To do this sometimes requires facing up to our sinful behavior and making choices to change our lives. We can only do this when we trust that the fire of God's love is not about destruction, but compassion, forgiveness, and a second chance.

May the Eucharist be nurturance for the foundations of our lives and a moment to take stock and to assess with honesty the fruitfulness of how, as a sign of the Christ's light within us, we live out our faith in our marriage, at home, at work, and in the world.

FOURTH SUNDAY OF LENT

JOSHUA 5:9a, 10–12
2 CORINTHIANS 5:17–21
LUKE 15:1–3, 11–32

What is so shocking about Jesus' parable of the prodigal son is that, as the story goes, everything about the Jewish culture of first-century Palestine set the boy up for a fall: He was greedy for his father's inheritance; we can assume he left the promised land for the far country where he squandered his inheritance recklessly; he ended up eating with the unclean pigs; and then he had the temerity to return and ask for forgiveness.

This was the least likable kid in town. He did not deserve to be treated better than a slave. That's what makes the boy's father so magnificent in love. He was derided by his faithful older son for this folly of the heart and he would have been considered a fool by his neighbors. And this is the model of compassion Jesus gives us to emulate.

There are many families who similarly fret over a child. They wander away from us in all sorts of ways, not just physically. In her poem "Missing," Máiréad Tuohy Duffy reminds us that the hope we have for our loved one's return is the same anticipation God has for us.

Missing?
Vanishing into the space of oblivion
In earth, sea or sky?
Who knows?
Gone into the wilderness
Of the unknown.
Leaving behind;
Fathers, mothers,
Brothers, sisters.
Bewildered Friends.
Watching, waiting,
Hearts aching,
Eyes peering,
Ears listening.
Minds hoping,
The door will open,
The vanished will return.
Like the prodigal son,
The father will say;
"Come into my open arms,
Oh! Child, how we missed you."

The context for the story of the prodigal son matters. The author of Luke 15 has Jesus responding to charges about the company he was keeping and especially those with whom he dined. In Jesus' day, one only ate with intimates and Jesus shared his table with losers. Three parables are given as an explanation for this practice: the lost sheep, the lost coin, and the lost son. In each case the shepherd, the woman, and the father go to ridiculous lengths to save that which is lost.

Who was admitted to the table of Luke's community was a huge issue. And it seems some things never change. The actions and words of Jesus, however, lead us to conclude the table is here for those of us who know the frailty of our lives enough to recognize our hunger and thirst for the Bread of Life and the Cup of Salvation.

Today's Gospel is not just about each of us being welcomed into the arms of our compassionate God, it is also a challenge for us to defend the right of the outcasts, the public sinners, and the losers who seek to turn their life around to be welcomed here as well. This is not just about the table of the Eucharist, either. To the degree that we help our country be more hospitable to the most defenseless, the poor, and the displaced then we live out the power of this parable.

Jill E. Penley could have been adapting some of the lessons from the parable of the prodigal son when she writes about the moment when we meet God face to face:

> God won't ask what kind of car you drove, but He'll ask how many people you drove who didn't have transportation.
>
> God won't ask the square footage of your house, but He'll ask how many people you welcomed into your home.
>
> God won't ask about the clothes you had in your closet, but He'll ask how many you helped to clothe.
>
> God won't ask what your highest salary was, but He'll ask if you compromised your character to obtain it.
>
> God won't ask what your job title was, but He'll ask if you performed your job to the best of your ability and with honesty and integrity.
>
> God won't ask how many friends you had, but He'll ask how many people to whom you were a friend.
>
> God won't ask in what neighborhood you lived, but He'll ask how you treated your neighbors.
>
> God won't ask about the color of your skin, but He'll ask about the content of your character.

May the Eucharist, then, help us live beyond our history, which so often colors those toward whom we can give the benefit of the doubt and show compassion and may it give us the courage and faith to be ridiculously generous, and magnificently loving.

FIFTH SUNDAY OF LENT

ISAIAH 43:16–21
PHILIPPIANS 3:8–14
JOHN 8:1–11

There is a tough phrase at the end of today's Gospel, "Go your way, and from now on do not sin again." It's like a sting in the tail, standing in contrast to the compassion of Jesus in his encounter with the woman. Yet, on closer inspection, it is the most important phrase in the story. And that's saying something, because this dramatic event is the only one in John's Gospel where Jesus confronts sexual sin, where only the woman is dragged from the scene of the crime to answer the charge of adultery. Is it any wonder that in some early manuscripts of John's Gospel this story was left out, its authorship questioned? The dangerous memory of Jesus' compassion toward the woman was too strong in the minds of John's community for it to be excluded, however, and so it remains as an inspired text for us to make our own. It is sometimes very important to hear Jesus say to us, especially in the area of our sexuality, "I do not condemn you."

So often, however, we want Jesus to leave it at that. But Jesus goes further. He tells it as it is. If any of us want life and want it to the full, we have to stop doing the destructive things that get us into trouble in the first place. It does not matter if it is drinking, gambling, eating, working, stealing, sexual dysfunction, being into pornography, being violent at home, or any other type of obsessive-compulsive behavior, there is little point in being sorry for the consequences of our weaknesses and not changing the pattern of behavior that leads us to ruin each time.

Twelve-step programs enshrine the wisdom of today's Gospel in how they help us to own up to the destructive behavior of our lives and yet give us hope to live beyond out worst moments.

Steps four to ten say:

Step 4. I have made a searching and fearless moral inventory of myself.

Step 5. I have admitted to God and to another the exact nature of my wrongs.

Step 6. I was entirely ready to have God remove all these defects of character.

Step 7. Humbly ask God to remove my shortcomings.

Step 8. Made a list of all persons I had harmed and became willing to make amends to them all.

Step 9. Made direct amends to such people wherever possible except where to do so would injure them or others.

Step 10. Continued to take personal inventory and when I was wrong promptly admitted it.

The thing I like best about these is that they are proactive. They alert us to the fact that the best pathway to healing and forgiveness is not to be passive, but to be active and admit our own faults and work to heal them. Some of us may have been given a tough hand from life's deck of cards, but we do not have to be passive victims, never able to change the cycles of destructive behavior. If the steps work and we trust today's Gospel, then we can be happy, healed, and forgiven because we heal and forgive others.

Jesus bestows great dignity on the woman by saving her from being condemned to death, but even more so he knows that it does not have to be like this and so challenges her to turn her life around.

May we hear the same challenge in this final week of Lent. No matter what we have ever done, sexually or otherwise, we are greater than our worst moments. Jesus loves us enough not to condemn us, but to give us the Eucharist so that we might find the strength and hope to stop doing the things that destroy us and to live a life that leads to peace and joy.

PASSION SUNDAY (PALM SUNDAY)

Procession: LUKE 19:28–40
ISAIAH 50:4–7
PHILIPPIANS 2:6–11
LUKE 22:14—23:56

The crowd who cheered on Palm Sunday proved to be an unpredictable lot. It took them no time at all to move from the cries of adulation of Palm Sunday to the derision of Good Friday, and back again, with frightening speed. What is most worrying, however, is that we can do the same just as easily.

Take, for example, many countries in our world where on the one hand the white majority tell the original inhabitants of the land that they have some claim on it and then change the rules when they begin to make such a claim. You don't have to look far for Calvary. Try being black in a white world.

We bask in the myth that our society is a land of equality, but then we do very little about racist politicians who seem to think that equality is primarily for white people born here of European origins, of Christian background. You don't have to search too far for Calvary. Try being Asian or African in a Eurocentric world.

We affirm that women and men are made in the image and likeness of God, but in the church and society we find new arguments to keep the boys in power and women only fractionally developing their God-given talents. You don't have to seek out Calvary. Try being a woman in a man's world.

We tell the gay community they may have been born with a desire for a same-sex partner and that no one should discriminate against them and yet we deny them basic rights for legal security and dignity. You don't have to hunt for Calvary. Try being gay in a straight world.

We sing the praises of in vitro fertilization and its associated technologies and proclaim how a thousand more couples are now "complete" as a result of having a baby, and yet last year we aborted countless babies. You don't have to explore far to find

Calvary. Try being a pregnant mother in an unsympathetic and death-dealing world.

The reality is that Palm Sunday is not a yearly historical pageant. It is the day when we hear proclaimed that our God knows what's it's like to be heralded on Sunday and condemned on Friday; our God loved us so much that he laid down his own life so that we might live; and our God showed us that the price of walking on palm branches is taking up the cross.

And how do we do that? How do we face all the Calvary's of our world and be Christ-like?

In the passion we are told that Jesus did five things:

He healed the ear of the High Priest's servant.
He spoke the truth to Pilate.
He empathized with the women of Jerusalem.
He forgave those who condemned him.
He had compassion toward the other criminal being crucified.

And here's the rub: In facing our personal passion and being with those who face their Calvary, we are called to do likewise.

If Holy Week means anything it means we end this week as we began it—processing. Walking away from inflicting pain to being a healer, desisting from lies and speaking the truth, resisting the temptation to judge and embracing empathy as our first response, and, always and everywhere, being generous with forgiveness and compassion.

No more and no less is asked of us if we are to follow the one of whom we sing, "Lord of earth, heaven, sky and sea. King of Love on Calvary."

HOLY THURSDAY

EXODUS 12:1–8, 11–14
1 CORINTHIANS 11:23–26
JOHN 13:1–15

The Passover and resulting Exodus are the defining moments in the life of Israel. For us, however, they can seem distant events that happened to "the Jews," and of little consequence to us today. On two levels, however, they are defining moments in our life too.

On the first level, as Christians we look to Jesus for salvation. His personal and religious identity was inextricably and proudly caught up with the Passover and the Exodus. This is one of the reasons why it is patently absurd for a Christian to be anti-Semitic. Such Christians end up hating the very religious tradition that formed Jesus, his mother, and stepfather, as well as all the apostles. If God chose our Jewish brothers and sisters as the people from whom the Lord would come, who are we to declare him mistaken? One of the worst things Christianity has done to the memory of Jesus is to strip him of his religious heritage. If we are sincere about ever getting to know the historical Jesus, the Jesus of the gospels, then it helps to have some devoutly Jewish friends to guide us.

On another level, the Passover and Exodus are now metaphors for what God does through Christ in all of our lives. Many of us know what it is like to be stuck, imprisoned by our body, mind, or soul—these places can be very dark indeed.

It's good for us to remember in the midst of the splendor of our Holy Thursday liturgy that the Passover in Egypt, and the Last Supper upon which it is based, were celebrated in the most desolate of circumstances. The Israelites were in exile and enslaved. Jesus was on the eve of his passion and death. But the Israelites and Jesus held on to the hope and faith that they would be freed from bondage in the first case, and that God would remain faithful to his Son in the second. For Israel, their hope and faith led to the Exodus. For Jesus, it led to the resurrection.

But there is one dramatic and important difference between the Passover and the Last Supper. The Israelites' freedom cost many lives, the firstborn son of every Egyptian family. By contrast, not one life was lost in the wake of the resurrection. In fact, the opposite is true: It gave all people the opportunity to know eternal life. God was so despairing of human death and the never-ending cycle of violence within which we are caught that Jesus went to his death so that death would be no more.

John's Gospel shows us how those who follow Jesus can break this cycle of destruction—we must serve one another, even our enemies. We get down on the floor and assume the nature of a slave so that others might discover their human dignity and worth.

You see, people who value themselves and have a healthy self-esteem do not need to perpetuate acts of physical, emotional, or verbal violence. They can express their love for others in acts of goodness and kindness, confident that this deepens, rather than diminishes, their human dignity.

No matter what situation we find ourselves in this Easter, but especially if we are in need of a sign of hope, Jesus comes to us, calls us by name, gets down and washes our feet so that we might be reminded how precious we are, and go find the way out of our enslavement. And once we are free, we can help him liberate others as well. May the Eucharist, this bread of freedom, help us to get free and stay free.

GOOD FRIDAY

ISAIAH 52:13—53:12
HEBREWS 4:14–16; 5:7–9
JOHN 18:1—19:42

A Jewish Holocaust survivor, Elie Wiesel, wrote in his book *Legends*, "You want to know about the kingdom of night? There is no way to describe the kingdom of night. But let me tell you a story... You want to know about the condition of the human heart? There is no way to describe the condition of the human heart. But let me tell you a story... You want a description of the indescribable? There is no way to describe the indescribable. But let me tell you a story."

This Good Friday let me tell you a personal story that captures what we find good about today.

On the morning of my twenty-fifth birthday, my mother was on the phone at dawn. "Your sister has had a car accident," she told me, "and we have to go to her." My sister, Tracey, had worked for three years with Mother Teresa in Calcutta. She had returned to Australia and worked for the Aboriginal people at Port Keats. She was young, athletic, and professionally competent.

As we flew to be with her, we were not sure how serious her injuries were. My mother and I warded off a sense of dread by saying, "We will get up there and Tracey will be sitting up in bed, having a drink and laughing at us for being melodramatic."

Tracey was not sitting up, she was not having a drink and we were not melodramatic in coming. She had two spikes buried in her temples like a crown of thorns and her arms were extended so that her immobile body was in the shape of a cross.

On October 23, 1988, Tracey became a quadriplegic.

The funny thing is that if we got to the hospital and were told that she had died, but that if she had lived she would have been a quadriplegic, we would have found death a comfort. We would have said, "How would she have coped? How would we have coped?" Instead, we saw someone we loved so much face Good Friday, with no Easter Sunday on the horizon.

In the weeks and months that followed, the nicest people said and wrote the most dreadful things. "It's all God's will and now you just have to accept it." "God has done this to Tracey so that he can do a powerful work through her suffering." "God only sends the biggest crosses to those who can bear them." "It's all a mystery that we will only understand in heaven." How can people believe in such a cruel, manipulative God who seems to punish the generous?

Tracey's accident has been the most painful theological lesson I have ever learned. Her Calvary has taught me that God does not send pain, suffering, and disease. God does not punish us. God does not send accidents to teach us things, though we can learn from them and, in the face of them, hold on to hope. God does not will earthquakes, floods, droughts, or other natural disasters, but God created a world that is less than perfect, else it would be heaven, within which suffering, disease, and pain are realities and where we make free choices—some of which are life giving, others are deadly.

The cross is not a symbol of a bloodthirsty God who would only be kept happy by the murder of his Son for human sin. But it is a symbol of martyrdom, of Jesus' sacrifice for the truth he lived, the life he offered to show how far God's companionship extends to us. Our God went to death so that death might be no more.

Tracey's Good Friday, and the many like it that she has lived since, reveal to me a completely compassionate God who grieves with us when we despair and is a companion to us in our darkest days. This utter solidarity with the human condition is the goodness we celebrate this afternoon and the hope with which we look for the light of resurrection in all our lives.

EASTER VIGIL

GENESIS 1:1—2:2; 22:1–18
EXODUS 14:15—15:1
ISAIAH 54:5–14; 55:1–11
BARUCH 3:9–15, 32—4:4
EZEKIEL 36:16–28
ROMANS 6:3–11
LUKE 24:1–12

The Easter Vigil is above all a ceremony of light, of Christ the Light raised from the dead, of the love that his light inspires in us, and how his way enlightens our lives.

Jesuit poet Peter Steele masterfully captures the Easter Vigil this way:

You might have thought that, with the invention first of gas light and then of electric light, there would soon be no candles left in the world. But as things stand, there are still millions of them.

Sometimes this is out of sheer necessity, but that is not why they wind up on birthday cakes or on Catholic altars. And above all it is not why the big Easter candle is first fashioned and then decorated.

A candle, wax and weak, is entirely fuel, designed to be consumed in order to give light. Candles used at ceremonies—birthday parties, Eucharists—show this process vividly. They remind us that if we want our own light to shine in the world, we will have to put something of ourselves into it: at least time, and usually intelligence, patience, and some love as well.

The great precedent for all of this is Christ himself, whose token is that Easter candle. But the Easter vigil in which it is first presented also offers the sight of many tapers or very small candles being lit from it. So it can go with us, even on dark days. To pray is to put the tips of our tapers into the blessed Fire.

Time, intelligence, patience, and love are such an accurately economical ways of summarizing what we have done over these five weeks of Lent, and what we celebrate at Easter.

We believe that God works in and through time, and so Lent calls us to spend our time well by spending ourselves for our neighbor in acts of sacrifice and goodness. And we have also listened to how, throughout time, God has worked to save his people, drawing us into an ever-intimate embrace. Because of the first Easter Day we have become God's sons and daughters, coheirs of the kingdom.

We believe that God creates and works intelligently, in an ordered way, so that we can discern his traces and follow them. And even though there remain in our lives seemingly random events and miraculous moments, a meaningful life is one where every moment, most especially the ordinary and humdrum, can hold God's presence.

We believe in a patient God, who calls us to be likewise. For many of us this is the hardest virtue of all. We are not called the "instant-gratification generation" for nothing. But the readings from the Old Testament are filled with longing, looking, and waiting, and Jesus goes to his death patiently hoping that the Father would have the last word after his death on a tree. He did. Patience pays off.

And we believe in Love. Love of a God who took our flesh, and was subjected to human violence, so that we could find the path to nonviolence. Love of each other that recognizes that Jesus' death and being raised to life was not for a select few, but for everyone. And whether they know it or not, or like it or not, we love others because they are our family in Christ. Love of ourselves because if you were the only person in the world Christ would have come and redeemed you.

This is the context in which we can speak of being consumed by the light of Christ, and we can spend ourselves as fuel so that Christ's kingdom can come. At this Easter Vigil, as we "put the tips of our tapers into the blessed Fire," may we be given the time we need to be the best person we are capable of being; develop our intellect enough to discern the right decisions in the ups and downs of our daily lives; pray for patience with God, others, and ourselves so that we can burn brightly for a lifetime, rather than flare and fade; and have the love that makes being consumed by the Light of Christ sound like the best invitation we have ever had.

Happy Easter.

EASTER SUNDAY

ACTS 10:34a, 37–43
COLOSSIANS 3:1–4 *or* 1 CORINTHIANS 5:6b–8
JOHN 20:1–9 *or* LUKE 24:1–12
Afternoon: LUKE 24:13–35

It is cheekily claimed that more people have seen Elvis since his death than those who saw Jesus after the resurrection. In Luke's Gospel it's difficult to work out how many disciples encountered the Risen Christ, but the number doesn't matter. The major difference between those who claimed to have seen Elvis and those who met Christ is what flows from what they say they saw. For the Elvis watchers, the focus is usually on them, and they get their fifteen minutes of fame. Rightly, no one takes them all that seriously. For the earliest witnesses to the resurrection, however, the focus of their encounter is almost always on Christ, their roles in the story of the Risen Christ have been passed on from one generation to another, and many of them died bearing witness to what they saw and came to believe.

The word *witness* appears twice in today's first reading from the Acts of the Apostles. It has become one of the most common ways of Christians talking about their relationship to Jesus. Mary Magdalene, Peter, and the others were the first "witnesses" to the resurrection. At our baptisms our parents and sponsors were told to "witness" to the Christian faith that they were professing so that we might learn how to live it. And sometimes we say we are trying by word and example to "witness" to Christ.

For us the word *witness* usually means that we attest to the truth of events from personal experience and knowledge. We regularly say that the best person to help a drinking alcoholic is a recovering alcoholic, a person who might inspire an obese person to lose weight is someone who has done it, and so on. The power of personal witness can hardly be exaggerated. And the same is true of Christian faith. It might be attractive to believe in Jesus Christ as Savior of the world as a good idea or as an engaging concept. But the best witnesses have firsthand access to the truth. They don't believe in the idea of the resurrection, but have had a personal encounter with the Risen Christ themselves, and are bold enough to proclaim and live it.

This may be why in the early church the word for witness and the word for martyr were one and the same. Anyone brave enough to publicly witness to the resurrection at that time ended up giving his or her life for it. In fact this is one of the two most compelling arguments for the reality of the resurrection. Within a generation after Jesus' death, people all over the Mediterranean world, most of whom had never seen Jesus, reported that they, too, had encountered the presence of the Risen Christ—that Jesus of Nazareth was not dead, but alive to them, too. The other compelling reason that is difficult to counter is that these same people not only believed in the resurrection, but also were prepared to put their lives on the line for the person they had encountered.

And nothing has changed. This Easter Day we are called to be witnesses to Jesus, raised from the dead, and alive to us here and now. This is no head trip, for in our own way we are meant to put our bodies on the line for it. In the Acts of the Apostles we are told this means two things: preach that death is finished and that, for us, life is Christ; and testify to the fact that we know we have encountered Christ because we have been forgiven and are in turn forgiving.

Let's not be fooled—going out from here to witness to life and forgiveness in Christ will have its costs in a world that is all too often given over to dealing in death, in all its forms, and addicted to revenge and retribution. So we, too, will have to pay a price for how we live and whom we challenge. But we have each other, we have the martyrs and the saints, and we have the Father who, in the power of the Spirit, would not let death have the final word over his faithful Son Jesus, and so opened up eternal life for all of us.

No wonder we stand and sing Alleluia! Happy Easter.

SECOND SUNDAY OF EASTER

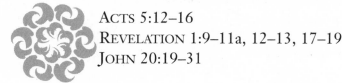

ACTS 5:12–16
REVELATION 1:9–11a, 12–13, 17–19
JOHN 20:19–31

Saying the Creed can be a sobering experience. Having said it all my life, I can still get stuck at various times and on various phrases, so I am always pleased that we say it as an assembly, and not as a solo. Most people I know prefer it that way too. There are, of course, some of us who get through it word perfect, every week. They are our rocks. The rest of us know most of it but need a hand with other parts. When all our weaknesses and strengths are put together we discover we can support each other through this monumental statement of Christian faith.

Welcome to "Doubting Thomas Sunday," a feast day for all of us who need each other to get through the Creed, and who need the assembly's strength when we don't know what we actually believe.

It would be nice to think we are always firm in our faith. Some people are, but many of us have moments of uncertainty and hesitation. Because what we share is faith, not certainty, these questions and reservations are entirely understandable. If we take them seriously enough to pursue some answers, then they can even be a path to a more mature and deeper faith.

And it always good to remember that in this passage it is not Christ whom Thomas doubts, but the church, the earliest Christian community. He won't buy the resurrection just because the others say so. He wants his own experience. And because the church remains faithful to him in his distrust of them, he has his own encounter with the Risen Christ.

John's Gospel is very interested in Thomas. In the other three gospels he is just named as one of the Twelve. In John, however, he is specifically spoken of three times and he is given a nickname, "Didymus."

It is Thomas who says to the others, "Let us also go, that we may die with him," as Jesus leaves for Lazarus's tomb. It is Thomas who responds to Jesus statement, "You know the way to the place where I am going," by saying, "Lord, we don't know where you are going, so how can we know the way?" And then it is Thomas who is the only one of the Twelve not present when they gather in the evening of the first Easter Sunday.

So John's portrait of Thomas is either as one who never seems to get what Jesus is talking about, or is in the wrong place at the wrong time. That's why he has become such an important figure for some of us—sometimes we don't get it either, and we think we aren't where the faith/action seems to be happening.

But this is to exclusively focus on Thomas's weaknesses. When the bold and stubborn Thomas gets it, he really gets it. The title John records Thomas as using when addressing the Risen Christ tells us everything.

Around the time this Gospel was written, Domitian was the Roman emperor. The same title John puts on the lips of Thomas for Christ the Lord, was what a Roman citizen would have used in greeting the emperor: in Latin, *"Dominus et deus,"* "My Lord and god."

It is hard for us to imagine how politically and socially subversive this phrase applied to anyone else other than the emperor was in the first century. This was the stuff of revolution. And 229 years after Domitian, that is precisely what happened, when Emperor Constantine the Great was baptized. That day he recognized that Jesus, who was wounded, crucified, and raised from the dead, that he alone is worthy of true worship, "My Lord and my God."

So, while Thomas consoles us in our doubts, he doesn't just leave us there, as though our doubts were fine all by their own. He also challenges us to seek out the answers, or at least be patient as they come. And Thomas stands as the patron saint of those who are prepared for the consequences of what they might find in the pilgrimage of faith. When we meet the Risen Christ our lives are changed, and so is our world.

Given that it is doubting Thomas's day, it seems appropriate for us to reflect on a question before we carry one another along throughout the Creed: When I have doubts of faith, am I open to life-changing answers, or at least am I in a place where I want the wounded Christ to find me?

THIRD SUNDAY OF EASTER

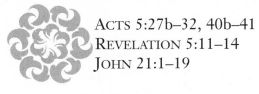

ACTS 5:27b–32, 40b–41
REVELATION 5:11–14
JOHN 21:1–19

The Shawshank Redemption, based on a novel by Stephen King, was the hit film of 1994. It is set in 1947, long before sophisticated forensic tests and DNA evidence, when justice could be tough, and wrong. That year Andy Dufresne's wife was having an affair. When he finds out about it he is enraged, but shortly afterward the couple are shot dead and Andy is arrested and convicted for the crime. He is sentenced to life in prison at Shawshank Penitentiary, run by the God-fearing warden Samuel Norton, who announces, "I believe in two things: discipline and the Bible. Here you'll receive both. Put your trust in the Lord; your ass belongs to me. Welcome to Shawshank." At first the bookish banker is treated cruelly by some of the guards and other inmates, and is regarded coolly by the better men in Shawshank. Andy Dufresne never tells his left hand what his right hand is doing. In time he is befriended by a fellow lifer, Red, who is the great fixer of the jail. He becomes his greatest admirer. He narrates this film. Red believes Andy is innocent. Andy tells Red that if ever they both get out of jail they will meet on the beach at Zihuatenejo in Mexico.

The longer we watch the film, the more we realize that Stephen King has modelled his story on the Gospel of John. It is, in many respects, a modern parable about John's portrait of Jesus. Andy, like Jesus, is an innocent man, treated harshly by the authorities of his day. He has to endure the condemnation and cruelty of the leading religious zealots who are keepers of law and order, while he inspires others to think of a world free of subjection and oppression where they can be free to live the life of which they dream. Like John's Jesus, Andy has big dreams and often talks in riddles, but he leaves clues for others to follow him in their quest for freedom.

In the last part of the film, after Andy has successfully escaped and the governor of the prison has been exposed for the hypocrite he is, Red is paroled after serving thirty-five years hard labor. He decides to go where Andy has gone and, just as Andy promised when they were together in prison, he finds that Andy has prepared the way for him to follow. The moving climax of the film comes as Andy and Red meet on a beach, embrace each other, and share food and drink to celebrate the new life both of them have discovered.

Stephen King understands John's portrait of Jesus very well. For all of Jesus' assuredness and composure throughout the Gospel, the sense of care and intimacy in the encounters with his friends is deeply moving.

In the Easter Gospel, Jesus returns to find his friends, who have fled from Jerusalem. In a parable about the growing numbers of the early church, the Eucharist, and the suffering they are enduring, John reaffirms that Jesus is intimately present in their following of him and their suffering for the kingdom. The only sense John can make of Jesus' death, the martyrdom of the apostles, or the persecution of the early church is to see them all as acts of love. "No one has greater love than this, to lay down one's life for one's friends."

And to those of us who have been caught up in the net of God's love, we are heirs to the same promises of Jesus' fidelity. Christ is intimately present to us in every act of loving sacrifice we undertake for him. He continues to send us out to tell people of the place that has been prepared for them at the banquet of life and he gives us strength to gird our loins for the times when life takes us to places we would rather not go.

Let's be grateful for this Easter season when we celebrate again that we have been set free from the prison of our fears and shown the way to live a life of sacrificial love and underserved redemption.

FOURTH SUNDAY OF EASTER

ACTS 13:14, 43–52
REVELATION 7:9, 14b–17
JOHN 10:27–30

The passages from the gospels where Jesus likens us to being sheep leave me a bit cold. I think I lose something in the translation from first-century Palestine to today. Most of the sheep I have ever watched may well be cute, in a woolly sort of way, but they are anxious creatures often running in packs in every direction, are notoriously stupid and difficult to manage or direct. So, on second thought, maybe the analogy to humanity is not so bad after all!

We, the people of God, can certainly be an anxious lot, a bit slow on the uptake and difficult to lead. It also true, however, that sheep are incredibly useful and adaptable animals. Think about all the places they have been taken throughout the world. In most places they thrive. With all due respect to the vegans, vegetarians, and animal liberationists, sheep have served humanity in multiple ways.

The point of the shepherd analogy in the gospels, of course, is about the importance of intimacy. A sheep in those days is similar to the central role some domestic cats and dogs have in our homes. They were members of the family. Shepherds in Jesus' day belonged to nomadic tribes that moved with their small flock throughout Israel. Every sheep mattered. Every sheep had a name. In an agrarian society every sheep was a vital economic unit. To lose one caused trouble not only to the individual, but also to the tribe. To lose a flock was financial ruin for a generation. As a result, when Jesus invokes the image of the shepherd he draws attention to the intimate knowledge and care the shepherd has of them.

In today's Gospel Jesus tells us that we follow him, not because we are too dumb to know otherwise, or because we are anxious or fearful of our alternatives, but because we know his voice, we know him, he knows our name. We follow Jesus' lead for no other reason than that throughout our life we have come to trust him and to rely on the intimacy of our relationship with him. In return he protects us and makes sure no one can steal us from his flock.

The possibility of being stolen away from the Christian family is a real one. We know many people who, for a variety of reasons, have left the fold and been seduced into pursuing other leads, whereas every Sunday we affirm that we cannot find a better way to live than following the Way, the Truth, and the Life which is Christ present here and now. Jesus was never under any illusions about what following his lead may cost, but he underlines how much we need each other to survive in this world. And we need his protection. We often like to feel so self-sufficient these days that we bristle when we hear how Christ "protects" us, but that is precisely what he does. The protection of the Good

Shepherd comes in the word, through the sacraments, in the church, and from the hands of all those who look out for us. And whether we realize it or not, we need protection.

Let's steal a few moments when we experience again the intimate and protective love of the Risen Lord, who knows and claims us as his own. May we respond by following his lead and enfold all our world in his care and welcome all his children into his flock.

FIFTH SUNDAY OF EASTER

 ACTS 14:21b–27
REVELATION 21:1–5a
JOHN 13:31–33a, 34–35

We've all seen those Hollywood films that begin with the reading of a will. Usually, all the warring relatives are sitting around a long mahogany table or desk as the lawyer for the deceased reads out, "The Last Will and Testament." The film's drama unfolds because whoever was supposed to get everything gets nothing and the Johnny-come-lately, the mistress, the newest wife, or the black sheep of the family gets the lot. Mayhem, and sometimes murder, follows in the story from there. Everyone ends up a loser.

In today's Gospel, Jesus gives his last will and testament, while he is still alive. Just. With the betrayer busy about his business, Jesus has a final few moments to make a last appeal to his disciples. Of all the things he said before in John's Gospel—profound, moving, and challenging things—it now comes down to this. And he wants them to get it. "I give you a new commandment, that you love one another…as I have loved you."

That's it. An entire life is summed up in one line. Like the Hollywood film, everyone is gathered around a table, but there is no lawyer present, and everyone receives exactly the same. There are no losers in the legacy. But murder and mayhem follow nonetheless.

It isn't just any old type of love that Jesus tells us is the guiding principle of the Christian life. It's not the distorted version of love that often dominates our thinking and actions today. We are told to love others as Jesus loves us. And what does that look like, and why it is "new"?

As important as the Old Testament is in enabling us to know the God of Jesus, there are times when God is portrayed as vengeful, condemning, and dealing in death. In the New Testament, however, we believe that to see Jesus in action is to see God in action.

There is not a page of the New Testament upon which we can read about Jesus taking anything away from anyone. He may have got justifiably angry, but he was never vengeful or condemning or dealing in death.

His love is tough at times, but an encounter with him was never destructive. His love for us was forgiving, healing, empowering, and life-giving. This is what makes this teaching "new."

The other inescapable feature of Jesus' love is that it is sacrificial. Within twenty-four hours of giving this final sermon he would be dead, refusing to compromise on being obedient to God's reign of peace, justice, and love in a violent, unfair, and hateful world.

Sacrificial love is not suicidal love. We can sort out whom we love fairly easily by naming to ourselves those for whom we would be prepared to die, or instead of. If we cannot name anyone, then we have some serious soul-searching to do about how self-preoccupied we have become. This might be fine for another type of believer, but not for the followers of Jesus. He loved us to the end and we are called to love one another to the end as well.

But death is not just about taking a bullet for someone. It comes in other ways too. We have a to die a little to challenge others to change for the better, to forgive, to heal, to empower the weak, to defend the rights of the marginalized, and to raise the spiritually and emotionally dead people we meet to new possibilities and opportunities.

Imagine if all the followers of Jesus lived like this? Imagine if we did? We would see the glory of God reflected in ourselves. And we can live like this, not only because Jesus told us we could, but also because it's the best and most lasting final will and testament we could ever leave the world. And everyone would be a winner, including us.

So let's go and do it!

SIXTH SUNDAY OF EASTER

ACTS 15:1–2, 22–29
REVELATION 21:10–14, 22–23
JOHN 14:23–29

Have you noticed how many books, films, television and radio programs harken back to yesteryear? Retrospectives are huge in the art world. We seem to enjoy the stuff of other generations more than our own. When musicians play romantic classical music in the first half of a concert and then contemporary classic music in the second half, many people have already left at half-time. Nostalgia is big business and we cannot get enough of it.

Nostalgia literally means "a yearning for home." And if our artistic tastes reveal anything about who we are at present, maybe the home we yearn for is where things are clearer, roles are more defined, accepted harmony is developed, and discord and dissonance are avoided—at least in public.

In today's Gospel, Jesus says that as a result of our love for him and fidelity to his word, the Father will come and make a home with us. The image of God as homemaker is, sadly, not very developed in Christian spirituality, maybe because too many undomesticated men have had too much of the say for far too long! But this is an image that tells us a lot for how and where we meet God.

The best homes are places where we relax because we are ourselves, we are known, and we know the others with whom we live. It's a common experience, for example, that when we have been away from our homes, as soon as we enter our front door we want to go to the bathroom. There is something intimate and familiar about our home that enables us to relax on many levels as we turn the key. Home is an earthy place where we don't get away with much and our vulnerability can be on display. Christian homes are particularly hospitable places, where Christ dwells to the degree that dignity, love, and forgiveness are present.

A home, however, is more than a house in which people live. Homes need work and attention. A friend of mine says memories rarely "just happen," they need to be created. That's the sort of attention to a family's life that turns a house into a home.

And this is the world in which God enters our lives. God wants us to be relaxed and vulnerable in his presence. We don't need to put on a show or say what we think God wants to hear—that's a theater where we perform, not a home where we know each other. Easter faith is about being comfortable and intimate, about being who we are, rather than the persona we would prefer God to see.

As with most of our homes, being at home with God has its ups and downs, days when we think we cannot bear to stay one more moment, other days when we could never imagine being anywhere else, and then most days when we are neither up nor down and we just get on with the routine of our lives. God the homemaker remains faithful through it all, offering the gift of Easter peace, sending us out to proclaim Christ's kingdom, welcoming us home eager to learn how everything went, and reassuring us always that while God is at home with us our hearts should never be troubled and we are not to be afraid.

For Christians, nostalgia is not about living in the past, it is about yearning for the sort of home where our heart truly is.

SEVENTH SUNDAY OF EASTER

ACTS 7:55–60
REVELATION 22:12–14, 16–17, 20
JOHN 17:20–26

This Sunday the church begins its annual week of praying for unity among Christians. Many of you will remember days, not that long ago, when children on either side of Bigotry Street threw stones at each other with taunts like "Proddy dogs," "Micks," or "Papists." Remember when Catholics couldn't go to the church to see their Presbyterian best friend get married or, dreadfully, when we treated Catholics who entered a "mixed marriage" as pariahs and humiliated them with a ceremony at a side altar or in the sacristy. Before the Second Vatican Council the world was simply defined as being Catholic and "non-Catholic," and in surprised tones we would declare, "She's not Catholic, but, still, is a very nice person." The Masons and the Catholics slogged it out in the teamsters and trade unions, the armed forces and the service industries. "Catholics need not apply" was not an unknown addendum to a job advertisement. And it wasn't long ago that we earnestly believed that all those outside the Roman Catholic Church were going to have a tough time getting into heaven.

Then it all changed. The Second Vatican Council ushered in dialogues and meetings. Now apologies are expressed, pulpits are swapped, and children play in Ecumenical Avenue. We now talk of coming together as one church and Christian Unity Sunday is an established feast on all our liturgical calendars.

It is hard for the younger generation to fully appreciate the pain of former days, where families were divided and employment, educational, or friendship doors were closed because you were a Catholic or you fell in love with a Lutheran. Much healing still needs to occur in many hearts before Christian unity becomes a reality.

In today's Gospel, while Jesus recognizes that the disciples will desert him, nothing can divide the Father and the Son. Their unity of mission, will, and love is what gives the churches renewed confidence to work at being one. One thing Jesus wants from us is to be united in our witness to his kingdom. Anything less than this is a scandal and diminishes the power of the gospel in the eyes of the world.

Working for unity among our fellow Christians does not mean we have to throw everything out and start again. But we have to leave behind that which no longer enables the unity, of which Jesus prayed at the Last Supper, to be achieved.

Thank God we know the hallmarks of this unity: sacrificial love, justice, compassion, forgiveness, truth, service, and charity.

A few years ago Pope John Paul II wrote movingly to other Christian churches asking them to imagine with him what a unified church would look like, and how the bishop of Rome could best serve that outcome. He made it clear that unity was not a question of other Christians "coming back to us." Ecumenism has gone well beyond that, replaced with dialogues, mutual respect, working together, sharing facilities and works for peace and justice. It is important for us to be reminded that ecumenism is not an optional extra in our Catholic faith. It is now a defined part of our identity, and we are all meant to do what we can to see the Lord's wish become a reality.

It always challenges me to remember that most of the disciples who Jesus predicts will abandon him came back together after the resurrection and were a unified witness to him in the world. Most of them ended up dying for our faith. May our following of Jesus and work for Christian unity be no less courageous and worthy of their witness.

ASCENSION OF THE LORD

ACTS 1:1–11
EPHESIANS 1:17–23 *or*
HEBREWS 9:24–28; 10:19–23
LUKE 24:46–53

A teacher told me recently that when she asked her fourth grade to draw a picture of the ascension, not unsurprisingly most of them did a fairly conventional portrait of Jesus rising up on a cloud. One of her students, David, who is a particularly gifted artist, had Jesus blasting off into the sky. Down the side of Jesus' pure white garment was the word *NASA* and David provided all the sound effects for how he imagined the scene of the first ascension. He concluded, without a hint of irony, that, "the ascension must have been a real blast!"

None of us can blame David for marrying our modern culture with an ancient story. In fact if some of us are honest, David's "space-shuttle Jesus" is not far from what we think as well. The ascension stories, however, are not primarily interested in how or when Jesus got back to heaven. John and Paul never mention it at all. Mark and Matthew have it happening on the same day as the resurrection and Luke has it occurring forty days after Easter on the same day as Pentecost. The one thing, on which all the New Testament writers agree is where in heaven Jesus went and where he is presently—at God's right hand.

Even to this day, being on someone's right is a place of honor. In the Older Testament being on the right hand of David, Samuel, or Elijah was to be the anointed and favored one, the true son or daughter. In telling us, then, that Jesus is now at God's right hand, the gospels use a formal phrase to announce that God affirms everything Jesus said and did on earth and that he is the way for us to follow.

Now, that can be all well and good, but Jesus goes one step further and that's why this feast is so important. Jesus taught us that where he is, so shall we be, that he was going to prepare a place for us, and that, in and through him, we will have life and have it to the full.

The feast of the Ascension is the day, each year, when we remember and we celebrate that, just as Jesus was welcomed to God's right hand, so, too, shall we be welcomed to the right hand of Jesus. This is his promise, this is our faith, and this is the hope we're called to proclaim to the world.

And let's be clear about the invitation. There is nothing we have ever done, are doing, or will do that will get our name removed from the invitation list to the feast of Christ's kingdom. The challenge is accepting that we have a standing invitation and living lives worthy of the love that places our name on the list. The feast of the Ascension announces that Jesus will faithfully accompany us, no matter how far we lose our way, and that by our fidelity to Christ we accept or reject the standing offer.

And because the ascension is an Easter feast it develops even further that there is nowhere, bar evil, where God does not dwell. Because of the resurrection and ascension we can find

God everywhere we want to: in our homes, our work, our suffering, our old age, our emotional, sexual, or financial turmoil—and even in our death.

Even though the writers of the New Testament are not too clear on the exact details of how the ascension happened, what we initially see in this wonderful feast is not what we get—thanks be to God, it's so much more.

PENTECOST

GENESIS 11:1–9 *or* EXODUS 19:3–8a, 16–20b
or EZEKIEL 37:1–14 *or* JOEL 3:1–5
ROMANS 8:22–27
JOHN 7:37–39

Last week, I was accosted by a fundamentalist Christian in the street. He asked me whether I had given my life to Jesus Christ. I have. He asked me if I spoke in tongues. I can, but choose not to. He asked me if I had made the necessary sacrifices for the Holy Spirit to come into my life. At this point I said my lifelong vows of poverty, chastity, and obedience for Christ were, I thought, a decent effort in that direction. Mind you, in saying that I had taken a vow of poverty I thought of my mother, who, on seeing Jesuit real estate for the first time, said, "If this is poverty, I'd like to see how you guys live chastity—it all seems pretty loose and fast to me."

The problem with our evangelical brothers and sisters is that they often think the Holy Spirit can be merely reduced to external signs. We know, however, from the first Pentecost and from our own experience that the Spirit works in both unpredictable and ordinary ways. The Holy Spirit, sent to live with us to continue to reveal God's truth to us, to advocate for us, and, in turn, to glorify us in Christ, seems to make a specialty of being present in the unexpected.

Some people wrongly claim that our time and place are the most wicked of all. I don't minimize for a moment the evil by which we are seduced and the traffic of death over which our world trades, but if we have Pentecost faith we will keep focusing on what exciting things the Spirit is doing in our own day. It is often a case of keeping up with her, and following her lead.

For most of us, seeing the traces of the Holy Spirit often happens retrospectively. It is only when we look back we see how, even in difficult and trying times, her presence can be found in our lives. For most of us it is a challenge to keep discerning the Spirit's presence. Poet Michael Moynahan expresses it this way:

> O Spirit of God,
> who's hidden
> Deep within the faces,
> Places, scattered thoughts,
> The strong and contradictory things
> That complicate and just confuse—
> The feelings of an aging heart,
> Draw near here now
> And counsel me.
>
> So many times
> I've longed and prayed
> Or looked for ways
> Of wading deeper
> into simple mystery....
>
> To love you
> Is no easy task.
> It costs
> (but who keeps count?)
> too much at times.
> Why must I constantly
> Court death
> And watch so many
> Golden thoughts and
> Sterling feelings
> Go up in smoke?
>
> Love means that I must
> Wander through the rubble

Of my squandered dreams
And in the fragile ashes
Of painful burnt-out memories
Find the tiny seeds
Of new beginnings…

God of every thought
Lord of my heart's desire,
In my search for you
I ask three things:
Give my knowledge clarity
Give my love intensity
And let my journey
Follow in your footsteps
So that my service
Can be patterned
After yours.

MOST HOLY TRINITY

 PROVERBS 8:22–31
ROMANS 5:1–5
JOHN 16:12–15

In the business world *empowerment* is presently a buzzword. Everyone is supposed to empower someone else. Even salespeople are told to "empower" their customers to buy. I guess they do.

This can seem very modern, except as Christians we believe that empowerment has been around as long as our faith. It's one of the hallmarks of the Trinity.

We hold that the Trinity is coequal, coeternal, and cosubstantial. In other words, the Father and the Spirit never get jealous if the Son gets more attention than they do. And the Son and Father are fine with charismatics who give the Holy Spirit the credit for everything. The Persons within the Trinity empower each other, and are equally present in every act of God in the world, be it in creating, redeeming, or making holy. One Person of the Trinity was not created by another Person. They just are, and always have been.

Some people say that this beggars belief, that the mystery of the Trinity is too much to deal with logically. The problem is, of course, that the Trinity is not a problem for our minds to solve, but a relationship to be drawn into, and to savor. In the power of the Spirit, through the gift of the Father in the saving love of the Son, we have found our way home—an eternal home of equality and substance. Not that we are coeternal, cosubstantial, or coequal with the Trinity, but through our baptisms we had been empowered by them to share in their inner and divine life, which, because they choose it this way, cannot help but overflow in goodness and creativity toward us.

Imagination, it seems, is the key to believing in the Trinity. There are lots of things in the world I can't explain—scientific things, genetic dispositions, why one human being would love another, how some people can forgive, or how good some of us are to others, asking for nothing in return.

I can't explain these things, but I can imagine them, because I have witnessed them.

Indeed, I can imagine a world where we speak the truth to each other gently and respectfully.

I can imagine a world where we share from our abundance with those who have nothing.

I can imagine a world where understanding takes the place of retribution.

And if I can imagine what others think is unimaginable about our world, I can also imagine an empowering God—Father, Son, and Holy Spirit.

Many people have tried to give us helpful images in regard to the Trinity. St. John of Damascus said the Trinity is a dance, a pas-du-trois. St. Ignatius Loyola described it as three notes in a single chord. St. Patrick famously used the three-leaf clover as a teaching aid to get the point across to the Irish, and St. Augustine thought the Trinity acted in unison in the same way that memory, intelligence, and will do within each of us.

All these images are helpful, but when I witness the life of the Trinity in action, the leap of faith is even easier. When I see

Christians treating others as equals, especially those they don't like, according them rights and dignity as children of God, then I can move beyond imagining the life of the Trinity, and experience it firsthand.

You see, if we dare imagine the Trinity, we can also imagine ourselves empowered by Power itself to be beacons of equality, exemplars of what's best in human nature, and with our feet on the ground turning our eyes to eternity.

BODY AND BLOOD OF CHRIST (CORPUS CHRISTI)

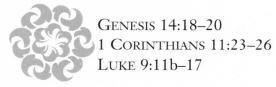

GENESIS 14:18–20
1 CORINTHIANS 11:23–26
LUKE 9:11b–17

The miracle of the loaves and the fish has to be one of the most action-packed episodes in Luke's Gospel. In five-and-a-half verses, Luke revisits Israel's history, narrates an extraordinary miracle story, and outlines the agenda for the kingdom to come on earth, as it is in heaven. Five-and-a-half verses.

There are six elements within the text that tell us that it is all about the "New Israel." First, we are told that the Twelve came to Jesus. That's shorthand for the twelve tribes, or the nation, of Israel. Second, we hear that the people were in "a deserted place," which would not have been lost on those who recalled Israel's wandering in the desert, and their complaints about the lack of food there. Third, seven gifts are presented to Jesus, always an echo of the creation story. Fourth, the five thousand sit down "in groups of about fifty." Fifty was the Jubilee number in Israel—a time for rest, renewal, and forgiveness. Finally, there are the twelve "baskets of broken pieces" leftover, another allusion to Israel, and what it should become.

Jesus in Luke's version of this parable tells us that the New Israel—that's us, the church—will be re-created into a community of abundance of food, forgiveness, freedom, and justice for all. But the sharing of this abundance comes at a cost; the pieces are broken and shared.

This Gospel on the feast of the Body and Blood of Christ tells us that it is not just the static elements of the Eucharist that are meant to be the object of our worship as much as what the broken "Bread of Life" and poured-out "Cup of Salvation" enable us to do, and become. If we really honor the gifts of the Eucharist we will be tireless in being broken for the sake of an abundance of food, freedom, forgiveness, and justice for all. Our worship at the altar is especially linked to, and is to be judged by, how we are re-created in being Christ's daily bread for the world.

Before the Jubilee Year in 2000 there was an international campaign across sixty countries to get the Group of Seven (G-7), as it was then, to "cancel the unpayable debts of the poorest countries by the year 2000, under a fair and transparent process." More than twenty-four million signatures were collected. Nearly every mainstream church in the world supported the campaign. The pope praised the initiative in his encyclical for the new millennium.

But there were many critics of the entire project, several within the church itself. How can it be that people who share the same Eucharist come to opposite conclusions about what it impels us to do? I think on this occasion one group may understand better the miracle of the loaves and the fish. In spite of the critics, by force of public demand the campaign for debt reduction was a great success. Nearly one billion dollars in international debt was cancelled, other debts were restructured, and the developed world's obligation to ongoing debt reduction is now a permanent feature of the G-8 summits.

In the spirit of the feeding of the five thousand, and in honor of the feast of Corpus Christi, I think Christ must smile when he sees such a creative and brave application to the world of his call to share abundantly.

I use the word *smile* deliberately. The word *miracle* comes from the Latin word *mirus* meaning "wonderful," which in turn comes from the Indo-European root *smer*, meaning "to laugh or smile."

As we celebrate this great feast, let's give Christ even more to smile about as we go to our sisters and brothers in deserted places, gather them together in groups of fifty, and re-create our world in the image of the New Israel Christ wants it to be. But we are not left to achieve it on our own. For such a task Christ has given us himself—body and blood, soul and divinity.

NINTH SUNDAY IN ORDINARY TIME

 1 KINGS 8:41–43
GALATIANS 1:1–2, 6–10
LUKE 7:1–10

Most of us have been there. Most of us have worried over a loved one's health so much that we would do anything to get them well. In our day and age this can mean travelling all over the nation or the world for a cure, praying for them as we have never prayed before, trying all kinds of therapies and remedies, and maybe making pilgrimages to certain places that we think might make them well, or to certain people whose fame precedes them.

In this week's Gospel the centurion was desperate, but what is so impressive is that he is not primarily anxious for himself. He is interceding for his beloved slave. We might wonder why. Our usual concept of a slave owner is that he or she sees their slaves as completely expendable. But here is man who loves his servant so much he will do anything to save him. This was no ordinary centurion. We are told in the passage that he was kind to the Jews and even built their local synagogue. The local elders were grateful for it, and admired him.

There are plenty of other fascinating details in this passage as well. The centurion and Jesus never meet. The Jewish elders go to Jesus in the first instance, and the Roman soldier's friends turn up on his behalf later, telling Jesus not to visit. The centurion gets cold feet. He starts out wanting Jesus to come to his house, but then he feels he is unworthy of such a visit and asks for a longer-range miracle. The phrase we recite during the Communion Rite, "Lord, I am not worthy to receive you, but only say the word and I shall be healed," is adapted from this story.

And then toward the end of this episode one of its best features unfolds: Jesus is surprised at the man's faith. He is genuinely taken aback at the depth and breath of a Gentile's faith in his ability to heal and save. Maybe he was especially surprised that this faith-filled Gentile belonged to the occupying army.

There are some Christians who think that Jesus could never be surprised. This argument runs that such was his divine nature that the full knowledge of God was realized in Jesus as well. The problem is that such knowledge would have compromised his human nature and made Jesus unlike us in another significant way, apart from being free from sin. The reality is that there is a difference between Jesus' profound insight into how to read events, people, and the human condition, and him having divine knowledge. The first is a gift we can discern in some other rare and extraordinary human beings. The latter belongs to God in heaven.

In this week's Gospel, then, we see an encounter that affects both Jesus and the faceless soldier. It has many things to tell us when we feel desperate. It doesn't matter how distant we feel from Christ—his companionship is only a prayer away. If we feel unworthy of his presence and power in our lives—ask some friends, here on earth and in heaven, to support us in our need and to pray with us. We don't have to do anything or go anywhere to experience the saving presence of God's love—we just have to have faith that Christ's word always accomplishes what it sets out to do.

And sometimes that accomplishment can surprise us so completely that, when we see its effect, in often unexpected ways, we know we are standing on holy ground.

TENTH SUNDAY IN ORDINARY TIME

1 Kings 17:17–24
Galatians 1:11–19
Luke 7:11–17

In her moving poem "Firstborn Sons and the Widow of Nain,"
Irene Zimmerman narrates today's Gospel in this way:

> Jesus halted on the road outside Nain
> where a woman's wailing drenched the air.
> Out of the gates poured a somber procession
> of dark-shawled women, hushed children,
> young men bearing a litter that held
> a body swathed in burial clothes,
> and the woman, walking alone.
>
> A widow then—another bundle
> of begging rags at the city gates.
> A bruised reed!
>
> Her loud grief labored and churned in him till
> "Halt!" he shouted.
>
> The crowd, the woman, the dead man stopped.
> Dust, raised by sandaled feet,
> settled down again on the sandy road.
> Insects waited in shocked silence.
>
> He walked to the litter, grasped a dead hand.
> "Young man," he called
> in a voice that shook the walls of Sheol,
> "I command you, rise!"
>
> The linens stirred.
> Two firstborn sons from Nazareth and Nain
> met, eye to eye.

He placed the pulsing hand into hers.
"Woman, behold your son," he smiled.

In the New Testament there are three people whom Jesus raises from the dead: Jairus's daughter in Mark 5, Lazarus in John 11, and the son of the widow of Nain in Luke 7. In each case Jesus is deeply moved by compassion, but there is a striking difference between the first two events and the widow's son. Jairus begs Jesus to come and lay his hands on his daughter so that she might be healed. Martha admonishes Jesus for not being there to prevent Lazarus's death, but then professes him to be "the resurrection and life." These scenes are in great contrast to the funeral procession that Jesus happens upon at Nain.

The widowed mother never asks for a thing from Jesus. All we know of her is her weeping, which is entirely understandable, of course, and not just because she has lost a child, but also because she has lost "her only son." In the patriarchal world of the ancient world her financial security and social protector has died. Life is about to become even harder and more precarious for her.

These details make the story even richer, and more applicable to us today. Because we are told in the gospels that there are places where Jesus could not perform a miracle "because of their lack of faith in him," we can be left with the impression that it is only when people profess the right words, or directly ask Jesus to do something, that he does or can respond. When we think like this, remember the widow of Nain. The most spectacular of all God's interventions in the world was given to a poor woman who didn't ask for it, and whose friends go on to recognize Jesus, not as the Messiah, but as "a great prophet." No doubt they were thinking of Elijah raising the widow's son in the First Book of Kings.

Sometimes we think we have to "walk the walk and talk the talk" to get God to listen to us. There are people within our Catholic community and outside it who never feel really at home or welcome among us because they can't "walk the walk and talk the talk" as they see some of us doing it. This is the Gospel for those of us in that situation, or whenever all of us find ourselves in that space. Remember the widow of Nain.

Remember that this story tells us that our God comes to us where we are, as we are, and is deeply moved by our plight. And the gifts Jesus brought to that widow that day are, we believe, the same gifts God continues to visit upon us now. God hears our cry and comforts us in our distress by looking out for what will be in our best long-term interests. God is interested in our spiritual, emotional, and economic needs. There is no dignity in dire poverty.

So when we think we have to get the words right for God to come and be present to us, or when we feel that God has abandoned us, or even if we sense that we are being left for dead, be consoled by the compassion of Jesus and remember the widow of Nain.

ELEVENTH SUNDAY IN ORDINARY TIME

2 SAMUEL 12:7–10, 13
GALATIANS 2:16, 19–21
LUKE 7:36—8:3

Today's Gospel contains one of the most important teachings in the New Testament, as well as one of the greatest insights into the human heart.

Jesus says that the sinful woman's "sins, which were many, have been forgiven; hence she has shown great love." Think about that, and what it means. Indirectly Jesus says that if this famous, but sadly unnamed, woman had not been forgiven, she could not have shown love. What Jesus does in this scene is celebrate with her that God's forgiveness enabled her to turn her life around, and go into her future in peace.

And what was true for the woman at Jesus' feet, is true for us—right here, right now. We can't pretend that we can love ourselves, or anyone else, if we are not about the business of forgiveness. Jesus teaches us, today, that we can *only* love to the degree that we have been forgiven.

This really is astounding.

Some of us have done things we wish we hadn't. Most of us have traits in our personality or character we wish weren't there. A few of us have done some very destructive things indeed—to ourselves, or to others.

Jesus announces this Sunday that there is no room for regret or shame in the Christian life, only knowing the sort of forgiveness that enables us to pick up the pieces of an unhealed past, have the courage to show what may seem by convention to be scandalous acts of love toward others, and move on into our future in peace.

The woman at Jesus' feet, who we should note is not Mary Magdalene, gives us an indication of how we might go about the task. The verbs tell the story.

Luke tells us that this extraordinarily courageous woman learns, waits, weeps, wipes, kisses, and anoints. There is something contemplative about all this. These are not angry actions, but rituals of someone who has claimed back her dignity in and through being forgiven. She doesn't need to hold on to her past, but can let go of it sufficiently so as to encounter God's saving love in Jesus, and so peacefully walk into her future.

Let's think of the things of which we need to be forgiven. Let's recall those parts about ourselves we say we hate, dislike, resent, regret, or will not or cannot forgive. These are precisely the hidden doors on which Jesus is knocking today. And while recalling them, let's learn about them, wait upon them, weep over them, wipe away our tears, and allow Jesus to kiss and anoint our wounded selves.

It isn't easy. And we can run away from this process pretending that it's too focused on me, and my psyche. But if today's story is to be believed, there is no other way to Christ-like love than through the hard nine yards of personal forgiveness.

And what this teaching does, of course, is set in train an entire way of living, for just as we love by the degree to which we have been forgiven, so too, we learn to stop hating, resenting, and

rejecting others, but rather love them because we have been forgiven enough to do so.

It would seem that only then will we have a chance of living
the sort of peaceful life that most of us crave.

The sinful woman came to Jesus at a meal. And so as Christ
hosts us at the eucharistic meal, may we have the same courage
that she had, and be worthy of her loving example and reclaim our
dignity, let go of our unhealed past, and begin to love ourselves,
Christ, and others as lavishly as he forgives and loves us.

TWELFTH SUNDAY IN ORDINARY TIME

ZECHARIAH 12:10–11
GALATIANS 3:26–29
LUKE 9:18–24

Today's second reading is considered to be the oldest baptismal
formula we have in the New Testament. The reference to baptism
is one indication of this, as is the invocation of the robe by which
we were all clothed in Christ, but even more so is what follows.
St. Paul goes on to give the community at Galatia a definition of
what these external signs should mean in the life of the community: "There is no longer Jew or Greek, there is no longer slave or
free, there is no longer male and female; for all of you are one in
Christ Jesus."

We need to own that our Catholic community has not been
worthy of this charge for a good part of its history, and we often
still fail to live up to this ideal. Frail and sinful human beings that
we are, we allowed multiple distinctions to appear among us in a
very short period of time. And some of them are still with us
today.

For example, we have accepted into our church order social
customs and other religious traditions that actively exclude
women from participation in ritual and decision making, declar-
ing them at various times in our history to be unclean, a source of

temptation, and misbegotten men. This worked itself out into terrible crimes against women's dignity, and even meant that some women were put to death in the name of God.

Tragically, the same can be said of the Jews, where a false reading of the passion stories legitimated waves of Jewish persecution over the centuries, and gave rise to anti-Semitism. And when we turn to slaves and free people, we have to own that at one stage the church taught that slavery was a divine institution, and so was very slow to stand with the emancipation cause.

So why concentrate on this bad news today? Because, as our Jewish brothers and sisters tell us, if we forget where we have come from, we are likely to commit the same sins again, and we need to take that momentum into our future as we become the inclusive community Jesus lived out, and St. Paul taught we should be.

But all of this has a cost, which is what Jesus tells us in today's Gospel: "If any want to become my followers, let them deny themselves and take up their cross daily and follow me." All too often we can hear this line as either a once-and-for-all moment, or as only applying to the big actions in our lives. I think, however, that it has as much to do with how we think and what our attitudes are, as much as it's concerned with what we do.

For example, choosing to let go of deep-seated racist, sexist, and bigoted prejudices might be the most telling way we could renounce our worldly selves, and take up the inclusive cross of Christ. And how do we know we have achieved this? Friends are normally a good indication about our resolve in this regard. Those we have in our home says so much about what and whom we include in our lives.

We can say we love people of color all we like, but having them as our friends changes the way we see the world. We can maintain that we want women to be equal, but have we ever had a long conversation with someone who thinks seriously about gender issues in the church and society? And while we might be very ecumenical in theory, actually having Lutheran, Jewish, and atheist friends is more valuable to us than all the best wishes in the world.

Let's pray for the grace to lose our life in such a way that we find it again in Christ, in whom there is no such thing as a Jew or Greek, a slave or free person, a man or a woman. There is in

Christ only one human family under God where everyone from pope to pauper is unconditionally loved and has equal dignity and status. That's the kingdom we're sent to build. May we be worthy if it.

THIRTEENTH SUNDAY IN ORDINARY TIME

 1 KINGS 19:16b, 19–21
GALATIANS 5:1, 13–18
LUKE 9:51–62

In his book, *Things You Get for Free*, Michael McGirr tells the story of going on pilgrimage to Rome with his mother. Maureen McGirr had always wanted to see St. Peter's Basilica. Michael records the big day:

> One of the features of a visit to St. Peter's is the modesty inspection. This is the kind of examination which most Australians on a visit to Bali would flunk. You aren't allowed to wear shorts or sleeveless garments. No swimming costumes, either, unless they have long legs and sleeves. No singlets. The modesty inspection has a point. It keeps out nudists and other undesirables....I would be more comfortable if the signs warned against coming in with a closed mind or an angry heart.
>
> When you get inside, however, St. Peter's strips you bear. Mum took a few steps forward into the cavernous gloom and stopped. I looked up into the dome that Michelangelo designed late in life: he never lived to see it finished. In that moment, hundreds of visitors rushed past. "What on earth are they trying to prove?" I wasn't sure if Mum was talking about the building or all the people rushing past. Officials were still clearing away the cheap plastic stacking chairs which come out for big masses. They were not part of the original design. I was distracted by the noise.

"When you think," said Mum, leaving her sentence unfinished…

"When you think what?" I asked…

"I don't know. When you think."

"What?" I was getting testy with her.

Mum drew in breath to say something important.

"When you think that Jesus had nothing."

It was a naked response. For seventy years, this building had stood as the physical centre of Mum's religion. This was her pilgrimage to Mecca. Yet her response was almost revulsion. I want to put a break on her reaction and jolly her along and tell her that Jesus would rather have had this as a monument than the Empire State Building or the Crown Casino.

No matter how much we try to ignore it, or play it down, the call to simplicity of lifestyle and detachment are important elements in the teaching of Jesus and the way he lived his own life.

In Luke's Gospel and in his second volume, the Acts of the Apostles, the obligations of the haves to the have-nots are regularly underlined. Scholars think Luke's Gospel keeps this teaching most alive because it was a community divided by wealth.

In today's Gospel this obligation is put in its starkest form. To "bury the dead" in first-century Palestine sometimes meant having to take on their responsibilities—farm, fishing, or family. To have "nowhere to lay one's head" gave as much freedom then as it does today; and to be detached, without regret, has always been a sign of God's kingdom.

Some preachers can blast off into what seems like loopy-land when they start drawing out lessons from this teaching. While Jesus' words have a radical edge that must not be blunted, if all Christians everywhere were to live this teaching literally we would constitute a family of happy but homeless people, surrounded by decomposing loved ones! There is no dignity in poverty and most people who are poor, while they can be rich in the best human values, do not want to stay poor. What they deserve, and what all Christians should want, is economic and social justice. We are not at liberty to follow Jesus and watch the rich get fatter and all-consuming while the poor pay the price for unchecked greed.

Some Christians are given the gift of living very simply, and to the degree that this gift brings life to them, and those around them, it is a wonderful sign of God's kingdom. All the rest of us, who struggle to embrace this gift, or a desire to ever want it, must face up to the challenge of Jesus' teaching here. But it's not just about money. We are also called to detach ourselves from memories, which can be cluttered with anger and revenge; from the demands of work, which keep us from being with those we love; and to be generous with our time, talent, hospitality, and compassion.

Previous generations strayed from the demands of this Gospel. Grand cathedrals, courtly behavior, and princely mansions were meant to reflect on earth the reign of God. These are our legacy, but may it not be said of us, what Michael McGirr says of St. Peter's, "any sense of the Divine completely disappears under the materialism of it all." Rather, may our generation show the kingdom of God most visibly in the way we live simply, fight for justice, are detached from everything, except the essentials.

FOURTEENTH SUNDAY IN ORDINARY TIME

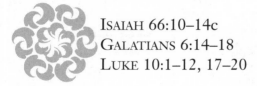

Isaiah 66:10–14c
Galatians 6:14–18
Luke 10:1–12, 17–20

A man was in his dinghy on a lake when a large yacht rammed him and his dinghy sank. As the man began to drown, the crew of the yacht threw him a life jacket, but the man yelled back, "I don't need help, for God will soon save me."

Straightaway another boat pulled up beside the man to haul him aboard, but he refused to go, saying, "I don't need help, for God will soon save me." Just then, the Air & Sea helicopter flew overhead and dropped a ladder, but the man pushed it away, yelling out, "I don't need help, for God will soon save me." And with that the man drowns. He meets God and angrily enquires, "Where were you when I needed you most? I kept believing you would save me and I've ended up here." "Don't blame me for your tragic death," replied God. "I sent you a life jacket, a boat, and a helicopter."

Sometimes today's Gospel has been used to talk about vocations to the priestly and religious life. While it can apply to these specific roles of service in the church, to exclusively read the laborers in the harvest as priests and religious narrows down too much the power of Jesus' message. His commission of the seventy disciples must be read over and against his commission to the Twelve. The seventy are called to be evangelizers, to go and prepare the way for Jesus to visit the surrounding villages and towns. This commission is for the whole community. It is the priesthood of all believers. The Twelve are later commissioned to serve as leaders of the community.

Through baptism we have all been commissioned to go out to live and proclaim the good news of Christ, to keep journeying on to all our sisters and brothers and prepare the way for Christ to come into their lives. The number of laborers for this harvest has never been greater. We have never had more Christians in the world than we have right now. If all of us, who have been baptized in Christ, were living out the gospel and bringing it to bear in our personal, family, social, and national life, then the world would be transformed. We seem to have lost our courage, our nerve for the task at hand. We have been consumed by sheepishness and daunted by the wolves.

Jesus reminds us that to live out this commission we need to depend on each other for support, hospitality, and kindness. He challenges us to travel light and stick together.

So let us pray for ourselves, the laborers who are putting in a hard day's work toward the harvest. Let us pray for the gift of faith and gratitude for the privilege of the commission. Let us also pray that all baptized people will live out their faith in such a manner that it prepares the way for Christ to come into every village and town. And let's ask for eyes to see the extraordinary flowering of vocations throughout the church and celebrate how grace comes in many shapes and sizes, even as a life jacket, a boat, and a helicopter.

FIFTEENTH SUNDAY
IN ORDINARY TIME

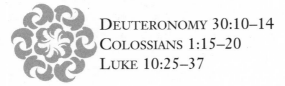

DEUTERONOMY 30:10–14
COLOSSIANS 1:15–20
LUKE 10:25–37

Margaret Thatcher once claimed that the parable of the Good
Samaritan showed Jesus' endorsement of the benefits of capital-
ism! The then British prime minister's argument ran that the hero
of this famous story is the one who could afford to pay for the victim's care. She surmised that the reason the Samaritan had the
wherewithal to do such a charitable act was because he worked
hard and saved his money wisely. Mrs. Thatcher said this central
Christian parable was a justification of her government's policies
demanding that unemployed people work for social security and
that they should be educated about saving their pennies.

Politicians should be careful of using the Bible to back up
their positions. It has a habit of saying the opposite of what they
think or want it to. Like many people, Lady Thatcher reads this
parable in terms of charity, and even then she got it wrong. Jesus
says it is a lesson in mercy. The difference matters.

It is not by accident that the phrase "as cold as charity" is still
current. Deciding on whom we will be kind to, just based on our
warm "fuzzies" and the glow of our purses, may make us feel
good; but it will result in a very wintry experience for the not-so-
lucky recipient. When we "do" charitable things, we can often
remain powerful and untouched by the situation of those our
money helps.

St. Thomas Aquinas, however, calls charity the mother of all
virtues. He argues it is more concerned with the feelings of the
heart than external action. Aquinas maintains that charity enables
us to sort through our desires, to see what we really want, whom
we actually love; it helps us use the other virtues to act accord-
ingly. Christian charity is not a feel-good moment; it is a life-
changing experience. Understood this way, the Good Samaritan

can be a great example of charity, but quite differently from that outlined in the Gospel according to Margaret!

For Jesus, nonetheless, he is a model of mercy. The Good Samaritan is not "good" because he has the money to act on what he sees. His greatness is that he has eyes to see it at all. To really see it. The priest and the morality-teaching Levite pretend it's not happening and walk on the other side of the road. But the most unlikely, the least liked person in Israel—a Samaritan—has the view of mercy.

Christian tradition teaches us that mercy and justice are intertwined. Thomas Aquinas says that mercy helps us hear, and justice calls for us to do something. The Samaritan does what he can at the scene of the crime and then he takes the victim with him. He not only sees, but judges and acts. In doing so, he breaks nearly every religious and social law in the book; but it doesn't matter. The virtues of mercy and justice enable us to see all sorts of things more clearly, even civil and religious laws that inhibit the justice of God.

This entire episode in Luke's Gospel is about the movement from an individualized faith, which can think that it is just "me and Jesus against the world," to a faith that goes out to the world acting mercifully and justly. This parable is about what we see, whom we love, and what we want to do about it.

The example of the Good Samaritan should enliven our charity, mercy, and justice; and it should challenge us to see clearly who needs to be carried with us on the gospel road.

SIXTEENTH SUNDAY IN ORDINARY TIME

Genesis 18:1–10a
Colossians 1:24–28
Luke 10:38–42

A farmer, a stockbroker, and woman who was a lawyer were standing in line, waiting for their chance at entrance into heaven.

St. Peter called the farmer first. "We have only one simple requirement for entrance here," St. Peter said. "You must spell *God.*" "Easy enough," said the farmer, "G-O-D." And he entered heaven.

Next, St. Peter called the stockbroker from Sydney. "We have only one simple requirement for entrance here," he said. "You must spell *God.*" "No problem," said the stockbroker, "G-O-D." And he went in.

Finally, the woman lawyer approached St. Peter. "Good riddance to the world," she said. "My whole life, I've tried to excel in a male-dominated society, only to continuously bump into the proverbial glass ceilings at every point. I can't tell you, St. Peter, how glad I am finally to be rid of male chauvinism."

"Well, you'll certainly find none of that here," said St. Peter. "I'm sure you'll enjoy heaven, if you can meet this one simple requirement for entrance. You must spell *Czechoslovakia.*"

One of the things I find reassuring about today's Gospel is that the church seems to have been wrestling with women's leadership since the very beginning. It's the issue that will not go away.

The story of Martha and Mary is a complex narrative. It can be read on at least two levels. The first level is extraordinary enough: It focuses on Mary, who assumes the position of the rabbi's student and is defended against any attack on her right to be there. As biblical scholar Joseph Fitzmyer tells us, in first-century Palestine, Jewish women were "not permitted to be taught the Torah, but only instructed about how they should live their lives in obedience to its demands. They were not permitted to touch the scriptures nor to take part in public debate or official liturgical ritual." (Fitzmyer: *Luke:* 892) From this context and against the practice of his own day, we can see the sort of freedom Jesus envisaged for women.

On another level, however, this story focuses on Martha. The writer of Luke's Gospel tells us that we are in Martha's home and that, with Jesus as special guest at table, she is serving the members of her household with care and devotion. Martha comes across as strong and outspoken. Mary, meanwhile, is passive and silent. It is likely this story is criticizing a call in Luke's community for women to move away from the leadership Jesus gave them and to adopt again the traditional roles to which the Jewish/Christians were more familiar.

At the Vatican on May 21, 2000, Pope John Paul II told a group of bishops from the United States, "The genius of women must be ever more a vital strength of the Church of the next millennium, just as it was in the first communities of Christ's disciples."

To that end today's story from such a community holds a key to our own dilemma. Just as Jesus broke through the gender boundaries of his own day, so too must we. We must renew our commitment to ending anything that degrades, exploits, or dehumanizes women throughout the world.

But more, it's time for the church to take some strong symbolic and practical steps to defend the leadership of women within our own Catholic community. For example, it would only take a couple of changes to canon law to clear the way for laywomen and men to be readmitted to the College of Cardinals. The last lay cardinal only died in 1876. Women could continue to assume high-profile positions in each diocese and also leadership roles within the Roman Curia, starting with those departments that deal with instructions and decisions that directly affect them; and the church could welcome the ordination of women as deacons.

These avenues would enable women to have even more options to demonstrate and realize the full extent of their genius, as the pope puts it.

At the Eucharist, then, let us recommit ourselves to using, in the best possible way for the mission of the church, the gifts, talents, and strengths of over half our community. May we learn from the earliest church that "the better part...will not be taken away from her."

SEVENTEENTH SUNDAY IN ORDINARY TIME

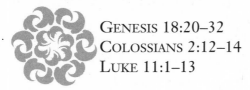

GENESIS 18:20–32
COLOSSIANS 2:12–14
LUKE 11:1–13

Did you know that Lincoln's Gettysburg Address was 250 words long? The man before Lincoln spoke for over an hour. The man who followed Lincoln spoke for even longer. Today, no one remembers what they said. Lincoln's two-and-a-half minutes, by contrast, changed the history of the United States and the mentality of the Western world.

This call to brevity is always a good challenge to preachers too! Luke's version of the Lord's Prayer, which has thirty-eight words, is another example of how a few sentences have changed history.

Around fifty years after the death of Jesus, Luke's Gospel was most probably written for the Christian community in Antioch, which was the political and cultural capital of the Roman Province of Syria. There are six major themes running throughout this Gospel: prayer, hospitality, compassion, forgiveness, the common life, and care for the outsider. Most of them are expressed in the thirty-eight words of this prayer.

We declare that we belong to God in the most intimate of ways, as members of God's family, and therefore we belong to each other. We pray that God's kingdom will come here and now, through our gratitude for God's generosity and forgiveness and so that we can be saved from evil.

I think Christians should keep saying this prayer with great urgency. In most Western countries today there are strong right-wing political movements that say they are for Christ or that they want our country to return to "Christian values." Many of their platforms and policies, however, are irreconcilable with the hospitality, forgiveness, compassion, common life, and care for outsiders found in the Lord's Prayer.

It is so easy to allow our faith lives to become compartmentalized. For some, religious belief and practice fits into a nice little box that has no discernible influence on the rest of their lives. Coming to church is a privatized affair. What we celebrate each Sunday is supposed to have an effect on all areas of our lives, every day. Though we can try to make ourselves feel better by turning religion into a weekly spiritual bonbon, that is not what Jesus and the martyrs of our faith gave their lives for.

Some Catholics argue that the church's teaching should be more publicly proclaimed and obeyed. In its social teaching, the church tells us that we should support political parties that best represent these key values in the gospel. The church has also taught us about refugees, immigration, gun control, violence, capital punishment, and the rights of minority groups. All Catholics are called to hold true to this teaching as well as to doctrinal matters.

Some Catholics complain that the church should not speak out on political issues. It is, however, the role of the church to help people form their consciences and to declare what it sees as evil, sinful, or harmful in society. Christ expects nothing less of all of us. And where the church has not done this, history has judged it very harshly, as in the church's relatively recent condemnation of slavery.

The old line goes, "Be careful what you pray because you might just get what you ask for."

Let's join then with all Christians and be worthy of the one prayer that unites us and, in the spirit of these thirty-eight words, pray fervently that all people everywhere will become one—in Christ—and under our one Father in heaven.

EIGHTEENTH SUNDAY
IN ORDINARY TIME

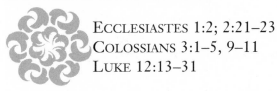

ECCLESIASTES 1:2; 2:21–23
COLOSSIANS 3:1–5, 9–11
LUKE 12:13–31

We only have to look at so-called reality television to see just how far some of our compatriots will go to be famous, to be wealthy, or to be part of the popular imagination. We should never be surprised when our media culture reflects this back to us. And by watching these programs, reading some newspapers and magazines, listening to the shock jocks and buying the merchandise, we need to be aware that we are part of the problem, not part of the solution.

In today's Gospel Jesus tells us just how deadly riches and greed can be. Our own experience tells how right he is: Think of how many children fight in the playground because everything they see "is mine," the families who have fought over an estate, the number of friends who have fallen out over even small amounts of money, colleagues who no longer speak to each other because of a failed investment, and nations who have gone to war to get what their neighbors have.

The issue with money is not in having it, because money, and the health, education, and welfare that flow from it, is a good thing, whereas poverty is an evil that God wants wiped off the face of the earth. The problem is what we do with money and what it does to us. Some Christians think that just because they are financially comfortable from legitimate earnings, they do not have to take any responsibility for the world's poor who are often stereotyped as being lazy, warmongering, and irreligious. These images may justify not sharing more of the excess we have, but it does not remove the moral obligation Jesus demands of us today. Of the world's 6 billion people, 1.2 billion of them live on $365 a year. We should try telling them they're lazy, warmongering, and irreligious! In an attempt to get rich quickly or to stay rich, most Western countries gamble away ten to fifteen times more money than they give to third-world development—money that might help foster markets with just wages, and so provide an incentive for work, curtail or prevent some wars, and help develop democracy.

When faced with the enormity of the world's poverty, the bad spirit can convince us that it is so large there is nothing that we can do about it. Not true. Every moment of consciousness and each act of goodness toward anyone anywhere is a victory for God's kingdom, and is God's will being done "on earth as it is in heaven."

No one can pretend, however, that throwing money around will solve the world's problems. Everyone who works on the frontline says that dignity is the biggest obstacle in the war on poverty. And dignity, as Jesus reminds us today, has very little to do with money or possessions. Each time we make a claim for our own dignity and we give dignity to people who do not even claim it for themselves, we contribute to the generous and just world Jesus wants. And sometimes that can be as easy as turning the channel on the radio or the TV.

Let's pray that we feel the sharp edge of the gospel and we accept its power to convert our hearts and minds. May we meet its challenges in regard to bestowing dignity upon the poor, and sharing our possessions with those who have a just claim on them.

NINETEENTH SUNDAY IN ORDINARY TIME

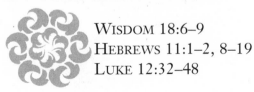

WISDOM 18:6–9
HEBREWS 11:1–2, 8–19
LUKE 12:32–48

As offensive as the Monty Python film, *The Life of Brian*, was to some Christians, the scene in which several competing messiahs try to convince the marketplace crowd that they are the real thing brilliantly and humorously captures Jewish expectations in first-century Palestine. Not unlike the fervor at the end of the last millennium, some religious people believed the end of time was close at hand. Far from selling his messianic wares at the market, however, Jesus crept in beside us and lived, suffered, died, and was raised from the tomb in a way no one anticipated. Even after his resurrection the earliest Christians believed Jesus would return very soon, so they could afford to live as if they were living in the last days. When this didn't happen there was crisis in the community. The earliest disciples, to whom much had been entrusted, had to hand on a faith in a more unpredictable God who does not fulfill all our expectations or run on our timetable.

Luke points out the greatest gift we Christians have received is knowing that Jesus is the Messiah, the Christ. What a relief to know we do not have to shop around anymore. From everyone to whom much has been given, however, much will be required, and so knowing who Jesus is only goes halfway. Living out the reality of the Christian life is the other half. Today's Gospel teaches us that our Christian life should be marked by five characteristics: that we willingly share with those in need; act justly; stay alert to the presence of God in the world; guard against those people or things that can rob us of our faith; and not abuse others, but live in peace. With or without a sense that Jesus is due back at any minute, the Christian life is meant to focus on the essentials.

Two thousand years later we are still waiting for Jesus' return and many of us live complicated lives that rob us of true happiness. Sadly, it often takes a tragedy for us to reassess what we have been given. In 1998 the Reverend Bob Moorehead in his book, *Words Aptly Spoken*, wrote this somber reappraisal of how he sees the world and what he thinks we should be passing on to the next generation:

> The paradox of our time in history is that we have taller buildings, but shorter tempers; wider freeways, but narrower viewpoints; we spend more, but have less; we buy more, but enjoy less.
>
> We have bigger houses and smaller families; more conveniences, but less time; we have more degrees, but less sense; more knowledge, but less judgment; more experts, but less solutions; more medicine, but less health.
>
> We have multiplied our possessions, but reduced our value; we talk too much, love too seldom, and hate too often.

We've learned how to make a living, but not a life; we've added years to life, not life to years.

We've been all the way to the moon and back, but have trouble crossing the street to meet our neighbor. We've conquered outer space, not inner space; we've cleaned up the air, but polluted the soul; we've split the atom, but not our prejudice. We have higher incomes, but lower morale; we've become long on quantity, but short on quality.

These are the times of tall men, and short character; steep profits, and shallow relationships. These are the times of world peace, but domestic violence; more leisure, but less fun; more kinds of food, but less nutrition.

These are the days of two incomes, but more divorce; of fancier houses, but broken homes. It is a time when there is so much in the showroom window and nothing in the stockroom.

We all know the world is not quite so neat, not so either/or, but these words focus the question well enough: What are the essentials of our life, or as Jesus puts it today, what is our treasure and where is our heart?

TWENTIETH SUNDAY IN ORDINARY TIME

JEREMIAH 38:4–6, 8–10
HEBREWS 12:1–4
LUKE 12:49–53

In our desire to affirm that the scriptures are inspired by the Holy Spirit, it can be easy to forget that they come out of the lived experience of a community of faith. Indeed, one of the things that is wonderful about our belief in God's revelation is that it occurs within human experience. Today's Gospel is an excellent example. Jesus predicts that one of the consequences of believing in him is that divisions will follow.

We can tell from the whole text of Luke's Gospel that these divisions were certainly a part of the earliest Christian community, which wrote this book, and that their faith in Christ led them to confront some very tough issues: how Gentiles inherit the promises made to the Jews; why the rich members of the community had special responsibility to the poor; the centrality of forgiveness in the Christian life; and what leadership role women should have in the earliest church. We know that fights over these issues and faith in Jesus as the Christ or the Messiah divided families and villages, cities, nations, and a religious tradition.

This Gospel is both a stark reminder of the costs involved in following Jesus and a comfort to us in the church today. Sometimes we can turn the Christian community into a "feel-good" society. If Christians at home, at work, in society, and on the international stage just go along with what is trendy or current because we're frightened of conflict or because we want to be seen to be part of the crowd, then we are not worthy of this Gospel.

Sometimes when we hear Jesus use the metaphor of a blazing fire we can see it as a violent image, but I am not sure if it has to be exclusively interpreted this way. Fire is sometimes necessary and good to clear out the layers of undergrowth, built up over time, that smother the soil of a forest and prevent new growth. Fire is a beacon that gives guidance and attracts attention. A blazing fire can attract everyone to its light, warmth, and power. So maybe this Gospel is a call to purge the weight of old growth that can stop fresh thinking. Maybe it gives guidance to us in the justice we are meant to live and the attention we must call to the needs of all God's children. And maybe it is a reminder that the life of our Christian community is meant to be attractive through its gentle power and warmth. If the price we pay for witnessing to any of these values is that we divide the crowd, so be it.

What's comforting about this Gospel is that it recognizes conflict as a necessary part of the Christian life. There are some who want to pretend that the followers of Jesus should never disagree with one another or with those outside the church. Conflict in itself, Jesus teaches us today, is an element of our commitment to the kingdom of God. What marks out the way we should disagree with one another inside and outside the church, however, is that the disagreement is conducted with charity, dignity, careful listening, and compassion. Christians always look to put the best possible interpretation on the opinions of those with whom we disagree and to be reconciled to those we have hurt, to heal divisions where we can.

May the Eucharist give us the courage to divide the crowd for the right reasons. May we be a blazing fire that casts light on darkness where people are exploited and injustice smothers the growth Christ wants to see in the human family. No one promised us that Christian faith was ever going to be a picnic!

TWENTY-FIRST SUNDAY IN ORDINARY TIME

 Isaiah 66:18–21
Hebrews 12:5–7, 11–13
Luke 13:22–30

A Buddhist, a Jew, and a Christian all die and get to heaven. Jesus asks each one, "If you could go back, what would you change?"

The Buddhist ponders a while and says, "There's so much violence in the world. If I went back, I'd try and stop people from going to war with each other."

The Jew thinks a bit and says, "There's so much poverty in the world. If I went back, I'd try and get people to share more of their wealth with the poor."

The Christian looks at Jesus and quickly replies, "If I went back, I'd change my doctor."

When it comes to religious faith, salvation has, rightly, always been the big issue. Who was going to be saved, how was it going to happen, and when will Christ return in glory have captured the imagination of each generation of believers.

The roots of this thinking can be found in today's Gospel. The earliest Christians, especially the Gentiles, saw that the Jews had been given every opportunity for salvation. They were the chosen people. They had the Law and the Prophets. They were looking for the Messiah. Jesus, however, did not come as they expected or act as they hoped, so they rejected him and his followers. Within a generation after Jesus' death, the Jews were persecuting the Christians and expelling them from the synagogues. The Christians took comfort from saying that in the salvation race the Jews might have begun as the favorites, but they had missed a step and were now coming last.

This way of thinking had a strong effect on the church. While we have always believed in the mercy and love of God, at different times we have been hostile to other religions, other denominations, and the secular world. We have often needed to express this in absolute terms about who was going to be saved and, more importantly, who was not!

The Second Vatican Council, however, reflected on the church's experience of working side by side with religious people and secular humanists throughout the world who were as committed as we are to justice, love, and freedom. In the *Declaration on the Relationship of the Church to Non-Christian Religions*, the bishops thought more generously about how God has a relationship with all people who in turn relate to God, even if they do not name it in the same way we are able to. The council did not draw back from believing that Jesus is the way to the Father, but it also affirmed that God can work in an infinite number of ways to assist people to salvation. It is church teaching now that our relationship to all people who share the best of our values must be characterized by acceptance, collaboration, dialogue, and charity.

This does not make salvation any less important. It just clarifies for us that it is God, not us, who does the saving and the judging. Christian salvation marks us out as a people who know who we are following, where we are going, how we are getting there, and why this world, and the next, matters to us. Salvation gives our lives meaning, direction, and purpose.

The way we live out this salvation should be irresistible to others. As the folk hymn sings, "They'll know we are Christians by our love, by our love. Yes, they'll know we are Christians by our love."

TWENTY-SECOND SUNDAY IN ORDINARY TIME

SIRACH 3:19–21, 30–31
HEBREWS 12:18–19, 22–24a
LUKE 14:1, 7–14

One of the most basic human responses to anything new is to ask, "What's in it for me?" We would like to think our motives are pure and our interests are for others, but there is often a nagging voice reminding us that selfish desires are never far from the surface. That said, we all know heroic individuals who care for sick spouses or children, who go to faraway places to give those in need their time and talent, or who stay at home and do the same in their local neighborhood. That's what makes them heroic. There is nothing in it for them; they are drawn by bonds of love or faith, or by a desire to create a better world.

There are at least two ways we can hear Jesus' words in today's Gospel. The first is as a strong challenge about social justice.

National boundaries mean nothing to God. All people are equal in God's sight, so the banquet Jesus refers to has implications for how we share the riches with which we have been blessed with others in the world. The poor, crippled, lame, and blind of our world are the majority of God's children who mainly live in the third world. They are our brothers and sisters. At the banquet of life Christians are called to give priority to the needs of these people, not only because they have a just claim on our resources, but also because they can't do anything for us in return. They purify our motives. When we link our concern, time, talent, career, and money with these children of God, we tame that nagging question, "What's in it for me?" with a firm reply, "Very little—except God's justice."

A somewhat comforting angle to take on this Gospel is more psychological. Many of us, when we come to God at any time, try to give ourselves a makeover so that we might be more acceptable to God. Today's Gospel reminds us that at Christ's banquet, however, it's not the poised and perfect who are most welcome, but the vulnerable. What does this mean for us who pray and celebrate the Eucharist? That God embraces those parts of us that are in greatest need of his love and healing—where we are poor, crippled, blind, and lame.

We know this is true because if Jesus is telling us to host the poor and broken at our tables, then as the perfect host he must do exactly the same with us at the eucharistic meal as well.

When I was a child we referred to our finest clothes as our "Sunday best" and we wore them proudly to Mass. Not only did we look good, we acted the part as well. Everyone was on best behavior for the entire parish to see. Now, I have nothing against dressing with care and behaving well at Mass; it can be a sign of our self-respect, our courtesy toward others, and our devotion to God. But is it truer that God cares about what's going on inside us. We can never hide from God, especially at the Eucharist, because we have been invited to be here, not as we would like to be, but as we are.

May the Eucharist, this taste of heaven's justice, give us renewed courage to think beyond our self and national interests, and show to others the hospitality of God that has been lavished on us. May we discover that, where faith is concerned, the real answer to "What's in it for me?" is "More than we can ever hope or imagine."

TWENTY-THIRD SUNDAY IN ORDINARY TIME

WISDOM 9:13–19
PHILEMON 9b–10, 12–17
LUKE 14:25–33

For some weeks now Luke has been telling us about the cost of discipleship. As a commentary on what was happening in his community and a preparation for what was to come, today's Gospel uses the hyperbole of hatred to drive home the point. For the earliest Christians a choice for faith in Jesus could be this stark and dramatic: Families split up and sometimes people who had loved each other turned their brother or sister, mother or father over to martyrdom. This is the context in which Luke's community produced this Gospel.

It is always good for us to recall that for some of our brothers and sisters beyond these shores the perils of public belief are still like those of Luke's community. Luckily for us the threat of death for our faith is only a very remote possibility. The power of this Gospel is that even if we are not faced with physical death, there are many other dyings that see us share in the cross of Jesus and follow in his way.

The verbs in this passage tell an interesting story: *carry, follow, estimate, lay foundations, sit down and consider,* and *give up possession.* It is a very tough list of things to do. Whatever our situation in life, this Gospel advocates that we figure out our priorities and live them out. In other words, we "say what we mean and live what we say."

We often think we could never live without most of the things to which we have become accustomed or attached. But we can. We know from people who have lived through some of the worst events of the last century that there are very few things that are essential to a happy life: human dignity, meaning and purpose, love of others, a sense of security. These are the essentials. Each person has a right to them and we have obligations to do our bit to see that they enjoy them. Everything else, as good as it might be, is icing on the cake. The problem is that we "want to have our cake and eat it too!"

As Christians we cannot have it both ways. We cannot say we are baptized into the life and death of Christ and not be prepared to sacrifice anything. If material riches come our way, with them comes an even greater obligation to share with the poor. If we have talents and energy we are called to put them at the service of improving the world in any way we can. If we want the hope of the resurrection, we have to first carry the cross. So riches, a better world, and hope come with a price.

Many of us, however, do not need to be reminded about all this because we carry crosses every day. For some it comes through mental, physical, or spiritual ill health. For others it can be in our homes where we have to deal with illness, dysfunction, or violence. It can be in our places of employment where we are overworked, undervalued, or bullied. Whatever our particular crosses may be we are one with all those who have "gone before us marked with the sign of faith" and who found Christ in the midst of their suffering. This Gospel promises us that Christ walks beside us bearing the burden of the struggle.

May the Eucharist give us eyes to see Christ present in our most difficult moments and make us more compassionate so we never add to the weight of another person's burden, but help carry it as best we can.

TWENTY-FOURTH SUNDAY IN ORDINARY TIME

Exodus 32:7–11, 13–14
1 Timothy 1:12–17
Luke 15:1–32

A bishop in a rural diocese was explaining to the confirmation class how he was the shepherd of the flock. Given that many of the children came from large sheep ranches, he decided to draw on today's Gospel as an analogy for his pastoral leadership. "I care for all of you like the Good Shepherd," he said. The students seemed consoled. Warming up, the bishop continued, "For instance, what would your fathers do if he lost one of his sheep?" The class was silent. The bishop asked again. The students were confused. The bishop got personal, "Michael, what would your dad do if he lost one of his sheep?" "Seeing we've 42,000 of them, My Lord, he'd let that stupid bugger go!"

Sometimes the power of the gospel needs a little help to become inculturated! If the bishop had done his homework, and understood the economic unit a sheep represented in first-century Palestine, he would have asked Michael about 420 missing sheep and got the answer he was after!

The Exodus reading and the Gospel from Luke could not provide a greater contrast in the images of God they present. Thank goodness we are children of the New Covenant, intimates of the Good Shepherd.

The Lord in Exodus, by contrast, is vengeful; his destructive anger only changes because of Moses' intercession. The idea that God "gets us" through disasters, illness, misfortune, and hardship is, tragically, still potent in Christian faith. At its worst it drives people away from the Good Shepherd who, by contrast, knows each of us by name, who will go to ridiculous lengths and risk everything to go after us and welcome us home. And just when we think we have left a vengeful God behind, it raises its ugly head.

A few weeks ago I met a devout Catholic couple in another city whose gay son has contracted HIV. His parents told me that they believed God sent this disease to their son as a result of his lifestyle. I wanted to weep at such terrible theology, not only because it cannot be reconciled with today's Gospel, but, also, when we follow this appalling line through, God's vengeance through HIV seems to have moved on from the gay community to heterosexual women and their children in sub-Saharan Africa. What did they ever do to be visited by such revenge?

There is a huge difference between God permitting evil in the world and God perpetrating such acts. For the record let's reaffirm that, although we can become better people for living through suffering and supporting those in need, God cannot send evil and terrible things upon us, because in God there is no darkness.

Our God is like a Good Shepherd who searches day and night for the one who needs him most, and rejoices when he finds us.

None of us is coerced into Jesus' flock, we're not victims of the Good Shepherd, we choose to belong, or we go along another path. But throughout our life and through a myriad of people and ways Jesus seeks us out, so that we may find the way, the truth, and the life.

May the Eucharist, then, enable us to let go of any residual belief that God is out to get us. May it sharpen our hearing to his call and help us to delight in his embrace. And may it embolden us, the church, to act as the Good Shepherd acts, to risk everything to be foolishly loving and compassionate as we actively seek out those who *most* need to experience God's saving love in Jesus Christ the Lord.

TWENTY-FIFTH SUNDAY IN ORDINARY TIME

AMOS 8:4–7
1 TIMOTHY 2:1–8
LUKE 16:1–13

A cheap jibe regularly levelled at the church is that while we preach justice and development for all people, we are one of the world's wealthiest multinationals. Sometimes Catholics are stung by this criticism. There's something healthy about that because there's always more we can, and should, do about our detachment from materialism. At the same time, however, our accusers should be reminded of three realities that spoil what they think is a good story.

The first is that in commercial terms the church is asset rich and cash poor. Many established churches through generosity and good planning have a large plant on decent real estate, but I don't know a diocese, religious order, parish, or church agency that has a generous cash flow. We rely on your goodness to keep going each year. Our real estate is, often, our only collateral for our borrowing—almost always done to improve the services we can render the people of God.

Second, our Catholic family's commitment to the poor is greater than any other comparable organization. Outside the United Nations and governments, Catholicism is the world's largest provider of education, health care, welfare, personal assistance, and third-world development; we have the largest and lowest-paid charitable workforce of any international group; and from the earliest Christians to this very day, some Catholics have loved and served the poor so faithfully that they have died with them, and for them. All of this is done in the name of our Catholic family. We should know it, and claim it as part of our own story too.

Third, the greatest asset we have, of course, is you—Christ's faithful people who witness day in and day out to the power of Jesus' life, death, and resurrection. Your commitment to making our world a more just and fairer place should never be undervalued or underestimated. Without fanfare or public acclamation many of you live out the generosity and goodness called for in today's Gospel.

Jesus' invocation of the master/slave relationship in regard to money is profound. How many people do we know who become very successful, but lose something essential in the process. They become enslaved by their success, but can lose their roots, their family and friends, and the best of their values. It's a lot to sacrifice for a big bank balance. For as Jesus asks us a few chapters earlier in Luke's Gospel, "What does it profit you to gain the entire world, but to lose your very soul?"

Money, in itself, is a value-neutral commodity. What defines its moral character is how and why we use it. For individuals and nations the rule of thumb in this area is an adaptation of Jesus' words in Luke 12, "Those to whom much has been given much will be required."

For Christians, who through the use of their God-given gifts and talents become successful and wealthier, then the obligation to share and be generous *increases* with every step up the ladder. But this doesn't put a damper on initiative for us; it defines the moral character of our hard work and good fortune. And reveals to us, and to the world, where our heart is, and what we really love.

May the Eucharist, this meal of God's poor, enable us to join in, and be proud of, the church's mission to alleviate poverty and to promote justice. And may it give us the courage to keep serving the one Master who sets all captives free, and fulfills the greatest desires of our hearts.

TWENTY-SIXTH SUNDAY IN ORDINARY TIME

AMOS 6:1a, 4–7
1 TIMOTHY 6:11–16
LUKE 16:19–31

Maybe the reason this Gospel story has become so famous is its extraordinary attention to detail—the regal colors of Dives's clothes, his exquisite tableware and fine dining. It all conjures up a vivid picture. At the same time Lazarus's world is equally well described. Begging at the gate, Lazarus's only companions are the dogs and his sores. Even giving names to both these characters adds to the power of the parable. These people are not just a rich man and a beggar. They are Dives and Lazarus, well known to everyone in the village. All these years later they are well known to us too. Not the actual characters, of course, upon whom the story could be based, but all the Lazaruses and Diveses in our own villages. It is an important task for us to decide which one of these characters we think we are.

A few years ago UNICEF, the United Nations Children's Fund, published a paper that creatively described the world as a village of one hundred people. Staying consistent with the international statistics UNICEF tells us that our global village looks like this. There are fifty-seven Asians, twenty-one Europeans, fourteen North Americans, eight Africans, four South Americans, and an assortment fills up the final four places. There are fifty-two women and forty-eight men, of whom only thirty are fair-skinned and seventy are dark-skinned. Ninety-one are heterosexual while nine are gay. Only one of us has a university education and yet six people in our village own 64 percent of our town's wealth and all of them are Americans. Eighty people live in substandard housing without electricity, clean water, and sewerage. Seventy of us cannot read and fifty suffer from malnutrition. And while we might be personally very generous in assisting the poor in a variety of ways, our Dives-like countries are not. The United States' third-world development budget works out at $67 per person, Australia $98, Canada $108 and the UK $112. And for all the moral scorn sometimes heaped upon Scandinavia, Denmark is the most generous country in the world, giving $649 per person last year.

This village analysis sorts out very quickly who Lazarus and Dives are in our world. As hard as life is for some of us and as much as we struggle financially, we are, comparatively, dressed in purple robes and feasting off fine linen.

The point of Jesus' story in today's Gospel is not to remind us that there are poor people at our gate. It is to implore us to listen and learn. Some Catholics want to vigorously uphold dogma and liturgical laws but do not seem to care one iota for the social teaching of the church, which instructs us that our love of God is truly found in deeds not words.

Given the way we keep repeating the sins of the past and we allow the rich to get richer while the poor die before us, it seems we Christians, who have had the benefit of the Law, the Prophets, and even a Man coming back from the dead, will not change the structures that enshrine global injustice. Why?

There is no way around it. Such a change would involve real sacrifice on our part and we are not prepared to pay the price. Jesus, however, reminds us today of the consequences in both of our selective deafness toward Lazarus's cry and our lack of action; our comfortable passivity has implications for this world and the next.

TWENTY-SEVENTH SUNDAY IN ORDINARY TIME

HEBREWS 1:2–3; 2:2–4
2 TIMOTHY 1:6–8, 13–14
LUKE 17:5–10

Today's Gospel highlights what a different world Jesus and the earliest Christians lived in by comparison with us today. Jesus and

Luke's community unquestionably believed in slavery. In all the Gospels Jesus regularly draws on the image of a slave to make points about duty, respect, or responsibility. In other passages, Jesus and St. Paul advocate for the just treatment of slaves or servants. It was an institution in their world that they never questioned. They never told the slaves to make a bid for freedom. They never told Christian slave owners to set their slaves free.

Like society generally, the church, for most of its history, followed this line. Much to our shame when the tide rightly turned against slavery in the eighteenth and nineteenth centuries, the church was, generally, very slow to be converted to the emancipation movement and take a stand against the colonialism and racism that slavery enshrined.

Our movement on the question of slavery is a wonderful study in the development of doctrine. Not all social realities that Jesus assumed in his day continue to be relevant to our world. It took society 1800 years and the church a bit longer still to see slavery for what it is—an assault on the children of God, both servant and master. It shows how we have to keep carefully discerning the movement of the Holy Spirit and God's guidance in the light of new thinking.

The image of the slave in today's Gospel is invoked to underline our response to God's goodness. It is good to recall that the word *redemption* literally means "buying back." It comes from the practice in the ancient world where there were two types of slaves—ones who were born or forced into slavery, usually for life, and others who paid off a debt or a crime by becoming a slave, usually for a period of time. The second type of slaves could be set free when someone else paid their debts, or the ransom their master now demanded for them was settled. They would, then, either be the slave of the purchaser, or set free completely. The metaphor came into Christian theology to describe how we, who are enslaved by our destructive behavior, gained a liberator in Christ who entered into a sinful world and subjected himself to its violence and death in order to set us free. Christ shows us that we do not have to live destructively anymore. Now claimed by the love of Christ, we are no longer slaves, but his friends, indeed through the redeeming work of Christ we have been welcomed into God's family.

Our work for God, then, is totally disproportionate to the gifts we have been given. Holding, as we do, that life, creation, all talents, and, in our case, security and peace are fruits of God's love, Jesus is right to highlight which side of the ledger is more generous.

To serve God in the world, in response to his invitation, is a privilege. We share in his creativity, compassion, hospitality, and care. And often, through us, others come to know God and make a judgment if Christian faith is sincere. As respondents to many surveys tell us, they may like who Jesus is and his teaching in the gospel, but the stumbling block for their joining us is the way they see that faith lived out in the church.

May the Eucharist, then, give us a sense of the dignity we have by being called the servants or slaves, friends and family of Jesus Christ the Lord.

TWENTY-EIGHTH SUNDAY IN ORDINARY TIME

2 KINGS 5:14–17
2 TIMOTHY 2:8–13
LUKE 17:11–19

The words *please* and *thank you* have to be two of the fastest disappearing words in our language. As Christians we believe that every person has the God-given right to human dignity. For us there is no such thing as the "hired help." Saying "please" and "thank you" is but one small way we remind ourselves that it doesn't matter whether someone is in paid employment or not. Each has human dignity, and deserves our respect. It costs us very little to be gracious and mindful of others, but it helps create a world in which people are never mistaken as commodities.

The story of the ten lepers, however, is not just about the courtesy of gratitude.

Until very recently, lepers were treated as outcasts. In Jesus' day, leprosy was considered a curse sent by God for an individual's or a family's sins. Lepers were ritually impure and made to live as religious outcasts as well.

In the ancient world if one touched a leper one incurred the same fate as the leper—exclusion from the community and the Temple.

What makes Luke's story even more extraordinary is that the leper who returns to say thank you was not just suffering from Hansen's disease, but he was also a Samaritan! Samaritans were mixed-race people from the north of Israel who were thought of as inferior and hated by the Jews of the south.

So this guy can't win a trick! He would have been rejected and despised by everyone, even the other Jewish lepers.

It's these details, lost on our modern ears, that reveal what Luke is really about in relating this story.

For what Jesus does is reject centuries of ritual taboos by allowing the untouchables of his day to approach him. He heals them, enables them to be welcomed back to the temple and into society, and draws attention to the fact that the poorest of the lepers, a Samaritan, is the only one who can recognize the source of the healing and has the humility to return and praise God for it.

This might be all well and good for Jesus, but what does it mean for us today. It means that in the Christian community there is no such thing as an unclean or untouchable person.

These days we need to hear this challenge in the church more than ever because we could be accused of having a modern list of untouchables. Apart from the recent celiac debacle, there are divorced and remarried people who want to participate in the sacramental life of the church. There are women who have had abortions, couples using contraception or in vitro fertilization, women who feel called to ordained ministry, and gay and lesbian Catholics who tell us that what they hear from different levels of the church is that no matter what they do the only place for them is outside the Temple and away from the community. We seem to be in the exposed position where some of our brothers and sisters can approach Jesus but not his church, where the servant seems to know better than the Master about who's in and out.

But Jesus comes to all of us this Sunday equally offering his gift of saving love. He challenges us to be with people who are marginalized and oppressed, even in our own midst, and defend their rights to dignity and participation.

And when we do this, we discover an extraordinary thing: that just as Jesus allows modern-day lepers to approach him, so too, we are similarly invited. In fact, it's the most leprous part of each of us that Jesus wants to touch and heal today. That's what the Eucharist, this meal of great thanksgiving, is all about. It's where Jesus, our host, declares that in the community gathered in his name, there is no such thing as an unclean or untouchable person. To be healed by him all we have to say is "please." And then have the grace and humility to say, "Thank you."

TWENTY-NINTH SUNDAY IN ORDINARY TIME

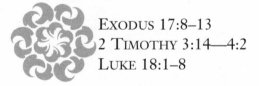 EXODUS 17:8–13
2 TIMOTHY 3:14—4:2
LUKE 18:1–8

Many years ago I remember hearing the story of a charismatic prayer meeting that went on all night. Apparently the leader was convinced that, "God wants to do a strong and powerful work here tonight and we have to show we are worthy." So he insisted that everyone stay until it happened. By dawn nothing had overtly occurred, so the leader declared, "God has worked hundreds of miracles here tonight—on the inside." He may have been right, but it sounded like mystical spin-doctoring to me! What worries me about this story is that it can portray God as a remote and severe figure we need to be convinced that we are serious about before he will be moved by our plight.

Today's Gospel is often used to support this idea. The persistent widow gets her way because she nags the judge into submission. While Jesus praises her endurance, he tells the disciples that God is *not* like the judge, but rather that God will quickly attend to our needs, rather than see us cry out all night.

There is a long and venerable tradition in the church that prayer can influence God's will. Our belief in the power of intercession is predicated on it. This tradition holds that God regularly and actively intervenes to effect good outcomes in the world. In this school God is waiting to be asked or have us ask others to petition him.

The problem with this school is how much an all-knowing, unchanging God changes his mind in regard to our petitions. Furthermore, God's interventions in the world are fine if all the decisions are running our way, but what happens when they run against us?

This approach can downplay free will. It can minimize our role, with God, to discern our options and choose carefully. If most of our petitions are focused on what God can do, it shifts all the responsibility (and the blame) on to God.

An equally long and venerable tradition in the church, however, is that prayer changes us. This tradition has had less airplay. Fasting, abstinence, and pilgrimages, for example, do not change God, but are meant to change the people who undertake them. These things can enable us to be more responsive or receptive to whatever happens in life. I think this tradition needs to be reclaimed.

The idea of prayer changing us changes our prayer—giving it greater dynamism and urgency. While we may not know the mind or will of God, we often know our own thoughts and desires. We can usually pinpoint what needs recrafting or reshaping in us so that we may live out the goodness and love of God more clearly. Confronting and converting these obstacles, with God, can see our prayer at its boldest and bravest. At these times we can enjoy God's healing and forgiveness. And because conversion is a lifetime process, Jesus encourages us not to lose heart but to pray always and hold on to faith even when the going gets tough.

Father John Powell once said, "God knows what we want and need before we open our mouths. In prayer, then, he does not need a performance from us. He longs for an act of love." May the Eucharist help us to move away from demanding that God change his mind or will to allowing his love to keep converting and changing us.

THIRTIETH SUNDAY IN ORDINARY TIME

SIRACH 35:15b–17, 20–22a
2 TIMOTHY 4:6–8, 16–18
LUKE 18:9–14

A leading multimillionaire had a near-fatal heart attack. After he recovered he was invited to appear on a national television chat show to reflect on the experience. At one stage the interviewer asked him, "Did you have a near-death experience after your heart attack?" The multimillionaire pulled himself up to his full height and exclaimed, "I was clinically dead. I went to the other side, and I am here to tell you there's nothing there!"

Leaving aside the contradiction inherent in how someone can encounter something that they choose to describe as nothing, my problem lay with the man's inability to see that the next life could be an experience, rather than a place. If this is true, then if I was him I wouldn't be boasting about the fact that his glimpse of eternity held nothing for him at all.

His response reminds me of the Pharisee in today's Gospel.

One of the pitfalls of personal success is the arrogance that sometimes comes with it. The Pharisee was, no doubt, a very good-living, devout man, but he made himself feel important by putting others down. He even did this in his prayer, reminding God of just how good he was in comparison to others. It's a wonder he went to the Temple at all because he doesn't seem to need

God. All he seems to need is validation. Like the multimillionaire, he trusts too much in his own righteousness.

On the other hand, it's a wonder that the tax collector turned up at the Temple too, but for very different reasons. Tax collectors were despised in Palestine. They were Jewish functionaries used by the Roman occupying army to extort the ferocious imperial taxes from the local community. No wonder he stays close to the back door of the Temple. He might have to beat a hasty retreat. But here he is in prayer recognizing the brokenness of his life and his need for God.

There's nothing wrong with being devout and successful. Conversely, there are plenty of dangers in doing a job that demands constant moral compromises, like being a tax collector for the Romans. What Jesus notices is what the life situations of both these men do to them. Hence the social outcast's humility shows up the haughty Pharisee. The tax collector becomes the model of right behavior for Luke's community.

For far too long we have thought humility meant putting ourselves down, pretending we were nobodies worthy of nothing. This is not Christian humility. Being humble doesn't mean we hide or minimize our God-given gifts, talents, or resources. It means we honor others by sharing our gifts, enabling them to benefit from the goodness of God entrusted to us. Humility comes the Latin word *humus*, meaning "close to the earth." The tax collector lived close to the earth and so he was open to conversion, to being lifted up by God. The Pharisee was so successful at being religious he was closed to it. He had altitude sickness from taking the high moral ground.

Most of us find ourselves somewhere in between these extremes. One of the best ways to make sure we remain humble is to be grounded in reality. It helps if we have friends who make demands on us. They might be economically disadvantaged, disabled, elderly, or sick. It's not necessarily easy to be with them, but that's the point. Our response to them keeps us grounded, draws out gifts we sometimes didn't even know we had, and, at very least, reminds us how grateful we should be for the gifts we have received. Others can tell a lot about us by the company we keep, and the people we shun.

May this weekly Eucharist ground us enough that we open ourselves to being converted again to put all our gifts and talents at the service of Christ's kingdom. In doing so, we can go home justified that we are working at being truly humble, and that as we look forward to the time when we go to the other side we can expect an eternity not just filled with something, but filled with life and life abundantly.

THIRTY-FIRST SUNDAY IN ORDINARY TIME

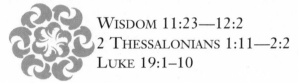

WISDOM 11:23—12:2
2 THESSALONIANS 1:11—2:2
LUKE 19:1–10

Philip was getting ready to graduate from university. For many months he had admired a beautiful sports car in a dealer's show-room, and knowing his father could well afford it, he told him he wanted this car as a graduation gift from the family. His father did nothing. As his graduation day approached, Philip awaited signs that his father had purchased the car.

Finally, the day after his graduation, his father called him into his study and told him how proud he was to have such a fine son, and that he loved him. He handed Philip a beautifully wrapped box. Philip opened the box and found a beautiful, leather-bound Bible, with Philip's name embossed in gold. He did not even take the Bible out of the box.

Angrily, he yelled at his father and said, "Is this it? With all your money you give me a Bible?" and stormed out of the house, leaving the Bible behind. Philip's family ran after him, but he jumped in his car and sped away. He refused to answer his mobile phone, even when his family kept ringing it for hours and hours.

Very late that night, when he had cooled down somewhat, he drove home to discover that his father had suffered a massive heart attack and died two hours before. His father had a history of heart disease. His furious and heartbroken mother told him to go and find the Bible that was the cause of the scene that morning.

He found the Bible right where he had thrown it down on his father's desk. With tears, he opened the Bible and began to turn the pages. He came to a bookmark where his father carefully underlined a verse, Matthew 7:11, "If you then, who are evil, know how to give good gifts to your children, how much more will your Father in heaven give good things to those who ask him!"

As he read those words, a car key dropped from the back of the Bible. It had a tag with the dealer's name, the same dealer who had the sports car he had desired. On the tag was the date of his graduation, and the words, "paid in full." Philip broke down and sobbed.

How many times do we miss God's blessings because they are not packaged as we expected?

This Sunday's Gospel is often called, "the little man's revenge." Zacchaeus was the least likely person in Jericho to host Jesus at dinner. In fact, as this marvelous story goes, that was the last thing on his mind as well. All Zacchaeus seems to have wanted is get a good look at Jesus who was on a "walkabout" in the village.

Jesus, however, seized the opportunity, given him by the actions of Jericho's chief tax collector, to teach everyone about how God's kingdom comes in extraordinary packages. Because of his job, the local Jewish community would have hated Zacchaeus, and yet Jesus does two things that welcome him into the family of God: He calls him by name, and dines with him. Jesus might have gone in the door of Zacchaeus's home, but he brings Zacchaeus out through God's door. He enables Zacchaeus to face up to his extortion and wealth and to claim his salvation.

It's the same with us. If only we have the eyes to see, the ears to hear, and the arms to embrace, Jesus comes to us through the most unusual people, times, and places. We are his family, he calls us by name, and he dines with us as often as we choose to accept his standing invitation to this table. But there's a price tag: We are meant to be different people for this encounter, generous with all we have to offer the world and transparent in all our relationships.

No matter how lost we are, how far up a tree we get stuck, or even when we are consumed with regret at the dreadful judgments we have made about the wrapping of God's gifts, Jesus calls us by name, invites us to his table, and tells us that salvation is near at hand.

THIRTY-SECOND SUNDAY IN ORDINARY TIME

2 MICAH 7:1–2, 9–14
2 THESSALONIANS 2:16—3:5
LUKE 20:27–38

It's not often that I'm speechless, but on the day Liz rang me to come see her in the hospital, I was dumbfounded.

I met Liz at the Easter Vigil ceremony at which time I received her sister, Ruth, into the church. I had met Ruth when she and her fiancé, Andrew, asked me to officiate at their marriage. Ruth was not much of a believer until she started going out with Andrew. As their love for each other bloomed, so her desire for faith deepened.

These loving experiences were connected.

At the reception following the Easter Vigil, Liz cornered me. She had a doctorate in molecular biology, and had long since given up any belief in Christian faith. Sadly, Liz felt science was in competition with faith, and that in this battle science won. Most of us know, however, that science helps faith-filled people explain the enormous complexity of God's creation. Science is a rich and constant source of revelation for some of us to marvel at God's handiwork throughout the universe, on the earth, and in us.

Liz could not understand how her equally accomplished sister had now embraced adult Christian faith. And so she was filled with lots of questions, and a good dose of resentment. And I got it both barrels at the party. I responded to her interrogation as best as I could, but Liz left our conversation unconvinced and unsatisfied.

A year later, Liz's baby son, Ben, was stillborn. She and her husband, Paul, understandably, were devastated, and they reached out to me, the only minister they knew. As we planned the funeral for their son, they needed to believe that his life and their relationship with him counted for something. They wanted to believe that they would see him again. To do so, Liz started on a journey of faith in God, who was with Ben in life and who received Ben into his arms at the moment of death. Faith in the resurrection of the dead was no longer a proposition to disprove, it was the essence of a loving relationship to experience.

Today's Gospel focuses on those nagging questions that plague us all from time to time: What will heaven be like? What will happen to me in the resurrection of the body?

Jesus answers this question in two ways: first, by an allusion to how the intimacy of marriage and the unity of God and the angels are akin to the love shared between everyone in heaven; and second, Jesus draws on the family analogy to explain heaven and the resurrection. He invokes the memory of Moses, Abraham, Isaac, and Jacob to show that their experiences with God affirm that eternal life for all of us is a reality. As the Gospel of Luke states: "Now he is God not of the dead, but of the living; for to him all of them are alive."

Jesus' words affirm something instinctive for most of us. If this life is it, if nothing exists beyond our time on earth, then there is a certain futility to our existence here, and to our relationships that mark the quality of our humanity. Not that atheists do not or cannot live fulfilled and meaningful lives. They do and can. Some of them are among the finest human beings on the planet, working to make our world a better place for this and future generations. It's just that we believe that there is also a spiritual connection between one generation and the next, and that every life, from those of highest achievements to those that are seemingly unproductive, has an inherent value and dignity because of our common origin and our common destiny. In God's family everyone is related and connected, in this life and the next.

At the end of the funeral service for Ben, after we sprinkled the little boy's ashes on a mountainside, we let go of nine white balloons—one for each month of his life on earth. We didn't look at the earth for long, but kept gazing into the sky, into the heavens. Liz, Paul, and I knew that Ben was alive to God and God to him. We stood there trusting in something we could not feel or touch, and could not rationally explain. There are plenty of those realities in science and faith. We tasted the resurrection of the dead not just because we needed to, but also because it was there for the asking—an encounter of love where randomness and futility count for nothing.

THIRTY-THIRD SUNDAY IN ORDINARY TIME

MALACHI 3:19–20a
2 THESSALONIANS 3:7–12
LUKE 21:5–19

Among the frightening things said by some Christian leaders in the United States following the bombing of the World Trade Center were "God turned away from America because we have turned away from God" and "God sent these acts as a wake-up call for us to live righteous lives and return to him." One went as far as to confidently assert, "Since 11th September we are living in end times."

We all have different reactions to shock and grief. When tragedy strikes on any scale, everyone asks, "Why is this happening to us?" But Christian ministers should know better and never resort to appalling theology to further their own social and political agendas. They give us all a bad name.

For as long as I can remember we have had Christians confidently predicting the end of the world. Whenever there is a tidal wave, cyclone, hurricane, earthquake, or other natural disasters, someone declares that "the end is nigh."

In the face of all evidence to the contrary, corporations spent billions over the Y2K bug, and we got apocalyptic sermons and end-of-time predictions.

We know from a variety of documents that people in the time of Jesus thought the world was coming to an end soon, and maybe Jesus thought so too. Given that Israel was being persecuted under an occupying Roman army and that their nation was in tatters, they seemed to have a better cause for this view than we do. In today's Gospel Jesus speaks to a demoralized people who thought, and some of whom hoped, that it would all be over soon. In such a context people are liable to follow the loudest voice to what appears the safest place.

After Jesus died, the earliest Christians thought the end would come quickly. This Gospel reflects the experience of this expectant first generation. But we're still waiting, and so we cling to Jesus' challenge not to be afraid, not to place our trust in things or institutions that we can see, but to hope and remain faithful through whatever suffering we may endure.

In today's Gospel Jesus tells us not to follow the doomsday prophets, those predictors of inevitable alienation. I think we should heed his warning very carefully indeed. But rather than focus on those who get off on the signs supposedly inherent in natural or man-made disasters, I think we should denounce and decry those who tell us that anyone is worthless, unlovable, has little or no human dignity, that its their way or no way, and that there is little we can do to change a death-dealing world.

For example, I once met a man who told me that when he was diagnosed with cancer the first emotion he felt was relief. He was forty years of age and his life would be over soon. He was prodigiously talented, attractive, lovable, and loving. But cancer gave him an honorable discharge from a life he didn't like living very much. To hope in a better future and to fight his disease, he had to confront the sign of his own self-loathing. In doing so he discovered that life was worth living in general, and that his life was worth living in particular. Thank God, on every level, he is more alive today than at any time in his history.

Even when life seems unbearable we have the anchor of Christ, who steadies us as we are tossed and buffeted by life's winds. And in the midst of the storm Christ keeps gently telling us that we are worthy, lovable, dignified, can live life our way, and that we can change the world for the better by how we change ourselves.

Today's Gospel is not interested in a timetable for disaster. It's about encouraging us to drop the anchor of hope overboard when the times get tough. At the Eucharist may we take into our hands the anchor of our faith that will enable us to endure in hope until the end of time—whenever it is!

FEAST OF CHRIST THE KING

2 SAMUEL 5:1–3
COLOSSIANS 1:12–20
LUKE 23:35–43

Recently I saw the digitally reworked film of Queen Elizabeth II's coronation. This was England at its most brilliant. The sense of flow, dignity, and beauty was quite overwhelming. I was struck by the moment before the crowning when the archbishop of Canterbury said, "Elizabeth Alexandra Mary, Christ has anointed you Queen of the United Kingdom and its dominions, of Canada, Australia, New Zealand and their territories, Head of Commonwealth and Defender of the Faith, by Christ's grace you are Queen for the glory of God and the just reign of his might."

The camera then panned around Westminster Abbey— dukes and duchesses, earls and countesses, anyone who was anyone was there.

But I became increasingly uncomfortable as I watched. While everything was said to be done in Christ's name, I could only think that Christ would prefer to be anywhere but there.

In ceremonies like it all around the world, Christ's kingship is often called upon to confirm that God approves of not only a particular monarchy or presidential campaign, but also of the entire social, economic, and religious hierarchy that seems to go with it.

Christians from their earliest days ascribed to Jesus the title of King. He is for us the fulfillment of what Israel was hoping for in the Messiah, or the Christ, literally, "the anointed one," the redeemer King who would defend the rights of the poor, and establish an everlasting reign of peace and justice.

The notion of Jesus as earthly King and an anointer of earthly kingdoms came to us when Emperor Constantine declared the Christian religion to be the faith of the empire in 313.

And yet Christ the King is not found in earthly wealth and splendor, but in submitting to the violence and death of our world so as to show us the way out of it—to break the cycle of the scapegoat, by becoming the definitive one, and announcing in the process that the reign of darkness is over.

It is patently clear from nearly every page of the Christian scriptures that the people who found this truth most attractive were those who lived on the margins of Palestinian society, including the thief who is capitally punished with Jesus.

I am not convinced comparable groups in our own day would be welcome or at home in the lavish coronation ceremonies conducted in Christ the King's name in the Westminster Abbeys of our world.

And here's the rub.

If we take seriously Christ's kingship, we cannot con ourselves into understanding it in terms of worldly status. Christ, surely, does not anoint any social or ecclesiastical system of personal privilege and wealth that is extravagant and disordered in its social relationships. In today's Gospel the good thief simply asks Jesus to "remember me." And Jesus tells him that being remembered by God is paradise. It's a wonderful way to understand the kingship of Christ. We know that Christ our King is not about earthly power, land, buildings, riches, or might. We know Jesus' kingship is not about lording it over us, or making us frightened of his compassionate judgment. The power of Christ the King is seen in his memory, holding every person in this world close, calling each one of us by name.

The test of those who live out the reign of Christ is not whether we are titled or monied, whether we are successful, or in *Who's Who*. No, our King calls us to follow him in remembering all people, regardless of who they are, and fighting for the dignity of each person.

And what's our reward for such work in bringing Christ's kingdom to bear in our world? Simply that Christ will remember us when he comes into his kingdom. So let's join our voice with all those who long for paradise and say, "Jesus remember me when you come into your kingdom."

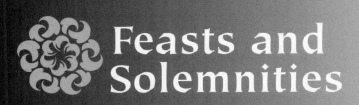

Feasts and Solemnities

MARY, MOTHER OF GOD

Numbers 6:22–27
Galatians 4:4–7
Luke 2:16–21

When the Council of Ephesus gathered on June 22, 431, it was by no means clear which way the bishops would vote in the matter of Mary being the mother of God. Indeed that council was not called to talk about Mary at all. It was primarily interested in whether Jesus was both truly human and truly God. In their deliberations about this matter two touchstones were established for orthodox belief: What do the people believe and how do they pray? This was a watershed moment. The theological sense in ordinary Christian belief and the way that ordinary people prayed, especially in the liturgy, were guiding lights for the bishops.

The vast majority of the bishops affirmed that their people believed that Jesus was truly God. But they also attested to the fact that their congregations believed Jesus was truly human. Why? Because while Jesus had done miraculous things, taught with authority, and been raised from the dead, they knew he also shared in the most important element of being a human being: He was born of a woman, Mary of Nazareth.

Strikingly, while the council fathers went on to define the union of divinity and humanity in Jesus, their deliberations did not put the issue to rest. It took another council, at Chalcedon twenty years later, to finally settle the issue of the two natures in Christ. What caused very little theological debate, however, was what Ephesus had to say about Mary, that she was the mother of God. The literal translation of the Greek proclamation is even more evocative: Mary is the *Theotokos*, the God-carrier. After the Council of Ephesus all sorts of hymns and poems were written in honor of the newly named mother of God.

In recent centuries Mary has become a battleground in Christian devotion. The Protestant reformers thought she was obscuring the centrality of Jesus in Christian faith. These days some Catholics complain that we never hear anything about her anymore. Others maintain that some people are overly caught up in her alleged appearances and communications. It's sad to think that what once united Christians now often polarizes us.

Pope Paul VI taught us that, if we wanted to recover a healthy devotion to Mary that is sane, Catholic, ecumenical, and inclusive, we should return to the scriptures. This is precisely what French Jesuit Didier Rimaud did in his poem, "There Is Nothing Told About This Woman." Following the post-Ephesus tradition, Australian Jesuit Christopher Willcock has translated this poem into English and set it to music. It is about the best contemporary Marian hymn around.

> There is nothing told about this woman, but that
> …she had once become engaged and an angel addressed her
>   and said: You are blessed among all your kind.
> ….she brought into the world, in the land of Judea, a son; for
>   some shepherds have passed on this tale.
> ….she searched for three long days for her child who was
>   busy elsewhere, and her heart then did not understand.
> …she at Cana was a guest, when her son changed water to
>   wine, so that all might believe who he was.
> …she was standing by the cross, when her son stretched his
>   arms out on high and met death with a thief on each side.
> …she was one in prayer with those upon whom tongues of
>   fire did descend, and the Spirit baptized them with flame.

The reason we celebrate Mary's memory on the first day of the year is because there is not an ordinary, everyday moment in the coming year when we cannot know the faithful love of God. The woman who carried God into the world shows us how her Son now carries us.

With Rimaud and Willock, then, let's lift up our voice and declare, "On this day all earth and all paradise join in naming you happy and blessed. Virgin Mary, blessed are you."

PRESENTATION OF THE LORD

MALACHI 3:1–4
HEBREWS 2:14–18
LUKE 2:22–40

For most of its history today's feast was a dual observation: The purification of Mary and the presentation of the Child Jesus in the Temple.

It's not that long ago that Western cultures had ceremonies to "purify" women after childbirth. These rituals have their roots in some appalling thinking about how the flow of women's blood defiles them and those who touch them. Maybe the only modern reclamation we could make of these rites would be to understand them as purification of the memory. After the selflessness of a pregnancy and the pain of childbirth, a mother could use such a ritual moment to reclaim her body. In any case, it is right and good that we no longer overly emphasize this side of today's feast.

The presentation of Jesus is more appropriate in modern society. Jewish law stipulated that within forty days of a child's birth the parents should present their baby in the Temple as an act of thanksgiving. In the Bible the number forty always indicates a time of formation. So forty days after Christmas the church has today's celebration. As Luke describes the scene, Simeon and Anna represent the Old Covenant. He embodies all those who longed to see the Christ. She embodies all those who prophesied his coming. In a few sentences Luke tells us that just as the Israelites entered the promised land after forty years in the desert, so now the time of waiting is over. Israel can receive the promised Messiah. The Old Covenant has been fulfilled and the New Covenant is established in Jesus.

The word *presentation* is used in two revealing ways these days. In psychology they talk about a "presenting problem." In medicine people are said to "present" with certain symptoms. In both cases, the word *presentation* is used to indicate that something more important lies beneath what is first observed. Further investigation reveals the deeper causes and the best course of action.

So to us. We present ourselves in the Temple knowing that God is intimately familiar with us. It is crazy that we should be anything but ourselves before him. But we sometimes go through the pretence of dressing things up, pretending otherwise, or putting on a show.

Today's feast reminds us that when we encounter the presence of God a range of responses are on display. Just recall the ones in today's Gospel: expectation, hope, frailty, thanksgiving, foreboding, puzzlement, love, and joy.

May Jesus' presentation enable us to let pass in peace any need to act before God, but rather embrace a new way of encountering God's presence, where we own just how we are, and not how we would like to be. When we do this we discover the possibilities of a rich, deep, and realistic relationship with God. We also find then that it's so much easier to discover, with God, the causes and the actions that will lead us to healing, fulfillment, and peace.

ST. JOSEPH, SPOUSE OF MARY

2 SAMUEL 7:4–5a, 12–14a, 16
ROMANS 4:13, 16–18, 22
MATTHEW 1:16, 18–21, 24a *or* LUKE 2:41–51a

It can be surprising to us today to discover that devotion to St. Joseph was a comparatively late development in the Christian church. We know that by the eighth century local churches had commemorations in honor of St. Joseph as husband of Mary, but these did not become a feast day in the Western church until the 1300s. After then devotion to St. Joseph takes off. Pius XI proclaimed St. Joseph patron of the universal church in 1870. Even then, it was another pope and another century that finally saw John XXIII in 1962 insist on Joseph's name being added to the list of saints in the Eucharistic Prayer called the Roman Canon. Blessed John XXIII had a vested interest in St. Joseph. It was his baptismal name.

One can see why the earliest church may have been slow to make a fuss of St. Joseph. He is never recorded as saying anything in the New Testament—not a word. The two things he is well known for in the Bible are his dreams and his actions.

In the scriptures dreams are highly valued forms of communication between God and humanity.

Joseph, the eleventh son of Jacob, is the famous dreamer of the Old Testament, as well as the interpreter of other people's dreams, notably the Egyptian Pharaoh. But he is not the only dreamer. King Nebuchadnezzar, the prophet Daniel, and King Solomon are just three more famous figures whose dreams have a dramatic impact on the destiny of Israel.

There are plenty of people who dream dreams and see visions in the New Testament too, culminating in the Book of Revelation. In Matthew's Gospel Joseph dreams twice: in today's Gospel where he is told not to fear taking the pregnant Mary as his wife; and later in learning of Herod's plans to kill Jesus, and then getting the all-clear to return home. But other characters have important dreams in this Gospel as well. The Magi are told in a dream not to reveal the whereabouts of Jesus to Herod, and Pilate's wife warns her husband to have nothing to do with Jesus.

There are a few curious features to God's revelation in all these dreams. God is not religiously discriminating as to whom he visits. Joseph is a devout and righteous man, but the Magi are Gentiles and Pilate's wife is a Roman pagan. The same holds true for Pharaoh and Nebuchadnezzar in the Old Testament. God visits whomever he needs to, to get the job done.

And it is this second feature of activity flowing from the dreams that is outstanding. In the scriptures these dreams were taken seriously enough for them to be the test of making decisions. In almost every case biblical dreams save lives or tell of how to guard and protect.

Today we can dismiss dreams as a fad of the new age, but that would be a mistake. Today's feast day tells us that, if God has created us with an unconscious and subconscious life of which dreams are a sign, then God has a purpose for this gift, and dreams can be used for good. Long before Carl Jung, dreams as a gateway to an inner mystical world had St. Joseph as their champion.

If we never take them seriously, if we decide that God cannot or does not talk to us through our subconscious world, then we will never know. But even then God visits whomever he needs to, to get the job done. So if we hear how we feature in other people's dreams, then maybe we should start listening. The scriptures tell us that ignoring dreams, particularly persistent ones, has destructive consequences—remember Pharaoh, Nebuchadnezzar, and Pilate.

Just as Matthew draws the parallels between the dreams of the Old Testament Joseph with Joseph of New, so we can see the parallels in our own lives too. St. Joseph went from being a dreamer to being the protector and savior of Jesus, the one who in turn would save the world. Where could our dreams be leading us? What protection and warning could they be providing for us?

It is not surprising that, when many people are unfaithful, addicted, unhappy at work, spiritually restless, or in emotional turmoil, they dream.

Like the scriptures, dreams need careful interpretation and discernment, but Joseph, the silent partner within the Holy Family, is testament to how a few words and great actions can save ourselves, our family, and even the world.

St. Joseph, husband of Mary, pray for us that we may be worthy of the promise and dreams of Christ.

ANNUNCIATION

ISAIAH 7:10–14
HEBREWS 10:4–10
LUKE 1:26–38

The announcement of a baby is still, for most people, a very happy event. And there are two things that unite nearly all announcements of babies everywhere in the world: They change lives and they are deeply physical affairs.

The annunciation of the Lord to Mary, and to the world, exemplifies this pattern. It changed Mary and Joseph's lives, and it has changed our lives too. And there is nothing in our accepted tradition to say that Mary had an abnormal pregnancy. Indeed to hold otherwise is to undermine the reality of the human nature of Christ. Jesus' presence in Mary's life, as in her body, was a deeply physical affair. And though none of us can know the same form of physical union Mary had with her Son, our relationship with Christ is nonetheless meant to carry the marks of a physical intimacy. This is the way God wanted it, because God knew it was what we needed.

Human beings can be a fairly sceptical bunch. Most of us believe in something when there is enough proof. On the whole this is no bad thing. There are enough fraudsters and charlatans in the world for us to be on our guard. Sadly for us, however, this same scepticism had entered our relationship with God. Despite the gift of creation, patriarchs and prophets, religious laws, revealed writings, and holy men and women, we had wandered far from God, and couldn't find our way home.

Today's feast celebrates that we're given our road map home, a spiritual MapQuest. It didn't come in the form of specific instructions on where to turn and for how long to drive. Free will rules that out. For better or worse, God wants us in the driver's seat of our own life. But God didn't leave us wandering either, and so in the midst of our need for evidence, God became one of us, one with us, "Immanuel," being tempted in all the ways we are, and even going to death, so as to announce death's demise. Our spiritual map quest came in the form of Jesus, the way, the truth, and the life. Christ is the proof of God's saving love of us.

So while we are not given precise instructions on how to act in every situation of our lives, we are told who we are to be, or who we can become. We are invited to model ourselves on him who was announced by the angel. And he told us that what we needed to do was love God with all our mind, heart, and strength, and to love our neighbors as we love ourselves. "On these two commandments hangs the whole Law and the Prophets too."

What does all that mean in our daily lives? In a nutshell, if we really understand the enormity of the annunciation, then it is meant to change us and affect our lives in a deeply physical way. On one level it already has. Most can't imagine being anything other than a Christian, a Roman Catholic, where there is already a certain language, way of praying, ritual life, and a worldview that informs the way we live. We cannot properly see its influence on us because we are too close to it. Take an atheist, Jewish, or Muslim friend to Mass one Sunday and they might help you understand what I mean. We take most of the Christian tradition's impact on our lives and the world for granted.

But there are always more ways in which we can become like Christ. Every time we speak, physically touch others, go to work, shop, travel, exercise, give to charity and share our goods, entertain ourselves, play sports, go on holiday, study, read, eat, and make love Christ should be "at home" in what we do or say. Not that we have to regularly think about this, but there are moments of choice in any or all of these areas of our lives that define who we really are, and it is at these times we might need to pray that Christ's life is so deeply grafted onto our own that our choices are faithful, loving, and hopeful.

The annunciation is not an annual historical pageant, wonderful as that feast might be. As with all feasts, it is an opportunity to reflect on what God has done for us in Jesus Christ, and to enter more deeply into the mystery of who God is calling us to be right now.

In what ways do I let Christ be born in me? And in what ways do I need Christ to be born in me?

JOHN THE BAPTIST

Vigil:
JEREMIAH 1:4–10
1 PETER 1:8–12
LUKE 1:5–17
Day:
ISAIAH 49:1–6
ACTS 13:22–26
LUKE 1:57–66, 80

The American political drama *West Wing* has been a huge hit on television in recent seasons. Well scripted, cleverly cast, and finely acted, it dramatizes events around the most powerful office in the world. This is one drama series that does not need to invent stories. With former White House insiders hired as consultants, *West Wing* explores important issues and demonstrates the process by which a public position is adopted. The best aspect of this drama, however, is that it portrays the power of the backroom players involved in the process. Every democracy, every institution, including the church, has people who are not the public face of the organization, but are very powerful in shaping what the group stands for and where it goes. A politician friend of mine says, "Congress or Parliament is theater sports writ large; real power and the important decisions are worked out in the back rooms, small offices, and corridors."

John the Baptist is the greatest of the backroom boys in the Christian story. When the gospels were written, the significance of John's role as a herald and mentor came to the fore. In first-century Palestine there may not have been parliamentary corridors for John the Baptist to strut, but his words and actions on the banks of the Jordan were powerful in recognizing who was to follow, what the Christian faith would stand for, and where it would head.

Is it any wonder, then, that the Birth of John the Baptist is one of the most ancient feasts commemorated in the earliest Christian Church? Its position in relation to Christmas is important too. By

354, the Christians had taken over the Roman celebration of the winter solstice as Christmas Day. John's birthday is on the summer solstice. From the summer solstice the northern hemisphere's sun declines in length and warmth until it reaches its nadir and is reborn at the winter solstice. Hence, John comes to prepare the way for the eternal light we celebrate in Jesus at Christmas. In Luke's Gospel John embodies the old covenant, made to Israel. Jesus, the new and everlasting covenant, made, not just to Israel, but also to all people everywhere, sees the power and warmth of God's love for us to burst forth for eternity.

Many biblical scholars now think that, for a period of time, Jesus was most probably a disciple of John the Baptist. John may have helped Jesus discern his special calling and to recognize his destiny. Whatever of that, we know that Jesus made a break with John in many ways and called his own disciples. Jesus does not wait for followers to come to him, he heads to the towns and villages—where the people are—and he speaks to them in ways they can understand. Jesus preaches to Israel first, but then to the Gentiles. Jesus rejects the harsh, ascetical life of the desert for spirituality of the everyday, and, unlike John, Jesus does not just preach repentance for sins, but preaches conversion through forgiveness and compassion. As Louise Pambrun puts it, John's ministry was "like the fast before the feast."

Like John, however, Jesus never wavered from the price that must be paid for faith in our just and merciful God. So this feast flags that we have six months to Christmas, not for shopping or any of the other excessive elements that have hijacked that day, but to recommit ourselves to living out a spirituality that values the everyday and the ordinary, that knows the power of compassion and mercy and is ready to pay the price for living it.

Today is the feast of backroom players. May all of them exercise their power with integrity. And who knows, maybe the real-life counterparts of *West Wing*'s Sam, Josh, and CJ will, one day, have their birthdays declared a public holy day. I bet they're quietly working on it right now!

SAINTS PETER AND PAUL

Vigil:
ACTS 3:1–10
GALATIANS 1:11–20
JOHN 21:15–19
Day:
ACTS 12:1–11
2 TIMOTHY 4:6–8, 17–18
MATTHEW 16:13–19

Have you noticed that away from the church we hear more about St. Peter than we do about St. Paul? It's because St. Peter regularly features in jokes about heaven, like this one:

> A man died and meets St. Peter at the gates of heaven. St. Peter says, "Before you meet with God, I thought I should tell you that we've looked at your life, and you really didn't do anything particularly good or bad. We're not at all sure what to do with you. Can you tell us anything you did that can help us make a decision?"
>
> The newly arrived soul thought for a moment and replied, "Yeah, once I was driving along and came upon a woman who was being harassed by a group of bikers. So I pulled over, got out my tire iron, and went up to the leader of the gang. He was a big, muscular, hairy guy with tattoos all over his body and a ring pierced through his nose. Well, I told him he and his gang had better stop bothering the woman or they would have to deal with me!"
>
> "I'm impressed," St. Peter responded. "When did this happen?"
>
> "Less than ten minutes ago," the man replied.

St. Paul doesn't feature in many funny stories, except for the children who got rather confused about his life and wrote in their term paper that "St. Paul cavorted to Christianity. He preached holy acrimony, which is another name for marriage. That a

Christian should have only one wife, which is called monotony. And in the end the natives of Macedonia did not believe in Paul, so he got stoned."

Peter and Paul symbolize two facets of our Christian community: mission and maintenance. Paul was the great missionary and Peter was the great leader who held together the earliest disciples. Both were crucial to the Christian community's expansion and survival.

The image of the missionary venturing out boldly to proclaim Christ to the world is so much more engaging than being a maintainer. But every organization or institution needs someone to provide a clear focus and vision, and to establish structures that will see the group survive past the first generation. To this day we need our Peters and our Pauls.

Peter and Paul did not always have an easy relationship. We know from the Acts of the Apostles that they disagreed about a fundamental issue in the earliest Christian mission: For whom was the good news of Jesus intended? Peter thought it was just for Jews. Paul argued it was for the Gentiles as well. What makes Peter's leadership so outstanding is that he not only listened carefully to what Paul said, but saw what Christ was doing among the Gentiles. He trusted that the working of the Spirit was bigger than he was, and that it included a man who never met Jesus and yet seemed to have a richer insight into where and how Christ was to be preached. That takes courage and humility.

Today we need to be careful that in Christ's name we do not bind things up so tightly that we leave no room for the Holy Spirit to challenge or surprise us. Having the courage and humility to "hang a bit loose" is not weakness. It can be about trusting that Christ's saving love is still at work in unexpected ways.

Peter and Paul show us what can happen when we cooperate with Christ in living out his love. Things we never dreamt of become possible. But their lives also show us the cost. Both of them died as martyrs.

We may not be asked to embrace martyrdom in our lives, but, in the way we run our race, we are challenged to keep the faith and proclaim Christ by how we live.

By doing so we are assured that when we come to heaven we will be greeted by Peter and Paul and with them we will behold the fullness of love for eternity—the Father, Son, and Holy Spirit.

TRANSFIGURATION

DEUTERONOMY 7:9–10, 13–14
2 PETER 1:16–19
Cycle A: MATTHEW 7:1–9
Cycle B: MARK 9:2–10
Cycle C: LUKE 9:28b–36

I recently had to teach Catholic grade-school children a class on the transfiguration. When I told them what we would be doing, they all beamed—which, given the subject matter, was an entirely appropriate response. It soon became clear, however, that the kids and I were not on the same page. As soon as I started to talk about Jesus and Mount Tabor, one girl said, "But what about Harry Potter?" What about Harry Potter indeed. When I last read the gospels Harry was not mentioned. I was then told that in J. K. Rowling's books when Harry, Ron, and Hermione go to Hogwarts School, they have to do a course entitled "transfiguration."

Most of us would have noticed that in recent years the church has accentuated much more the humanity of Jesus. We can see why. For a long period, the divine nature of Christ was often overemphasized, sometimes to the danger of us thinking of Jesus as God parading around in human form. With new biblical tools now at our disposal scholars started recovering the equally important human nature within Christ.

But there can be danger the other way as well. Christ can be seen as a man, albeit a good, noble, and sacrificial man, but simply one of us.

The feast of the Transfiguration holds both extremes together. Mark, Matthew, and Luke, who all recount this event, tell us that Jesus was metamorphosed before the eyes of the three disciples. At Tabor Jesus' divine nature was seen directly and immediately by them, which is why this feast was once called the Manifestation of Divine Glory.

Trying to describe the indescribable, the evangelists use the shorthand of the Old Testament to set the scene: the mountaintop religious experience, a cloud that covers them there, and the glory of God revealed through dazzling light.

But the transfiguration is not like the other events in the lives of Moses and Elijah, whose memory and support is invoked. For just as Peter, James, and John might like to stay on Mount Tabor, they have to come down the mountain and start another journey with Jesus to another mountain, to Calvary.

But the disciples have been changed forever. They know that to behold the glory of God they don't need a mountaintop light show. They know that to look at Jesus is to behold the glory of God, to see the divinity of Jesus in and through his humanity, the uncompromised and uncompromising love of the world's only complete human being. One early commentator said Christ's transfiguration was like the opening out of a beautiful rose.

It's the same with us. We don't have to feel cheated because we have no access to Jesus, as had his disciples. Nor do we have to keep looking for our own version of Mount Tabor, as important as religious experiences are. What we need is an ever-deepening faith to believe that the glory of God found expression in Jesus of Nazareth, Christ the Lord.

Unlike Harry Potter we don't need a course on transfiguration. It's caught not taught. To catch it we always keep our eyes firmly on what Jesus does, so that when we are overcome with the enormity of the Christian mission given to us in baptism, we can get up off the ground, not be afraid, take up our cross, and follow Christ to the glory of his resurrection.

ASSUMPTION OF THE BLESSED VIRGIN MARY

Vigil:
1 CHRONICLES 15:3–4, 15; 16:1–2
1 CORINTHIANS 15:54–57
LUKE 11:27–28
Day:
REVELATIONS 11:19a; 12:1–6a, 10ab
1 CORINTHIANS 15:20–26
LUKE 1:39–56

On the August 15, 1975, the entire parish council of a village outside the capital of Chile was arrested by the military police. For months the villagers tried to find out where the men had gone and why they had been taken away. Abduction, torture, and illegal imprisonment were daily realities for Chilean people under General Pinochet.

Word arrived in November that the corpses of the parish councillors could be found in Santiago's morgue. My cousin, Catherine, an Australian nun working in that parish, took the mothers of the eight men to the morgue. Catherine later wrote to me, "There were over 300 corpses piled high on each other and the mothers had to roll someone else's son over in an attempt to find their own."

As the mothers searched they began to weep loudly, realizing how evil we can be toward one another. As they wept they prayed the rosary. As one mother, and then another, found her son, they called out more desperately, "Holy Mary, Mother of God, pray for us sinners now, and at the hour of our death."

Catherine's letter continued, "For years I rejected devotion to Mary because I felt oppressed by the way generations of men in the Church presented her—blue veils, white skin, always smiling, a perpetual virgin and yet also a mother, an ideal I could never achieve, but one to which I was told I should aspire. In the experience of the village mothers, however, the distortions of who Mary was for a poor and suffering world faded away. Far from feeling distant from their devotion, I found myself praying with them, knowing that Mary was with us in our shock, anger and grief. One of the women told me, on the way home, that Mary knows what it's like to bring a child into the world and claim his dead body in her arms."

Fourteen years later, in 1989, Catherine died in that village of hepatitis. Her family had been trying to get her to come home for months, but she lied about how ill she was and said that she could get everything she needed there. The only consolation Catherine's family got was when a letter arrived from the mothers in the village. When it was translated into English it read, "We want you to know that we were with Catherine when she died. We would never have let her die alone for she was one of our children too. We often prayed the rosary with her. She seemed to like that, thumbing the beads she used ever since she bought us back with our boys. We have buried her next to our sons and put on her tombstone the line she asked us to inscribe, "Mary my friend, my companion and mother of the poor, pray for me."

The writer of Luke's Gospel has a similarly earthy picture of Mary. There's nothing sentimental and pious about the Magnificat. In this hymn Mary proclaims that God, through Jesus, will show strength through scattering people's pride, will tear down the mighty from their thrones and raise up in the poor in their place. God will fill the hungry and send the rich, who have not shared, away empty. In this the promise of salvation will be fulfilled for *all* people.

And so Mary is in union with all of us who feel the poverty and unworthiness of our humanity. Like her, God calls us to face down our fears and take up the same mission—to remain faithful to the kingdom Jesus proclaimed no matter what, whether it's in our relationships with our family, colleagues, or friends, at home, at work, or in searching for the bodies of our children in a Santiago morgue.

The feast of the Assumption tells us that it is possible for humanity to be assumed into God, that God will remain faithful to us as we are faithful to God. And not understating the special honor Mary received, we affirm that she prefigures the joy that can be ours in the life to come.

This is why now is not the time to move away from a rich devotion to Mary, so let's reclaim the sanest, most inclusive and Catholic of heritages that makes room for a poor woman to say something to our poverty and to a poor and suffering world.

TRIUMPH OF THE CROSS

 NUMBERS 21:4–9
PHILEMON 2:6–11
JOHN 3:13–17

It's said that if we laid out end to end all the parts of the "true cross" found throughout Europe today, it would stretch from Rome to Jerusalem! Today's feast has its roots in such piety, and it is an extraordinary story.

In 326 the emperor Constantine's mother, Helena, at the grand age of eighty, set sail for Jerusalem to find the cross of Jesus and his tomb. To her satisfaction she found the site of the Holy Sepulchre and established a church on the site, which is venerated as such to this day.

The true cross was more elusive. It was claimed that the leaders of the Jews had hidden the cross in a Jerusalem well. One of the Jewish leaders told the empress Helena in which well to look. The story goes that they dug for days and found three crosses. They weren't sure which one was the true cross, so the bishop of Jerusalem, St. Macarius, sent the crosses off to the bedside of a dying woman. She touched the first two crosses to no effect, but on touching the third cross she immediately recovered. St. Helena had found the true cross.

The true cross remained in the Church of the Holy Sepulchre in Jerusalem until the early seventh century when the entire city was looted by the Persian king, Chosroes II. He took the cross back to Persia. In 628 Emperor Heraclius II overthrew the regime in Persia and carried the cross, first to Constantinople, his capital city, and then in the spring of 629, to Jerusalem.

Today's feast, the Triumph or the Exaltation of the Cross, commemorates this triumphant return of the holy cross to Jerusalem.

On the one hand it's a rather ghoulish tradition that pays so much attention to the instrument of torture used to kill Jesus. The only modern equivalent we might have is the pilgrimage people make to the ovens of Auschwitz and Dachau. No one goes there as a mere tourist. These are places at which we remember past evils so that it might never happen again.

In a similar way this is what today's feast calls us to focus on too. The triumph of Jesus' cross is that in it, through it, and beyond it, he has shown us how to let go of the evil that can trap us in the most destructive of behaviors, and embrace a life that is loving, just, and good. We see in the cross the price to be paid for living our humanity to the full, for sacrificial and saving love, and for confronting evil head-on. To the degree that we do these things, we share in the cross as well, and in the final and never-ending triumph of Christ's resurrection.

Whatever jokes might be made about how far the fragments of the true cross might reach today, the love between Father, Son, and Spirit for all people around the world who suffer reveals the degree to which our God wants us to know his solidarity with our lot.

The cross stands as the sign that God does not condemn us, nor want us to perish, but that the Son came to us, and suffered, died, and was raised so that we might know the way that leads to love and eternal life.

ALL SAINTS

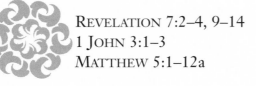

REVELATION 7:2–4, 9–14
1 JOHN 3:1–3
MATTHEW 5:1–12a

Do you remember the old hymn, "Faith of Our Fathers"? These days we would, of course, want to explicitly name the extraordinary faith of "our mothers" as well. But do you recall how we once used to stand and sing

> Faith of our fathers living still
> In spite of dungeon, fire and sword.
> Oh how our hearts beat high with joy...
> If we like them could die for thee.
> Faith of our fathers, holy faith,
> We will be true to Thee 'till death.
> We will be true to Thee 'till death.

In one of his letters St. Ignatius Loyola tells us we should never pray for something we don't want, because we might just get it. Let's think about what we ask for in this hymn: that if need be we will die for our Christian faith.

For the first four hundred years of the church's history, Christian women and men could be dead at lunch for taking the waters of baptism at dawn. It is on the basis of their fidelity and sacrifice that we gather in freedom and peace.

Since most of us are wimps when it comes to pain, all we can hope and pray for is that, given a similar context, we may have the grace to witness to our faith in whatever way is demanded of us. It remains true that when most of us hear about the faith of modern-day martyrs we are still deeply affected, our own faith is challenged, and our values are shaken up. Mothers and fathers are still dying for the faith that we so often take for granted.

All Saints' Day has its roots in the early church's "Martyrs' Day," attested to by a hymn written in 359 by St. Ephraim. It was called All Saints' Day in the seventh century.

A saint is someone who the church believes is in heaven with God. Wrongly, we often think saints are perfect, but in fact their greatest witness is how they coped with the ordinary difficulties of life and how they reflected in a variety of ways the love of God.

For most of us sanctity and martyrdom will not come in dramatic ways. The daily routine of looking after a sick child, spouse, or parent, of living with a mental, physical, emotional, or spiritual illness, the scourge of being unemployed, homeless, or addicted, and the feeling that we are unlovable brings with it the reality of sharing in the lot of the martyrs and saints.

All Saints' Day is the feast when we commemorate all those we know who may never be publicly proclaimed on the canon, or list, of saints but who nonetheless are in heaven. Some of them may only be known to God. Others are people whose love, sacrifice, and fidelity we have seen for ourselves and who have inspired us. Sometimes they can be our own mothers and fathers.

These, too, we believe belong to the great multitude of witnesses who went through their own persecutions and found the blessings within their daily lives. They saw God in this world and are now fully alive to him in the next.

In this Mass may we have the grace to live a holy life that, in ordinary ways, demonstrates the extraordinary power of God working in us. In doing so, in our sacrifices, forgiveness, and love may we remain faithful to the women and men who are our saintly heroes and pray that we remain faithful to the gospel of Christ as they did.

"We will be true to Thee 'till death. We will be true to Thee 'till death."

ALL SOULS (CYCLE A)

(SELECTED READINGS)

All Souls' Day has it roots in the sixth-century Benedictine tradition of praying to the dead. It was a way of recognizing the human bonds that go beyond death. By the tenth century this feast was about praying for the dead, that they might know the merciful love of God.

It's appropriate today for us to think about what a soul is. In an increasingly secular society it's interesting to note that the word *soul* persists in ordinary conversation. Many nonreligious people use this most religious of terms to describe another person.

We often hear how others are lonely, distressed, or lost souls. It can be said that someone has a "beautiful soul" or that a piece of music, a painting, or other work of art "stirred my soul." We describe mellow jazz as "soulful" and still alert others to distress by an SOS, "save our souls." These uses of the word reinforce St. Thomas Aquinas's teaching that the soul makes us human, that it sets us apart from other animals.

Nearly all the great religions of the world believe in a soul, or its equivalent—something that survives the annihilation of the body in death. I have come to the opinion that whatever else might characterize the soul, memory is an integral part of it.

I have done several funerals of people who have suffered from Alzheimer's disease. These are rarely very sad occasions because the family invariably says that they "lost" their loved one months or years before. Why? Because increasingly their loved one couldn't remember anyone or anything. We hold to caring for the body from the womb to the tomb because we believe that human dignity must always be respected. There are now theories about how even the memories of the circumstances of our conception and birth have a bearing on the way we live our lives. It is also apparent that even when people seem to have lost their memory, or are unconscious, there is some recognition of some things at a very deep level.

Soul as memory means that when I meet God face to face, I will remember who I am and how I lived, and God will remember me. It's also a comfort for us to think that we will be reunited with those we have loved who have died before us, because we remember each other.

And what's best about a "remembering soul" is that it is purified. In the old catechism we used to say that heaven was the place where we are perfectly happy with God for eternity. If we think of purgatory as a stage rather than a place, then it's possible to reclaim it as a moment when we see the fullness of God's sacrificial love for us, and recall our sometimes-destructive behavior toward ourselves, others, and the world. Purgatory can be a moment where our memory is purified so we can be eternally happy with God in heaven.

So let's remember at the Eucharist all those "departed souls" we have known and loved over the years, that they might pray for us that we never forget God's saving love and live lives worthy of it.

ALL SOULS (CYCLE B)

 (Selected Readings)

Have you noticed a major change in the way we conduct funerals these days? The ritual hasn't changed, but our language has. Where we once spoke of "commending our sister or brother to the mercy of God" or "praying for the departed's immortal soul," we now sound much more confident about where our sister or brother is.

I was struck by this during the homily delivered at Pope John Paul II's requiem Mass. There, Cardinal Ratzinger moved in the direction of saying that the pope was now enjoying heaven. I don't disagree with him, but it was a change of emphasis. And it has an impact on a feast such as the one today.

Once, All Souls' Day was about praying for our deceased relatives and friends who might be in purgatory. We prayed that they would be "released" soon from a place of purgation and admitted to heaven. Those were the days when we considered getting into heaven was very tough, it was for the select few, so we usually had a lot of people to pray for.

Given today's readings, our newfound confidence in God's compassion toward the dead is entirely justified. The prophet Isaiah tells us of a God who will destroy death, wipe away our tears, and save us. St. Paul is even more confident. If we place our faith in Christ and his resurrection, he argues, we will not be let down. And John's Gospel reminds us that God's fidelity to us has been in place since the beginning, and that darkness will never overcome the light of God.

So we have strong reasons to have confident faith. But if everyone immediately enjoys heaven, then All Saints' Day and All Souls' Day are the same feasts. But they're not. And they shouldn't be either. Yesterday we celebrated our publicly known and privately treasured saints. Today, we pray for the publicly notorious and privately known sinners.

I truly believe with confident faith in Jesus Christ that God would not deny heaven to the many people we know who faithfully, lovingly, and hopefully lived their lives as best as they could. The scriptures give us confidence to know that God does not concern himself with small matters. But what of the individuals and societies whose behavior destroys other people? What of those who never repent of child abuse, physical and emotional violence, being a serial adulterer, and murder? What of those who refuse to share from their excess with those who have nothing in our world? And what of those who don't care or don't want to know about the fallout from their apathy or the consequences involved in the luxury of ignorance? None of these people, none of us, is ever too far from the compassion and forgiveness of God, but I am also convinced that God takes our free decisions on serious matters very seriously.

The problem is that we think of heaven, hell, and purgatory as places where we do time. Yet they may also be experiences or states.

Whatever these realities are like let's pray for the powerful and the meek, whether they had been on the world stage or in our homes, that they may now realize the consequences of their sinfulness in contrast to the gracious love of God.

And may we resolve, by how we live our lives, to show that it's possible for a loved sinner to make amends where possible and confidently look toward the infinite mercy and compassion of God.

ALL SOULS (CYCLE C)

(Selected Readings)

Funeral eulogies are some of the most difficult forms of address to which I have to listen. It's not just that they are often too long and try to say too much, it's that they often have a tone that is at odds with what the church says about death.

When people eulogize their family or friends these days, there is often a lack of faith that God has destroyed death. As part of our death-denying Western culture where we want to always look youthful and be immortal on earth, death is painted as wrong, or a complete surprise, as though it just happened, full stop. As painful as death is, we know that we will see our brother or sister again, that the Christian funeral is a moment to say, "See you later," rather than a definitive "Good-bye."

The Christian position on death is very clear. We believe that in Christ there is no death; it has been destroyed.

God tells the prophet Ezekiel to say that, when he encounters the valley of dead bones, God will breathe life into them and they will revive. He instructs him to tell us that God does not stand at gravesides weeping, but opens them and leads our dead to the promised land. And St. Paul tells us what heaven looks like—imperishable, undefiled, and unfading. Then in today's passage from St. Luke's Gospel Jesus encounters death, and without being asked or invited, calls an end to it.

As with All Saints' Day, All Souls' Day recognizes that death is no more. For those who hold firm to faith in Christ, we live as if death is finished, while also knowing that what we do in this life affects how we will be in the next.

Traditionally, the emphasis on All Souls' Day was on what we could do for the dead. People sometimes lit many candles, went to more than one Mass, and visited a few churches to "get souls out of purgatory." It was a serious time to realize that the living have an important relationship to those who have gone before them.

The problem with a lot of our practices on All Souls' Day, however, was that the emphasis was on what we did for the dead, even to the point that in some forms of popular piety, it seemed that God's merciful love was in response to, or dependent on, our actions and prayers. Salvation in all its forms and ways, however, is dependent on God's activity alone.

These days, All Souls' Day is an opportunity to thank God for those who have died, and to commend some of our family and friends to God's mercy and forgiveness, while praying for healing of memories and the gift of peace.

It's good for us to recall that the church is a community of saints who were sinners, and sinners who did saintly things. Celebrating that in Christ there is no darkness, death, or destruction, we can do no more generous thing than pray for those who have departed this life, especially anyone who has died alone, unloved, or unmourned.

It would be nice to think that when our turn comes to meet Christ our Savior, we will be supported by our family of faith on earth, whether they ever met us in this life or not.

Eternal rest grant unto them, O Lord, and let perpetual light shine upon them. May they rest in peace. Amen.

DEDICATION OF THE LATERAN BASILICA

 EZEKIEL 47:1–2, 8–9, 12
1 CORINTHIANS 3:9–13, 16–17
JOHN 2:13–22

Many Catholics are surprised to discover that St. Peter's Basilica is not the cathedral church of Rome. Try as pilgrims might, they cannot find the bishop of Rome's *cathedra*, or chair, in that church.

Sometimes they think it's the high Baroque sculpture of the Chair of St. Peter behind the high altar. Other times some people assume it's the portable chair in which the pope sits when in St. Peter's. Neither is true.

The cathedral of Rome is the Church of St. John Lateran, and here we find the bishop of Rome's cathedra. Dedicated, or made holy, to Christ our Savior in the fourth century, it is here the pope comes on various liturgical occasions during the year, and when he wants to speak especially to the people of Rome, the members of his own local church.

On any given day in the life of the universal church there are probably several local churches observing the anniversary of the dedication of the cathedral in their diocese. The Dedication of the Lateran Basilica is a universal feast because it reminds us of our local bishop's communion with our bishop of Rome.

Sadly today, sometimes we find people who think that they can choose between their local bishop and the pope. This is many things, but it's not Roman Catholic. Whatever personal devotion we might have for a particular pope, our loyal affections toward him are of no consequence in terms of being in communion with him. How we establish our communion with the pope is through our communion with the local bishop, who celebrates the same Eucharist as, and with, the bishop of Rome.

It's easy to see how some people get this wrong. In years gone by, the church emphasized the role of the pope so strongly we could be forgiven for thinking of the pope as the chief executive officer of the church, and our local bishop as a branch manager. The pope ordered, "Jump!" and we just asked, "How high?" The problem with this rather monarchical model of papal authority is that, given the whole history of the church, it is relatively recent.

This is why the Second Vatican Council, while clear about the essential governing, teaching, and legislating roles the pope has in the church, was careful to recover more ancient thinking about the pope's leadership. The council showed that governing, teaching, and legislating always has a context. It taught that the pope exercises his leadership as first among the bishops, as the universal pastor, the sign of our unity, and as the one charged to teach, guard, and defend the faith of the whole church through the way he confirms his brother bishops in the similar tasks they have in their respective local churches. Even the root of the word *obedience* means "to listen carefully."

So on this feast we celebrate our unity amidst our diversity, as we focus on the mother church of all Roman Catholic churches. May we gain from it a recommitment to our local bishop, who is also a successor of the apostles, and respond to the present pope's recent call to help him imagine ways in which his office of service can be a greater sign of Christian unity for the world in the future.

And may we always remember in the spirit of today's Gospel that the Church is not defined by bricks and mortar, but that the glorified body of Christ is made of people who live out his saving love in the world today.

IMMACULATE CONCEPTION

GENESIS 3:9–15, 20
EPHESIANS 1:3–6, 11–12
LUKE 1:26–38

At its simplest level, this feast says that God does his homework. Mary was not invited to be the mother of Jesus without any preparation. As any of us might expect of this definitive intervention in the world, God prepared Mary so that she might have the requisite gifts for her mission. Though of a vastly different order, we can see that from our conception, too, we have all received certain gifts from God. Some of us have the potential to become brilliant musicians, academics, sportsmen and women, or we have the innate courage to become campaigners for justice, development, and peace. By nature and grace, God prepares all of us to change our world for the better.

What we learn from the personal gifts we have received from God casts light on today's feast. For Mary and for us, our God-given gifts are only part of the equation. The other part is our cooperation with God and personal commitment, which sees us realize our potential.

Even though today's feast focuses on the singular and extraordinary gift Mary received for her mission in the world, there is nothing about the Immaculate Conception that takes away her free will. Mary could have said no to the individual invitation to be the mother of Jesus. Indeed, it is an even more powerful moment for us to reflect on the fact that faced with a choice Mary said yes, and risked everything in an extraordinary partnership with God.

Like a musician, an athlete, sportsperson, or justice campaigner who realizes his or her full potential in this life, Mary went on to realize the fullness of the spiritual gifts she was given. And like some of us who strive to achieve perfection in our particular areas, we know it comes at a cost. It did for Mary as well. Without knowing where the mission would lead her, she gave herself to her Son, and to us, so that we might discover the freedom of faith she was blessed to enjoy, and the redemption to be found in Jesus the Lord.

In today's Gospel, Mary's first reaction to the news of her mission is to be frightened or perplexed. It is such a human moment, where, despite her nature and grace, she needs reassurance that she can do it. That's often true for all of us as well. Far too often fear has the last word in our lives, limiting the dreams we have, and our determination to see them fulfilled. Mary shows us that even in the face of what other people might think, and what we might think of ourselves, we can be bold and courageous with God.

So on this feast let's thank God for a poor teenager in Nazareth who believed in promises and gifts given by God. And may it remind us of the inherent talents God has given all of us, in significantly individual ways, to bring his kingdom to birth in the world of the here and now.

May Mary the mother of God, and our mother in faith, pray for us that we might be worthy of her witness.

SACRED HEART OF JESUS (CYCLE A)

DEUTERONOMY 7:6–11
1 JOHN 4:7–16
MATTHEW 11:25–30

The devotional life of the church reveals as much about us, as it does about God.

St. Margaret Mary Alacoque may be credited with popularizing the Sacred Heart, but the devotion certainly predates her. It's described as early as the eleventh century and recorded in the visions and writings of many saints thereafter—Gertrude, Mechtilde, Francis de Sales, Francis Borgia, John Eudes among them.

Almost always, large-scale public devotions in our church rise to counter a theological position. When St. Margaret Mary had her religious experiences, France was in the grip of the Jansenist heresy. Among other things, Jansenism placed great emphasis on individual responsibility for sin, and the difficulty of obtaining Christ's mercy, whose true humanity was played down.

In this context Margaret Mary sees that the wounded, suffering heart of Jesus expresses his love, intimacy, and forgiveness for us. It comes as no surprise that part of her revelation was that the popularizing of the devotion should be given to the Jesuits, who were also the loudest opponents of the Jansenists.

The fact that the devotion spread like wildfire in the latter part of the seventeenth century says something about how necessary the revelation was for the church. The *sensus fidei* won again.

Public devotion to the Sacred Heart has certainly waned since the Second Vatican Council. But that's only because the council absorbed the best elements of it—the celebration of Jesus' humanity, his suffering and death as an expression of his love for us, and the Eucharist as the most intimate of moments where Christ is broken and poured out in love so that we reproduce this pattern of sacrificial love in our own lives.

Let's pray then that by what we say, and more so by how we live, we proclaim to all people the breadth and length and height and depth of the saving love of God made visible in Christ Jesus the Lord.

SACRED HEART OF JESUS (CYCLE B)

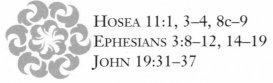

HOSEA 11:1, 3–4, 8c–9
EPHESIANS 3:8–12, 14–19
JOHN 19:31–37

Nearly all peoples in the ancient world thought that the heart rather than the brain controlled the body. They concluded this because they could feel their hearts move, and they saw that when it stopped, death followed. In the prescientific world the heart was given mystical properties.

The various descriptions of a heart come down to us today. We still talk about people who have "big hearts," are "warm hearted," "heartless," or have "good hearts." We can even have "full hearts," or be "brokenhearted." These metaphorical uses of the word point to a presence or an absence of love. And the best example of that comes on St. Valentine's Day, the feast day of an obscure Roman martyr that took over the day dedicated to the Roman pagan festival of love. To this day, February 14 is covered in hearts.

Today we know that the brain is the organ that defines life and death, love and hate, and guides our choices, but the heart remains a strong as ever as a symbol of love.

The problem with the secular world's take on love is that it often and simply equates love with romance and sex. In the Christian tradition we are all for faithful, loving, and happy sexual relationships and we encourage anything, including romance, that might keep them fresh and committed. But we think love means much more than romance and sex. So much more.

In Hosea we hear that the love of God just keeps hanging in their with us even when we push God away. In St. Paul's Letter to the Ephesians we hear that God's love cannot be measured, weighed, or valued. It is boundless and priceless. And in St. John's Gospel we hear that as Jesus' heart stopped beating, out of love for each of us, God's heart burst open with gifts of salvation and resurrection.

The feast of the Sacred Heart uses an ancient metaphor to remind us of a God who is incomprehensibly loving and jealously regards us as his own. There is nothing we can do to earn this gift, and even if we reject him, God will never stop loving us.

The challenge of this feast is that for those of us who have accepted his love, we are called to be as generous, faithful, and sacrificial in our loving as Christ is toward us.

In that spirit may we pray that God will "create in us a clean heart and put a steadfast spirit within us." Amen.

SACRED HEART OF JESUS (CYCLE C)

EZEKIEL 34:11–16
ROMANS 5:5b–11
LUKE 15:3–7

A few years ago Father James Martin, SJ, edited a book called *Contemporary Catholics on Traditional Devotions.* One of the best essays in the book is by Christopher Ruddy on reclaiming devotion to the Sacred Heart of Jesus. It begins:

> 72 times a minute. 4,320 times an hour. 103,680 times a day. Almost 38 million times a year. Over 2.6 million times in the course of an average life. Fist-sized, the human heart beats powerfully and durably. It must be sturdy enough to contract and send fresh blood throughout the entire body, elastic enough to collect spent, deoxygenated blood. Too much hardness or softness of heart, and it dies. Only a

healthy heart—strong and supple—can give and receive lifeblood....

Devotion to the Sacred Heart of Jesus has suffered cardiac arrest in recent decades. It has been dismissed as superstitious in its apparent guarantee of salvation to those who practice it, as masochistic in its emphasis on making reparation for Jesus' own suffering. Its popular iconography is—to put it generously—saccharine, kitschy, effeminate and grotesque at once. This decline in devotion is all the more striking because of its pre-eminence in the first half of the 20th century, when so many Catholics families had a picture of Jesus and his Sacred Heart displayed in their homes, and when Thursday night holy hours and first Fridays proliferated in parishes. Like many forms of heart disease, such atrophy could have been prevented through a healthy diet—in this case, Scripture and tradition.

Dr. Ruddy goes on to talk about how devotion to the Sacred Heart is all about moving from having a heart of stone to having a heart of flesh.

In today's readings we hear how the metaphor of a heart of flesh should play out in our lives. In Ezekiel God is a shepherd who searches, seeks, rescues, guides, binds up, strengthens, and feeds. The Gospel keeps the shepherd metaphor going but adds that Jesus will risk all the other sheep in the fold for the sake of the one who is lost. And St. Paul tells the church in Rome, and us, that we didn't have to find our own way out of our destructive behavior, but, rather, God came and found us where we are, as we are.

The Sacred Heart of Jesus is not about outdated piety. It says that falling in love is at the very center of our God. And that we should "fall" for each other because God has fallen for us.

Thomas Merton put this better than anyone in his book *Love and Living*: "Love is our true destiny. We do not find meaning of life by ourselves alone—we find it with one another. We do not discover the secret of our lives merely by study and calculation in our own isolated meditations. The meaning of our life is a secret that has to be revealed to us in love, by the one we love. And if this love is unreal, the secret will never be found...we will never be fully real until we let ourselves fall in love—either with another human person or with God."

May this feast help us fall in love with God and one another all over again. Amen.